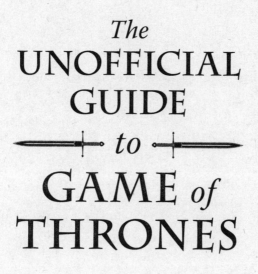

The
UNOFFICIAL GUIDE
to
GAME *of* THRONES

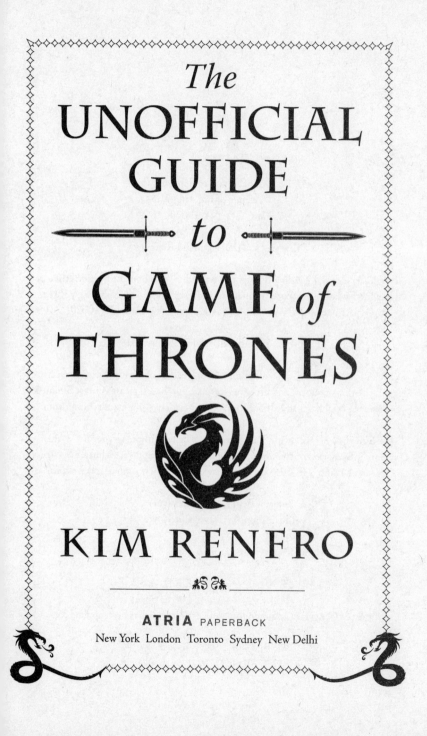

The
UNOFFICIAL
GUIDE
to
GAME *of*
THRONES

KIM RENFRO

ATRIA PAPERBACK

New York London Toronto Sydney New Delhi

ATRIA
PAPERBACK

An Imprint of Simon & Schuster, Inc.
1230 Avenue of the Americas
New York, NY 10020

First Atria Paperback edition October 2019

ATRIA PAPERBACK and colophon are trademarks of Simon & Schuster, Inc. For information about special discounts for bulk purchases, please contact Simon & Schuster Special Sales at 1-866-506-1949 or business@simonandschuster.com.

The Simon & Schuster Speakers Bureau can bring authors to your live event. For more information or to book an event contact the Simon & Schuster Speakers Bureau at 1-866-248-3049 or visit our website at www.simonspeakers.com.

Interior design by Jason Snyder
Illustrations by Devin Elle Kurtz

Manufactured in the United States of America

1   3   5   7   9   10   8   6   4   2

Library of Congress Cataloging-in-Publication Data has been applied for.

ISBN 978-1-9821-1640-8
ISBN 978-1-9821-1641-5 (ebook)

For Mike, the Father of Cats, Brewer of Coffee,
Protector of Sanity, and Keeper of My Heart

CONTENTS

◇◇◇◇◇◇◇◇◇◇◇◇◇◇◇◇◇◇◇◇◇

INTRODUCTION

earest reader,

First, a warning. This book is filled from front to back with spoilers for the entirety of *Game of Thrones*. So if you are a super-new fan who hasn't yet seen the whole show and wants to experience it fresh, please gently place a bookmark at this page and return to it only once you've finished the series.

My hope is that you are standing in a bookstore or library or even your own home, drawn to the page you are reading right now because you, like so many millions around the world, love *Game of Thrones*. Whether you read George R. R. Martin's A Song of Ice and Fire (ASOIAF) series starting in 1996 or binged the first seven seasons last year and then tuned in to HBO for the big finale, I am grateful you have found yourself here, reading my book.

I first learned about Martin's work in 2011, along with much of the world, because of HBO's adaptation. From the first episode, I could tell this was something I would love. Kingdoms! Outcasts! Boromir! Wolf puppies! Sex! It was all I needed.

I also realized I needed to read the books upon which this show was based. As an avid Harry Potter fan, I knew the vast differences between a visual adaptation and a novel was treacherous territory for me. But if I loved what I saw on the screen, the odds were high I would love the source material even more.

I purchased slightly worn copies of the four ASOIAF books that were then available. I devoured the first chapters of *A Game of Thrones*, and instantly knew I was holding something special in my hands. Soon I became that inconsiderate, reckless brand of New Yorker who walked down sidewalks while reading a book, nearly stepping into intersections or brushing shoulders roughly with strangers as I scanned the pages.

I bought the massive hardcover copy of *A Dance with Dragons* as soon as it was available. Toting that beast around the subways along with my textbooks was no easy feat, but I couldn't contain my reading to the apartment.

At the same time I was falling in love with Daenerys Targaryen and Jon Snow and Arya Stark, I was introduced to Reddit. "The front page of the internet!" they called it. At first I just called it "a cesspool of misogyny," but soon saw the value beneath the loud hordes on the main page's threads. I learned how there was a subreddit, or subcommunity, for nearly every interest or hobby one could possibly have. Naturally, there was one for A Song of Ice and Fire. That little page, /r/asoiaf, soon became my addiction. I read every discussion thread, awed by the little details and foreshadowings I had failed to notice as I sped through the novels on my first time.

It was among those unfurled conversation chains that I first learned about "R + L = J"—the theory about Jon Snow's parentage so popular and perfect it was effectively treated as fact. It was also there that I learned my first big lesson in navigating the internet for spoilers. At the time, discussion posts on /r/asoiaf had to be marked with the acronym of the book you wanted to discuss, so people would know to avoid threads about books they hadn't yet finished. I was pretty far along in *A Storm of Swords* when I stumbled upon a thread titled something like "[ASOS] A question about Roose Bolton." Well, I had my own questions about Roose Bolton. Maybe this would help. I clicked on the post, despite having not yet finished the book. The thread opened, and the first line was basically "So when Roose Bolton stabbed Robb Stark in the heart and betrayed the Northern army . . ."

I actually screamed. You think watching the Red Wedding was bad? Or reading it in *A Storm of Swords* as Martin masterfully builds up to the horrible scene? That was nothing compared to the pit in my stomach as I realized I had just spoiled for myself one of the biggest shocks of the series. But this was the first of my many forays into the spoiler-filled world of both A Song of Ice and Fire and the *Game of Thrones* fandom. My obsession with the books, and by proxy the show, knew no bounds.

In January 2014, I graduated from Hunter College and quickly registered at a temp agency. They placed me at a digital media company called *Business Insider* to fill in as an administrative assistant.

I soon made myself a valuable part of the growing team. My days were spent stocking the kitchen with snacks and seltzer and setting up Mac Mini computers for new hires, all while I observed the hustle of a newsroom. The temp job became permanent, and for the first time in my life I was introduced to a behind-the-scenes understanding of journalism and digital media and online content creation. One day, when I was adding sodas to the kitchen fridge and chatting with an editor about the coming weekend, *Game of Thrones* came up. We started swapping opinions on the show, and how it differed from the books. He was confused and surprised by how much I knew about, well, *everything* to do with Martin's world of characters and HBO's adaptation.

"If you ever want to write something for *Business Insider* about the show, let me know," he said.

And my whole life changed.

In my spare time outside of office assistant duties, I began writing articles about Martin's plans for the book series or ways HBO's adaptation had changed up characters or roles or hinted at important prophecies and twists. The company grew, and new teams were created. As the person responsible for setting up all new hires' computers and restocking the kitchen, I knew anyone and everyone at the company *and* what job openings were being posted.

When I read the description for a new entry-level reporter role on the "Culture" team, I applied for the job. Within three months, I was officially a full-time reporter for the company, covering not just *Game of Thrones* but other internet culture trends and entertainment news.

Now Los Angeles is home, and I've found myself guesting on podcasts and participating in events like Con of Thrones and often in a daze of writing anything and everything *Game of Thrones* related. I inadvertently started down a new path on the day I watched that pilot episode, even if it took years for that change to manifest itself.

And I know I'm not alone. This show changed thousands of lives, bringing love and jobs and friends and joy to so many incredible fans around the world. This book is here to help give back a little piece of the joy and celebrations the fandom has brought to my life. Can the lasting impact of a cultural behemoth like *Game of Thrones* be understood within the immediate minutes, hours, days, or even months after that final episode aired? As Tyrion Lannister wisely tells Jon Snow in the series finale, "Ask me again in ten years." Maybe then I'll have the best words to describe how much this roller coaster of a show has meant to my life.

For now, come along with me in an exploration of how *Game of Thrones* was created, how it changed pop culture, and the deeper meanings contained within some of the most magnificent hours of storytelling ever seen on television.

—Kim Renfro, *INSIDER* entertainment correspondent

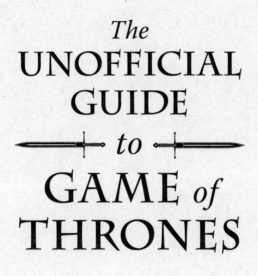

The
UNOFFICIAL
GUIDE
to
GAME *of*
THRONES

CHAPTER ONE

◇◇◇◇◇◇◇◇◇◇◇◇◇◇◇◇◇◇

The
GREAT DIVIDE

On the night of June 2, 2013, a chasm of pain and misery materialized in front of an unsuspecting television audience. Millions of *Game of Thrones* fans had spent more than two years obsessing over the grim politics of Westeros and falling in love with knights and lords and ladies and outcasts alike. They hadn't noticed HBO was barreling them toward a cliff's edge the whole time, like lambs to the slaughter. But the rest of us knew, and sat back, popcorn in hand and camera phones out, to watch the blood spill and the tears flow.

"Red Wedding" is such an innocuous phrase. It means nothing. But now it means everything to *Game of Thrones* fans. Ever since that fated night, this pair of words has taken on a cultural weight almost no other television show in history can lift. Author George R. R. Martin had changed fantasy storytelling long before he turned his story over to David Benioff and D. B. Weiss so they could change television. But on that June night, the entire world was finally fully clued-in on the mastery that is *Game of Thrones*. The invisible rift that had sat between the book-readers and show-watchers was stitched back together.

From then on, we entered a new phase of pop culture. There was everything before the Red Wedding, and then everything after. There was a past when *Game of Thrones* might have been lost in the shuffle of prestige television's heyday, and the future where HBO's big risk on a fantasy series would be remembered as one of the greatest decisions ever made in Hollywood.

The novels in Martin's A Song of Ice and Fire (ASOIAF) series were already topping bestseller charts before *Game of Thrones* came along. But tens of millions more people would not have known the stories of Daenerys Targaryen, the Unburnt and Mother of Dragons, or of Jon Snow, the secret Targaryen prince kept hidden in plain sight, if it weren't for David Benioff and D. B. Weiss. Those fans wouldn't have shed tears over the execution of Lord Eddard Stark, nor sat, mouths agape, as they realized his son and wife, Robb and Catelyn, were doomed as well.

When HBO announced the episode titles for the third *Game of Thrones* season, Martin's longtime readers knew at once what was coming. The ninth episode was called "The Rains of Castamere," the name of the infamously ominous Lannister song. The lyrics of "The Rains of Castamere" tell the story of Lord Tywin crushing a lesser house beneath his heel when they dared challenge the Lannisters of Casterly Rock. In both the books and the show's version of events, Catelyn Stark only realizes the festivities of her brother's wedding are about to take a perilous turn when the Freys' hired musicians begin playing "The Rains of Castamere," signaling Tywin's machinations even though he was nowhere near the castle.

Knowing what was coming for the show-only fans, ASOIAF

readers banded together, both online and in the real world. They were determined to let the show's audience experience the horror of the Red Wedding in the same way they had in the books: shocked, angry, heartbroken, and going from heartily invested in the young King in the North to freshly grieving for Robb and Catelyn and what felt like the entire House Stark cause.

Book-readers went through this gauntlet of grief with Martin's third novel, *A Storm of Swords*, when it was first published in 2000. Ask anyone about the experience of reading Catelyn Stark's point-of-view chapter, starting with the drums pounding, pounding, pounding, and they'll feel a sick churning in their stomachs. They'll tell you about throwing the book across the room in anger, or gasping so loud they startled their sleeping cat.

Only the most astute of readers would have seen the Red Wedding coming. No other book series had begun its run with the surprise execution of its presumed protagonist, only to carry forward with a new hero, that former protagonist's son, and then give him the axe, too. What kind of sadism was this? What twisted sense of justice? What self-sabotaging writer would do such a thing?

This is Martin's genius. Many of his characters are gray, and their prospects are bleak. Heroic characters die not in glory but in cold blood at a dinner table and all because of very human missteps. The heart and truth and valor lurking within them is captivating. Losing Ned Stark hurt. Losing Robb and Catelyn hurt more, because they represented our best hope for vengeance. Martin knew the moment he planned out Ned's death that his son would have to follow, but the story was carefully built to lull us into a sense of security before he pulled the rug out.

The signs were all there with Robb's series of mistakes and misfortunes, but audiences and readers alike were duped by the tropes of fantasy we thought the story would follow. Martin's devoted book-readers had taken extra care over the previous three years not to spoil the coming shock. "Red Wedding" wasn't even typed out in full on fan discussion forums like Westeros.org and Reddit; it was shortened to "RW." Some news outlets picked up on the fact that *something* bad was about to happen, but it was anybody's guess as to what new devastation was on its way.

Benioff and Weiss had been purposefully building toward this moment in the series from the start. Like the rest of us, they were hooked on Martin's writing from the moment Jaime Lannister pushed little Bran Stark out a window. But they knew if they could sell *Game of Thrones*, and convince HBO to renew the series for at least three seasons, they would make it to the Red Wedding and everything would change. If they could get there, they knew they'd have the world convinced that A Song of Ice and Fire was the greatest story ever told.

"When we read the books, we knew we just wanted to get to this scene and do this holy-shit moment justice, that throw-the-book-across-the-room moment," Weiss said at a 2016 San Diego Comic-Con panel.

With a few loaded crossbows, a few more daggers, and a twist to the heart, "The Rains of Castamere" brought together two factions of the fandom. Book-readers prepared for the aftermath of millions of people around the world finding out Robb, Catelyn, Grey Wind, and the entirety of the Stark army was obliterated. The people in the know were ready to be a shoulder to cry on, but first they would have a bit of fun with their show-only comrades.

Within hours of the silent credits rolling on the episode, videos began circulating online showing people, in real time, watching the

Red Wedding unfold. Some crafty readers, simmering with anticipation of the shared grief and horror, took out their cell phones and recorded the trauma washing over their loved ones like so many shocks of cold water. In one such video, a shirtless man lays on a beige carpet. He rolls over onto his back and looks into the camera, his expression both accusatory and impressed.

"You guys knew about this?" he says, his voice cracking with what could be either high-pitched emotion or the sound of a person's reality collapsing in on itself.

This clip was shown during an episode of *Conan* on June 5, when Conan O'Brien welcomed guest of honor George R. R. Martin. He sat the author down and had him watch a compilation of *Game of Thrones* fans reacting to "The Rains of Castamere."

"The episode on Sunday melted people's minds," O'Brien said. "My eyeballs melted out of my head. The reaction was stunning. And I was thinking, 'What is it about this show *Game of Thrones?*' And I realized you get us to really care about characters, love them, think that they're central to everything, *and then you kill them!* You sick bastard."

Martin sat wearing his signature cap with a turtle pin, a symbol of the little dime store turtles he had as a boy, kept in a terrarium with a miniature castle. The small creatures died often, as was their lot, and so Martin would dream up stories of wars and royal family infighting to explain the turtles' high mortality rate. Decades later, faced with the kind of success no author dares to imagine, Martin sat beside Conan O'Brien as a guest of honor, hands folded across his stomach and chuckling at the late-night host's indignation.

Despite the humor embedded in Martin's major television appearance, the author talked at length about the emotional challenge of writing the Red Wedding. "I've gotten a lot of mail from readers, many of them saying it was brilliant, but others saying they couldn't read past that, and they were giving up on my book, it was too painful," Martin told a fan during an *Entertainment Weekly* Q&A in 2007. "But it's supposed to be painful. It was painful to write, it should be painful to read, it should be a scene that rips your heart out, and fills you with terror and grief. That's what I'm striving for."

We may laugh now at the "Red Wedding reaction" compilation videos, showing women with their hands over their mouths, curled up unsuspectingly on couches and beds, but the dreadfulness of it is always there. The terror and grief live in our bones. It was a betrayal not just from Walder Frey, but from Martin himself.

The Red Wedding was a thousand *thousand* times worse than Albus Dumbledore getting blasted off the top of that tower. More gutting than Gandalf letting go of that ledge, disappearing into the abyss below. More horrifying than Dexter finding Rita in that bathtub of blood. More stunning than Omar Little dropping to the floor of that convenience store. And yes, the Red Wedding was more shocking than anything else that would happen on *Game of Thrones*. Even the execution of poor, dead Ned.

The horror didn't just come from Benioff and Weiss's bold choice of starting off the massacre with the stabbing of an unborn child in its mother's womb (a specific slice of brutality *not* found in Martin's novels), but from the nonstop slaughter that followed. This wasn't a fight. Not even a bit of fisticuffs. Just death, death, death. And then a quick break as we see Arya. Oh, right—she's watching Grey Wind die. And back to death. It was a massacre of unparalleled proportions, a scene so laden with emotions that we didn't even need a somber background score. As the credits rolled, the audience was left sitting in silent contemplation of how point-less this all really was.

Of course, what goes down must come up. That's how *Game of Thrones* works, even if the peaks were hard to see while we were laid so low in the valleys. It took four years, but our thirst for vengeance was quenched when Arya returned to that wicked castle and sliced open Walder Frey's throat. Our hearts soared when Jon Snow stood with a tentative pride before the lords of the North as they hailed him as their king, just as his brother (er, "brother") had done.

As the series marched toward its end, a truth became clear. *Game of Thrones* was the last show of its kind. For decades, before VCRs and then DVR and then on-demand and then streaming, appointment-viewing television was how the world consumed shows. But by the time the final episodes of *Game of Thrones* were set to air, no other show could command a live audience of tens of millions of people. Instead, for most other programs, people watched at their own pace. Sometimes live, other weeks they'd catch it a few hours later, or maybe the next morning or on Thursday when they had a free night. They'd binge old seasons of series on Netflix or HBO Now or Hulu. But not *Game of Thrones*.

By the end of its run on HBO, *Game of Thrones* was the Super Bowl of scripted television. It wasn't just TV—it was a worldwide event happening live in your living room every Sunday for more than a month. Sure, you could opt out of watching. But if you went that route you were sure to wake up the next morning to an onslaught of spoilers. There was no avoiding the tidal wave of conversations, both on- and offline, about the events of the episode. You had to sit down and watch *Game of Thrones* at 9 p.m. ET on HBO, or else suffer at the hands of the zeitgeist. No other television show was achieving that kind of public fervor in 2019.

To know how that rabid fandom evolved, we have to travel further back in time before the Red Wedding broke hearts on that spring evening. We must go back to the days when the Mother of Dragons and King in the North and grumpkins and snarks were just an inkling of an idea in one man's mind.

CHAPTER TWO

FORGING GAME *of* THRONES: A FATEFUL MEETING

When George R. R. Martin set out to write A Song of Ice and Fire, he likely knew full well the thousands of pages of material would be unadaptable for television. In fact, he's often said he designed them that way.

Martin spent almost a decade working in television in the eighties and early nineties, cranking out pilot scripts and helping adapt other people's written works for the small screen, including a revamp of *Beauty and the Beast* and episodes of *The Twilight Zone*, both on CBS. But Martin's overactive imagination steered his TV writing into territory that simply wasn't feasible for a cable network budget. He was over it.

"There were *constant* limitations," Martin said in a 2014 interview with *Rolling Stone's* Mikal Gilmore. "It wore me down. There were battles over censorship, how sexual things could be, whether a scene was too 'politically charged,' how violent things could be."

He recalled a fight over the violence he was writing into an episode of *Beauty and the Beast*. "The Beast killed people. That was the point of the character. He was a *beast*," Martin said. "But CBS didn't want blood, or for the beast to kill people. . . . It was ludicrous. The character had to remain likable."

Martin began his professional writing career in the 1970s with published science-fiction short stories and eventually published his first novel, *Dying of the Light*, in 1977. By the early 1990s, after his stint in TV writing with a sprinkling of sci-fi/horror novel writing on the side, Martin decided to return to writing fantasy books, where there would be no cap on the magical creatures, epic battles, or nuanced internal narration of the characters he was dreaming up. One day a scene came into his head, fully formed: a young boy on his pony, watching an execution before he and his brothers would find direwolf pups in the snow.

And so Martin crafted a new world, his *own* world. One unrestrained by budgets or extras or the notion that high fantasy was a niche market. His world was a medievalesque planet where seasons lasted for years and stories of heroes and magical beings fell to mythology. A world where an exiled teenager hatched dragon eggs with blood magic across the sea from an unstable kingdom too distracted by political squabbling to notice a coming threat looming beyond an immense wall made of mystical ice. Martin conjured up knights with intricate heralds marching into bloody battles fought in the shadows of looming castles. His was a world of ice and fire, of beauty and fantastical terrors.

In 1993, Martin sent an outline and the first thirteen chapters of a new book idea to one of his literary agents, Ralph Vicinanza. Photos of the three-page letter were photographed and tweeted out by a UK bookseller in 2015. The tweet has since been deleted, but the letter outline remains famous among die-hard fans of Martin's work.

"Here are the first thirteen chapters (170 pages) of the high fantasy novel I promised you, which I'm calling *A Game of Thrones*," Martin wrote in the letter. "When completed, this will be the first volume in what I see as an epic trilogy with the overall title, A Song of Ice and Fire."

His letter promised a rotating cast of characters, many of whom would die. From this letter, the very start, Martin knew he wanted us to feel as if every character was at risk of dying in any given chapter.

"Even the characters who seem to be the heroes," Martin wrote. "The suspense always ratchets up a notch when you know that any character can die at any time."

When it comes to the origins of HBO's adaptation and the elements at play that led to Martin signing over the rights to his story, it's essential to start with exploring how Martin's initial seedlings of ideas changed significantly in the thirteen years following this pitch. As he began writing this seemingly unfilmable series, Martin's imagination quickly outdid itself, and the planned story started branching out in ways he at first did not expect.

Three years after the initial trilogy outline was laid out in the letter to Vicinanza, Martin changed his mind and decided he'd write *two* trilogies. The six books would be separated by a five-year gap of time passing between each trilogy (in order to give the younger cast of characters time to age up).

A Clash of Kings followed *A Game of Thrones* in 1998 and was the first of the series to appear on the *New York Times* bestseller list. The third volume, *A Storm of Swords*, was published several months behind schedule, in 2000. It was even more popular than its predecessors.

The second trilogy was initially scheduled to launch in 2002, but Martin ran into unexpected issues with his blossoming storylines and unwieldy page counts. Publishers had asked him to keep the next volume under 1,200 pages, but the working text was already longer than the previous book.

He wound up abandoning the five-year jump, and also took a friend's advice and divided the plotlines of the fourth novel into two separate books whose chapters would take place at approximately the same time. This meant that the fourth book, *A Feast for Crows*, featured the plotlines of characters like Brienne of Tarth and Cersei Lannister but contained no new chapters showcasing fan favorites such as Tyrion Lannister, Jon Snow, or Daenerys Targaryen.

A Feast for Crows debuted in June 2005 and was an instant bestseller. But despite its immediate sales success, the volume is often lamented among people as the worst of Martin's published series. This is likely because of the long delay in publishing combined with the perceived "missing" storylines of beloved characters.

The book came with a caveat, published at the end of its final chapter, saying the fifth volume would likely arrive by the end of 2006. Also, the new plan was now for a total of seven books in the series.

"Tyrion, Jon, Dany, Stannis and Melisandre, Davos Seaworth, and all the rest of the characters you love or love to hate will be along next year (I devoutly hope) in *A Dance with Dragons*," Martin wrote in early summer 2005 in an afterword published in all copies of *A Feast for Crows*.

As you can already tell, the landscape of A Song of Ice and Fire was in a near constant state of flux—even before the idea of a TV show was introduced.

As Martin had been plodding along with A Song of Ice and Fire in the nineties, he signed a deal with a management company called Created By, helmed by Vicinanza and a man named Vince Gerardis. Vicinanza was Martin's literary agent in charge of handling all the foreign-rights deals for his books going back almost twenty years. But now Vicinanza would work with Gerardis specifically to get clients' science-fiction and fantasy works turned into movies and TV shows.

And so word was spread about the potential opportunity for A Song of Ice and Fire to be optioned by a lucky producer or screenwriter. As Martin revealed in *Inside Game of Thrones*, a book about the HBO series by Bryan Cogman, calls were coming in from interested parties by the time *A Clash of Kings* was published in 1998.

Most of the people approaching Martin and the Created By team were eyeing A Song of Ice and Fire for a set of feature films. None of the meetings had Martin convinced, though. He privately told Gerardis that he thought HBO was the only potential home for the series, but that he didn't have the time to write the scripts (though he did have the résumé to pull it off himself).

A Song of Ice and Fire began steadily picking up notoriety as the novels won literary awards and climbed the bestseller charts, and more inquiries about optioning the rights to the story started streaming in. This was helped by the fact that several major advancements had been made in special effects and computer-generated imagery (CGI) since Martin first began penning the saga that made filming the "unfilmable" possible.

The first of Peter Jackson's Lord of the Rings film trilogy

premiered in 2001 to resounding praise from critics and movie-goers alike, and showed what was possible in fantasy storytelling. Suddenly producers and executives realized there was an untapped market for epic fantasy series outside the scope of normal serialized television.

As the Lord of the Rings films continued making waves in Hollywood, scooping up Academy Awards in record-breaking fashion, people continued to approach Martin with proposals for movies based on A Song of Ice and Fire. Martin turned them all away, knowing he didn't want to cut corners if his epic universe was ever going to make it onto a screen.

Then Gerardis found David Benioff. Though how exactly Gerardis came across the then thirty-five-year-old author and screenwriter is still a small mystery, we do know Benioff spoke with Gerardis on the phone in January 2006. Benioff hadn't heard of Martin or A Song of Ice and Fire, but the pitch was tempting enough. He told Gerardis he'd be interested in reading the books, and shortly thereafter nearly four thousand pages of the ongoing fantasy story arrived at his home.

Benioff devoured hundreds of pages of *A Game of Thrones* before calling Dan (D. B.) Weiss—one of his oldest friends and a fellow writer/fantasy-obsessive. Weiss voraciously read A Song of Ice and Fire, and knew it was a match made in writer heaven.

"If a large part of your livelihood is adapting source material for the screen, you're always on the lookout for deep characters, a beautifully crafted and compelling story, passion, violence, intrigue, humanity, and all the ambiguities that come with a fully realized world," Weiss said in HBO's first edition of *Inside Game of Thrones*. "You never find them all in the same place. Except we did. It was exhilarating and terrifying."

Benioff and Weiss had met in 1995 while studying literature at Trinity College Dublin. The pair bonded over being outliers in the academic environment while grinding out their respective theses.

"We were two American Jews in Dublin, with no Irish roots of any kind, obsessed with Irish literature and trying to find a functional gym in Dublin in 1995, which is not something that most Irish people in 1995 were all that preoccupied with," Weiss told *Vanity Fair* during a 2014 interview.

Benioff's debut novel, *The 25th Hour*, was published in 2002. He eventually adapted it himself into a screenplay for a movie directed by Spike Lee and starring Edward Norton. Weiss wrote his own debut novel, *Lucky Wander Boy*, around the same time. It was published in 2003, the same year he worked on his first collaborative project with Benioff—a movie script for an adaptation of Orson Scott Card's *Ender's Game* (the iteration Benioff and Weiss wrote was never used by the studio).

These writing efforts and experience adapting a book to the screen were likely what had drawn Gerardis to Benioff in the first place, and he in turn brought in Weiss. Though they later told Collider News the pitch from Created By was for a series of ASOIAF "feature adaptations," Benioff and Weiss agreed with each other that TV, and specifically HBO, was the way to go if an adaptation was to be made. They had no idea Martin had been thinking the same thing.

Gerardis scheduled a lunch meeting between Martin and the two writers at the Palm restaurant in Los Angeles in the early months of 2006. Everyone at the table was in agreement that A Song of Ice and Fire couldn't have the movie treatment like Harry Potter or Lord of the Rings. It had to be television, and if it had to be television, then it had to be HBO.

"We had to convince him it was a TV show and then convince him that we, who had never produced a minute of television in our lives, were the people to do this television show, that we were the people for him to give his child to," Weiss said, reflecting on the day in a later interview with *Vanity Fair*. "The first was very easy, because he knows television and he knows film storytelling . . . that part was a relatively simple conversation. Convincing him that we were the ones to do the job took the rest of the three-and-a-half-hour lunch."

For Martin's part, he had to be certain that his unfinished series was in safe hands. The midday meeting spilled over into the afternoon and eventually the evening.

"We talked right through lunch and then everybody from lunch left and we were alone in the restaurant, they started resetting all the tables for dinner, then the dinner crowd started to come in and we were still talking," Martin recounted during a 2013 Emmy Awards panel. "I did ask them a few pointed questions to determine whether they had actually read the books or [not]."

This knowledge test was tossed at Benioff and Weiss unannounced, but thankfully they had already spent hours discussing A Song of Ice and Fire with each other and were prepared.

"At the very end of that lunch, he said, 'Who's Jon Snow's real mother?'" Benioff told *Vanity Fair*. "And it was very much like a test question. It wasn't like, 'Ha-ha!' He asked it and stared at us . . . we made a guess, after a nerve-racking silence."

"We gave an answer—a shocking answer," Weiss confirmed at the 2013 Emmy Awards panel. "At that point, George didn't actually say whether or not we were right or wrong, but his smile was his tell. We knew we had passed the Wonka test."

Just over a decade later, Benioff and Weiss would use the penultimate scene of the seventh season finale, "The Dragon and the

Wolf," to confirm that Jon Snow was in fact the son of Lyanna Stark and Rhaegar Targaryen—not Ned Stark and a mystery woman, as much of the realm (and Jon himself) believed. But back in 2006, with only four volumes of A Song of Ice and Fire published, this fact was still just a fan theory, albeit one of the most widely believed predictions circulating among readers of Martin's books.

Weiss and Benioff had clearly done a close reading of the novels and had picked up on the many contextual clues placed in Ned Stark's point-of-view chapters that would lead a careful reader to understand the implied truth about Jon Snow. Benioff and Weiss would wait until their 2019 appearance on *Jimmy Kimmel Live!* to reveal that the name they gave Martin at that consequential lunch meeting was "Lyanna Stark," but fans long assumed this was the "shocking" response they took a chance with. In Martin's recollection of the afternoon, he indicates the two future showrunners got full marks.

"They gave me the right answers, so we shook hands and they took the ball and ran with it," Martin said at the 2013 Emmys panel. "And next thing I knew we were in business with HBO."

In March 2006, Benioff and Weiss gave the first pitch to Carolyn Strauss at HBO, and the television series *Game of Thrones* (the "A" was dropped from Martin's novel title) was set in motion. Martin had turned over the optioned rights to HBO and Benioff and Weiss, trusting them with his literary offspring.

But what neither Martin nor Benioff and Weiss could have predicted at the time was that the next book in A Song of Ice and Fire wouldn't arrive on schedule that year. Nor the year after that. Instead, Martin would find himself tangled up with plotlines and overlapping characters and battles and epic ideas. The fifth novel, *A Dance with Dragons*, didn't come out in 2006 as Martin had hoped and put down in writing in that now-unfortunate afterword of *A Feast for Crows*.

Instead, as the years passed and Benioff and Weiss worked on getting the first version of the pilot filmed, Martin toiled away and rewrote chapters and reworked outlines until he finally turned in the manuscript for *A Dance with Dragons* in 2011. Much had changed by then, including the unexpected death of Vicinanza. He was sixty years old when he died of a cerebral aneurysm.

"The HBO series that we are all so excited about would not exist without the efforts of Created By," Martin wrote in a LiveJournal post. "It was Ralph and Vince who brought the books to David Benioff and D. B. Weiss, and spearheaded the complex rounds of negotiation that followed. Ralph was to be co-exec producer on the series. It saddens me to think that he will never get to see it."

A Dance with Dragons was published in July 2011, just months after HBO's *Game of Thrones* premiered to an audience of two million people. At the time he agreed to the deal with HBO, Martin thought he was light-years ahead of Benioff and Weiss, and therefore had plenty of time to publish the final planned three books.

But he would not complete another installment in A Song of Ice and Fire until after the show had overtaken his published works and aired its finale in 2019 to a new record audience for HBO: 18.4 million viewers, more than nine times the number of people who tuned in for the pilot (and that doesn't even count the millions of likely pirated streams).

Benioff and Weiss, the two men to whom Martin had trusted his life's greatest work, would be the ones to carry a version of the ending to A Song of Ice and Fire over the finish line first. But before they would get there, progress back in the late 2000s would hit an unexpected road block with the disastrous first try at making a *Game of Thrones* pilot.

CHAPTER THREE

The PITCH and the "PIECE of SHIT" PILOT

In 2006, a few weeks after their crucial conversation with George R. R. Martin, it was time for Benioff and Weiss to convince HBO of the idea for *Game of Thrones*. They set up a meeting with then HBO Entertainment president Carolyn Strauss and her senior vice president Gina Balian.

"We had been warned that Carolyn was a tough pitch and we shouldn't expect her to laugh at any of our jokes," Benioff and Weiss later told Multichannel News. "So when she cracked a smile midway through the meeting we felt like we'd won the golden ticket."

The Writers Guild Foundation Shavelson-Webb Library has a digital copy of a document aspiring TV writers should be required to study: the "show bible" for *Game of Thrones*. This forty-five-page document includes a pitch letter, addressed to "Carolyn, Gina, and Michael" (who are assumed to be Carolyn Strauss, Gina Balian, and the then soon-to-be head of programming, Michael Lombardo). Benioff and Weiss had never worked on a TV show before, let alone created one, but they wrote a mission statement brimming with enthusiasm, vigor, and an impressive showing of unearned confidence.

"The source material, our vision for it, and your experience with turning such visions into unforgettable series all point to one thing: *Game of Thrones* is a television phenomenon waiting to happen," the pair wrote in the letter.

The show bible also made comparison between Martin's work and *The Brothers Karamazov*, the epic philosophical novel by acclaimed Russian writer Fyodor Dostoevsky, published just before his death in 1879. Benioff and Weiss wrote that "there was no film in [A Song of Ice and Fire], any more than there is a film in *The Brothers Karamazov*" and said that "shoehorning it into a three-hour package would be an act of vandalism."

The pair also compared Martin's work to having the "character depth of *Lion in Winter*," a 1966 play by James Goldman, and "the drama and epic scope of *War and Peace*," the seminal 1889 work of Russian author Leo Tolstoy.

Regardless of their literary comparisons, one thing was clear: "This is an HBO series."

The mission statement also smartly touches upon HBO's past hits (*The Sopranos*, *The Wire*, and *Deadwood*) and a key void that existed in the market back then, the one they were primed to exploit—the epic fantasy.

"People are hungry for *Game of Thrones*. They are starving for it, and when we give it to them, they will wolf it down," Benioff and Weiss wrote. "When we give them this show, they will lose their fucking minds."

Benioff and Weiss were presciently aware of the gold mine they were perched upon, with a full blessing from George R. R. Martin to start digging. The show bible takes playful swipes at popular onscreen fantasy, too. Benioff and Weiss promise HBO there will be "no long-bearded wizards" (as featured in Lord of the Rings), "no invisibility cloaks" (the magical object made famous in Harry Potter) and no "glowing grimoires" (a book of magic spells, as seen in the Halloween classic *Hocus Pocus*).

"In short, none of the things that can make fantasy feel creaky, corny, or kiddie," Benioff and Weiss concluded.

In early articles hyping up *Game of Thrones*, many reporters and critics cite HBO and Benioff and Weiss giving the tagline: "It's *The Sopranos* in Middle Earth." And this clever move of combining a known HBO triumph with the newly resurrected fame of Tolkien's Lord of the Rings fantasy world paid off.

Aided by their comprehensive breakdown of the compelling cast of characters and outline of the pilot episode, the mission statement convinced Strauss to give them a retainer to write the pilot. But by the time Benioff and Weiss were ready to start shooting the first iteration of the pilot, two years had passed and Strauss was out at HBO.

According to a March 2008 report from *Deadline*'s Nikki Finke, part of the reason behind her exit was a decline in uber-successful HBO shows.

"'Everyone felt this was the right time,' an insider told me about her firing," Finke reported. "Because the pay channel has lost all its sizzle. Heck, HBO hasn't had a new hit series in, like, forever."

Little did HBO know the mother of all TV shows was sitting on their backburner thanks to Strauss, who left her role at HBO and became one of the executive producers credited on *Game of Thrones*. Though HBO's team didn't realize it, Strauss had been one of the first people at the company to see the potential in what would eventually become HBO's most successful series of all time. With Strauss's firing, *Game of Thrones* was left in the hands of new co-presidents Richard Plepler and Michael Lombardo.

As explained in *Fast Company's* "Oral History of How *Game of Thrones* Went from Crazy Idea to HBO's Biggest Hit," Plepler and Lombardo were the perfect pair to greenlight the series. They had already begun investing in fantasy programming with their first out-of-the-norm venture, the vampire drama series *True Blood*. Thanks to the early signs of success for *True Blood*, as well as the Oscar haul of the Lord of the Rings trilogy, Plepler and Lombardo were as ready as they'd ever be for a show like *Game of Thrones*.

Benioff and Weiss sent them the script for the pilot and an updated pitch letter with the complete outline of the first season, and hoped they were ready to take a new kind of risk with big-budget, high-fantasy programming.

There were two compelling parts of Benioff and Weiss's pitch for *Game of Thrones*. First was the then radical idea of killing off a main character. Martin's novels were riveting, and not just thanks to the lush scenes of sex and violence and magic, but because he had crafted narratives where no one—not even the core cast of heroic protagonists—ever felt safe.

The second key aspect of the pitch was a focus on the political intrigue and drama that would be driven by power struggles more than magic and mythology.

"These are not two guys that are interested in telling a story about dragons," Lombardo recalled thinking. "They didn't come at this because they were interested in visual effects. They were really, profoundly, emotionally moved by the story of these warring families and about the thirst for power and love and validation."

(Almost a decade later, Benioff and Weiss would confess to *Entertainment Weekly* that part of this pitch wasn't exactly truthful. "The lie we told is the show is contained and it's about the characters," Benioff told *EW*'s James Hibberd in 2018, ahead of the series finale. "The worlds get so big, the battles get so massive.")

Plepler and Lombardo were ready to dive in, but the waters would quickly grow choppy. The BBC had originally signed up to be a production partner with HBO for the show, but the company pulled out at the last minute. This left HBO (and therefore Plepler and Lombardo) with the full monetary responsibility for what would eventually become a $10 million pilot.

"I knew this was a big swing for us—to pull this off on a TV budget," Lombardo told *Fast Company*. "Because even though people talk about our big budgets, we didn't have the money Lord of the Rings had to pull this off. And I think the consumer had a certain bar in their mind of how something had to look to have the feel of authenticity. You really had to transport yourself into a world that felt real even though it was a mythical world. And that takes money and expertise, and, so, we were aware of that."

With Plepler and Lombardo's blessing, Benioff and Weiss headed to Northern Ireland to set up shop and spend several months filming the first-ever *Game of Thrones* episode. Dozens of costumes were made, sets were built, castles and moors and other natural landscapes were overrun with filming crews. Wolves were brought to the set, White Walker prosthetics were designed, and the Iron Throne was built.

By early 2010, after three years of perfecting their script and seven months of filming overseas, the neophyte showrunners had the first cut ready to go. In a Santa Monica studio, the two showrunners sat down with Scott Frank, Ted Griffin, and Craig Mazin—all fellow script writers and good friends whom Benioff and Weiss trusted to give an honest review of their *Game of Thrones* pilot.

As the episode came to a close and Jaime Lannister shoved Bran Stark out of a tower window, it was immediately clear that something somewhere had gone horribly wrong. Craig Mazin looked at the two inexperienced showrunners and spoke truthfully: "You guys have a massive problem." This grave pronouncement was noted (literally, in Sharpie and in all caps, on a pad of paper) by Benioff and Weiss, who realized they might have just blown it.

"Watching them watch that original pilot was one of the most painful experiences of my life," Benioff said during a live recording of Mazin's podcast, *Scriptnotes*, along with Weiss. "I mean, it's probably like appendicitis and that."

One of the biggest errors that came to light was how the pilot had failed to establish Jaime and Cersei Lannister as siblings, let alone twins. The whole final climax of the pilot occurs when young Bran Stark discovers Jaime and Cersei having sex, thus revealing to the audience that the queen and her brother are engaged in a covert incestuous relationship. But nobody in the viewing room understood the Lannister-sibling relationship, nor why that would lead to the presumed murder of a child.

More generally, the pilot seemed to be doing a poor job of establishing the very large cast of characters and their relation to one another—both familial and geographic.

"Craig [Mazin] didn't really have any brilliant ideas except he told us 'change everything,'" Benioff said. "And we believed him, because he was right."

Shortly after this first crash-and-burn trial run of the pilot, the two new showrunners had to repeat this horrific viewing process with HBO president Mike Lombardo. HBO hadn't yet signed off on a full first season run of ten episodes, so this was a major test.

"We needed to get to series," Weiss explained in a later *Vanity Fair* interview. "Mike came in. He had had enough waiting. And I was just staring at Mike's face. It was like a horror movie. Not Mike's *face*—which looked great—but his expressions."

Though Weiss remembers it as a horror story, Lombardo's own recollection of the first pilot was told more gently in the oral history published in *Fast Company*.

"The pilot was okay," Lombardo said. "It wasn't great. The casting was really good. We ended up reshooting, I don't know, 80 percent of that pilot, 90 percent of that pilot, but by that time we were in. We knew there was something amazing and we learned from our mistakes."

Lombardo was able to focus in on one key problem happening within that first attempt at a pilot.

"The weakness was that the show needed more scope," he said. "It screams for scope. You need to feel the landscapes of the different kingdoms, so it was a visualization and an execution that we learned from, and we learned to do it on a budget that made sense for us."

Plepler wasn't in the same room as Benioff and Weiss when he first saw this pilot with an all-caps "MASSIVE PROBLEM," but he was much more optimistic about the prospects of the show based on this hour of footage.

"We were told by someone who watched it with Richard that when it was done, he stood up and pumped his fist in the air, which was very far from our own reaction to the pilot we had shot," Weiss told *Fast Company*. "To his credit, he saw through the mistakes that we couldn't."

And so in early 2010, four years after meeting George R. R. Martin for the first time, Benioff and Weiss had to wait patiently to see if their shared dream would become a television reality. Weiss says it took around four months after the first pilot was turned in for the HBO executives to greenlight the full series.

"HBO was really on the fence about whether or not they were going to let this go to series," Weiss told *Variety* in a later interview. "And those were four of the longest months of both of our lives—sitting there thinking every day that this thing that was a once-in-a-lifetime opportunity that's never going to come by again, and we fucked it up. It would be one of those big fish stories, those one-that-got-away stories, you'd be telling for the rest of your life."

In spite of that first-lap stumble, Lombardo and Plepler decided to charge forward. On March 2, 2010, news outlets were buzzing with reports that HBO had officially greenlit *Game of Thrones*. Benioff estimated that an astonishing $10 million had already been spent on the first iteration of the pilot. According to the *Hollywood Reporter*, HBO eventually shelled out a total of $20 million before the final version of the pilot was completed. The entire first season was greenlit with a new $50 million total budget, and orders for reshoots were given.

"So what happened was, they said, 'O.K., the pilot's not so good, but we're just going to go ahead and make season one, and you'll reshoot the first episode while you're doing season one," Benioff told *Vanity Fair*.

"To be given the opportunity to do something like this one time is a pretty rare gift," he said. "To be given the opportunity to do more or less the exact same thing twice is an extremely rare gift."

Benioff and Weiss knew the responsibility and trust that was being handed over to them by both HBO and George R. R. Martin.

"In 2010, [Plepler] ordered a very expensive show set in a genre alien to pay TV, from two guys who had never written or run a show before, and whose first attempts at writing and producing the *Game of Thrones* pilot had fallen well short of expectations," Benioff and Weiss told Multichannel News years later. "And knowing all those things, he supported our show, and took a serious, potentially ruinous risk in doing so. Because he believed in it."

That belief wasn't doled out with zero caveats, however. Weiss and Benioff would later admit that it was clear they had to earn HBO's trust back in the year after they initially bombed the pilot.

"That first year felt very probationary," Benioff told *Variety* in 2015. "It was like, 'All right, these guys are probably not very good at this. Let's see what they can do. We've already sunk a lot of money into this pilot. Might as well get one season out of it.'"

As anyone who has taken an Econ 101 class will tell you, HBO subscribed to what's known as the Sunk Cost Fallacy, in which people will choose to continue spending money on something they think is bad because they've already sunk enough value in it, and they figure it'd be an even bigger waste of money to quit and walk away. Thankfully this fallacy isn't always correct, and we are forever indebted to HBO for not following behavioral economic theories to a T.

And perhaps no one can sum up the turnaround achieved by Benioff and Weiss better than that same friend, Craig Mazin, who first said they had a serious problem on their hands. Benioff and Weiss invited Mazin along to HBO's *Game of Thrones* premiere event in April 2011. Back then the premiere was a smallish affair, nothing over-the-top or celebratory in the way future red carpet premieres would be.

"One of the moments I will never forget is being invited to the premiere of the first season where they showed the first two episodes of the series," Mazin said on his *Scriptnotes* podcast. "So I went in just thinking, well, I'm going to see how this goes. And I sat there, and this show unfolds ... and I am stunned. Stunned."

Mazin told Benioff and Weiss on the podcast how shocking the pilot turnaround was.

"I very specifically remember walking out and you were there, and I said to you, 'That is the biggest rescue in Hollywood history,'" Mazin recalled. "Because it wasn't just that you had saved something bad and turned it really good. You had saved a complete piece of shit, and turned it into something brilliant. That never happens."

With their first big blunder out of the way, Benioff and Weiss had to wait and see if the world would become as captivated by George R. R. Martin's imagined universe as they had nearly six years prior.

We now know with the gift of hindsight that it worked the second time around, but why?

"Every single department stepped up," Benioff later told *Vanity Fair*. "As Dan was saying, certainly we hadn't done it before. I don't know if anyone had done this type of genre on this type of scale ... the difference between what we had originally shot and what you see in season one is dramatic."

For the first version of the pilot, Benioff and Weiss had hired director Tom McCarthy to be behind the camera. As McCarthy explained to the *AV Club* in a 2011 interview, he took the gig because he was between jobs and it would be a new challenge (McCarthy had primarily worked in film prior to this, including the breakout indie movie *The Station Agent* starring Peter Dinklage).

McCarthy said he had "very little" impact on the look and feel of the pilot, and by the time Benioff and Weiss realized they needed to reshoot the bulk of it, McCarthy was busy with another project and unable to return for another run.

"I couldn't do it. And I just didn't feel connected to it," McCarthy said. "It wasn't a big decision. It felt right."

"I think if you're going to do series television on any level, and if you want to enjoy it, you really have to understand the parameters of what you're doing, and have your team in place, and have your support network," McCarthy said. "I think the great shows, *The Wire, Sopranos, Six Feet Under*—I think there was a very clear understanding of whose show it was, and I think those guys who made those shows, there was a singular vision there."

And so McCarthy walked away, and Timothy Van Patten took over for reshoots of the pilot, and also directed the second episode of the debut season. In addition to a new director, Benioff and Weiss worked with casting director Nina Gold to get new faces into several key roles.

All of Catelyn Stark's scenes were reshot with new actress Michelle Fairley instead of Jennifer Ehle, who had decided to leave the project after reconsidering the lengthy time commitment. The role of Daenerys Targaryen was also recast, and the now famous Emilia Clarke stepped in for *Pride & Prejudice* and *The Tudors* actress Tamzin Merchant.

Martin was very active on his blog, then hosted on LiveJournal, at the time. He announced several of the changes there. One actor swap has become more meaningful in hindsight: the recasting of Ser Waymar Royce. He is the lordling in charge of the Night's Watch ranging mission that opens the entire series and goes horribly, deadly wrong.

"David and Dan and HBO have decided to reshoot the prologue sequence from the pilot," Martin wrote on *Not a Blog*. "For the very best of reasons, I think: to make it better. I've seen the pilot, or at least a rough cut thereof, and I thought the prologue sequence was quite good, actually. But this will be the opening scene of the entire series, the first introduction to the world of Westeros for millions of viewers, so 'quite good' was not good enough. We want to make it great."

Martin then explains how the reshoots become an issue when "life moves on and so do actors." One such actor was Jamie Campbell Bower, a young actor who Martin said "everyone loved" as Ser Waymar, but he had landed a role on the Starz *Camelot* series by the time HBO needed to do reshoots.

"Unfortunately, Jamie's shooting schedule with *Camelot* conflicted with our own, so there was no way he could come back and reprise his performance as Ser Waymar," Martin wrote. "But we wish him luck with his new (much larger) role ... and who knows, if *Game of Thrones* should happen to have a longer run than *Camelot*, maybe one day he can come back and play another (much larger) role for us."

By January 2019, nearly a decade later, *Camelot* was long gone and HBO had made new casting announcements for the first *Game of Thrones* prequel series, then in its pilot stage. One of the actors who landed a part was none other than Jamie Campbell Bower, making Martin a bit of a blogging prophet.

In addition to recastings, Benioff and Weiss reworked almost the entire pilot script. We know the details of what was changed between versions of the episode thanks to the Shavelson-Webb Library, where both a version of the original script from Benioff and Weiss and a new version (penned in 2010) are available for public perusal.

In broad strokes, the original pilot script pulls swaths of

George R. R. Martin's first chapters of *A Game of Thrones* onto its pages, often word for word. But the new version is a clear concession on Benioff and Weiss's behalf that some things don't translate straight from page to screen. They realized they needed to spoon-feed information to the audience and better explain the relationships between all of the characters and locations.

The original pilot opens precisely as Martin's first prologue chapter does, with three Night's Watch rangers (Ser Waymar Royce, Gared, and Will) beyond the Wall and already in the middle of tracking wildlings. However, the aired pilot begins with our three doomed rangers crossing beneath the Wall and beginning their journey north.

Benioff and Weiss were taking Lombardo's advice and giving the pilot a better sense of scope. By showing Castle Black and the Wall right away, the cold open is given a better sense of location.

Another change came with the description of Will's discovery of the wildling corpses and the White Walkers themselves, referred to as "Others" in the first script but White Walkers in the final version (Martin uses these terms interchangeably in the books).

When Will sees the corpses in the final pilot, their bodies are mangled and arranged in a pattern, something Benioff and Weiss invented for the show. Their script indicates that this was a "witchy mandala" designed to send a message and show that the White Walkers were not mindless animals. The change allows for Benioff and Weiss to establish that the White Walkers are sentient, inhuman beings with a culture and purpose.

And both versions of the script make it clear that the White Walkers speak a language humans cannot understand. Again, this is something Martin alludes to in his books when the Other speaks

MAESTER'S NOTES

The first attempt at a pilot had a different opening credits sequence than the one we've come to know and love. Benioff and Weiss originally used a raven flying with a message as the opening, showing the bird soaring over various locations. For the final pilot, Benioff and Weiss hired Angus Wall at the Santa Monica design firm Elastic to create the new opening credits sequence. As *Vanity Fair* reported, Wall had previously been hired by Carolyn Strauss (ex–HBO executive turned *Game of Thrones* producer) to do the credits for *Carnivale* and *Rome*.

Wall took this early idea of a raven flying over the various spotlight locations and re-imagined it as a digital camera's perspective with machinelike, da Vinci–esque inspirations. This is where we get the cogs of castles and sigils and the final shot of the astrolabe rotating around the sun with engravings that show the battle for the throne between the stag (Baratheon), lion (Lannister), wolf (Stark), and dragon (Targaryen).

By putting the map into an inverted sphere shape, the Elastic team was also helping Benioff and Weiss solve their challenge of properly establishing the geography of Westeros and Essos.

and Will thinks the voice sounds "like the cracking of ice on a winter lake."

The small tweaks only increase from there. Many of the changes are centered around Benioff and Weiss making more room for expository dialogue, like adding in Ser Waymar Royce telling Will he'd be executed "as a deserter" if he abandons his post. This happens again with the inclusion of a new opening Winterfell scene with Jon telling Bran that their father is watching the boys train, but specifically saying "and your mother" in order to tell audiences about Jon's bastardship.

Another obvious example of this spoon-feeding can be seen in the changes made to Cersei and Jaime's first scene together in the throne room. Benioff and Weiss rearranged this whole section to better establish the Lannisters' rivalry with the Starks, with Jon Arryn's death being the inciting event that will bring the two families in closer proximity. Here we get more pointed dialogue that tells the audience about Cersei and Jaime's sibling relationship, as well as her marriage to King Robert.

The scene kicks off with a not-so-subtle line from Jaime as he walks up to Cersei and begins with "As your brother..." Benioff and Weiss's friends had completely missed the sibling link between Cersei and Jaime for the first go-around, so they changed this scene's dialogue to make it extra clear that Cersei was married to the king, Jaime was her brother, and the two siblings had a secret big enough to get themselves killed if King Robert ever found out.

Not everything was redone, though. The copy of the 2010 script at the Writers Guild Foundation library has sections underlined by Benioff and Weiss to indicate where they planned on using old footage. The first of these recycled scenes comes nearly twenty-two minutes into the aired pilot, where we see a raven flying toward Winterfell with a scroll tied to its leg.

The second snippet of footage Benioff and Weiss managed to rescue from the first pilot is the shot of Bran climbing the walls of Winterfell and watching the king's party approaching the castle.

Once the travelers enter the Winterfell courtyard, we get another bout of exposition when Arya tells Sansa, "That's Jaime Lannister, the queen's twin brother!" as he takes off his helmet and looks around, and then later in the scene she asks Sansa "Where's the Imp?" as a way for the episode to lead into Tyrion Lannister's introduction.

Tyrion's R-rated brothel scene features the sex worker named Ros, played by Esmé Bianco. Nearly ten years later, Bianco carries an earned pride for having one of the only scenes that wasn't axed after the first pilot's filming.

"I was originally just called 'the red-headed whore,'" Bianco said during a spotlight panel at the second annual Con of Thrones in 2018. "I didn't have a name at that point. And I was only meant to do this one scene with [Tyrion] . . . and they reshot almost the entire pilot with the exception of my scene with Peter [Dinklage]."

You'll notice how Tyrion's hair is very blond and straight in this entire scene. In the books his hair is described as so blond "it seemed white," and so Benioff and Weiss tried out a wig on Peter Dinklage for the first version of the pilot. But by the final version, his natural hair was back. You can see his hair change within the pilot.

During the Con of Thrones panel, Bianco also revealed it was Martin who suggested her character be given a name. He was more closely involved with production back in those days, and when Benioff and Weiss continued to write scenes for Ros (who doesn't exist in the books), Martin pointed out she should be called something other than "red-headed whore."

The other scenes saved from the "piece of shit" pilot include Ned and Robert's conversations in the crypts (Sean Bean's hair looks a tad greasier in those original scenes) and shots from the feast at Winterfell when Ned speaks with both Benjen and Jaime. Once again you can tell thanks to the change in Sean Bean's hairstyling.

The first run of the pilot's feast scene included Jaime and Ned talking about the Mad King, Aerys II Targaryen, and how he executed Rickard and Brandon Stark. Instead of cramming this into the pilot, Benioff and Weiss moved the exchange to the third episode of the season, "Lord Snow." That way when Ned and Jaime speak bitterly of the Mad King and Ned's father in the throne room, it helps contextualize the events of Robert's Rebellion.

Given how much of the first season of *Game of Thrones* relies on an unfolding understanding of Robert's Rebellion and the way it impacted our various lead characters (Ned, Cersei, Jaime, Catelyn, and Littlefinger, to name just a few), it's no surprise that Benioff and Weiss first tested out the possibility of using flashback scenes.

One of the most legendary aspects of the unseen pilot is a flashback scene that showed Ned's father and brother killed on the orders of the Mad King. A small flash of this scene made it into two of the early *Game of Thrones* promotional videos and trailers released by HBO.

In the footage, which lasts barely a second, a man who looks an awful lot like Ned Stark is struggling against a rope tied around his neck (rumor has it the man in this scene was Sean Bean's body double, which is why he so resembles the Ned we've come to know). Blood covers his face, and he's clearly in anguish. In the blurred background of the shot we can see the Iron Throne and a blond king upon it.

Book-readers knew the details of this scene intimately: Brandon Stark (Ned's older brother) stormed into the city following Prince Rhaegar's "abduction" of Lyanna Stark and demanded the prince fight him. Brandon wanted answers about his sister's whereabouts, but the Mad King arrested him and then summoned Lord Rickard Stark to answer for his son's perceived crime of plotting to kill the prince.

Upon Lord Rickard's arrival, Aerys had both men sentenced to death in a heinous manner. He had Brandon tied to the floor with a rope around his neck and his sword just out of reach while Lord Rickard was dressed in full armor and strung up in the air above a burning fire. Brandon strangled himself while trying to reach the sword so he could cut his father down, and Lord Rickard was roasted alive in his own armor.

Because of the small snippet of footage HBO released showing Brandon's death, we know this flashback scene was filmed (at least part of it) for the first season of *Game of Thrones*. But Benioff and Weiss chose to stay far away from the flashbacks and dreams as vehicles for exposition.

"The decision to not include flashbacks was made right off the bat," writer Bryan Cogman said in an MTV interview. "The principle reason for that is a logistical and budgetary one . . . We already had the biggest cast in, maybe, TV history."

According to Cogman, during that first season of filming they simply didn't have the budget to cast a whole additional generation of players for the "nineteen years earlier" flashbacks.

"The other reason is, that's a perfect example of what works in a book that doesn't work on TV," Cogman continued. "The book does brilliantly flash back through memory, and through people telling stories of the past. If you were to just take those passages from the book and do them onscreen, you would be doing a flashback every five minutes! It would be very jarring, and very difficult to sustain the momentum that you want to sustain."

So the scene with Brandon's and Rickard's deaths was cut, and instead Benioff and Weiss relied on exposition through dialogue to explain the history of the intersecting rivalries between Houses Stark, Lannister, and Targaryen. But those early promotional videos are still available on YouTube, which means that every once in a while a still frame or slowed-down GIF of the scene makes its way online and into fan conversations about "what could have been" when it comes to the show's pilot.

Daenerys's wedding to Khal Drogo had to be totally redone thanks to the new casting of Emilia Clarke in the lead role. George R. R. Martin had made a cameo in the original version of this scene, which was filmed in Morocco. But the whole section, and therefore his cameo, was axed.

"It was, sad to say, left on the cutting-room floor," Martin said in a *Daily Beast* interview ahead of the first season premiere. "It was during Daenerys' wedding and I was a Pentoshi nobleman in the background, wearing a gigantic hat."

Though Benioff and Weiss planned on making it up to Martin by incorporating a new cameo into the fourth season, the appearance never happened.

Last but not least, the episode returns to Winterfell one last time, and we get our final salvaged scene from the original footage. Tyrion (blond again) sits next to the Hound (whose burned-face prosthetics are recognizably different from the future episodes) and Theon Greyjoy crosses the courtyard to hand Ned his gloves. Here we have yet another look at Ol' Greasy Ned, and you can see that Alfie Allen's Theon hair is much more blond than it appears in the rest of the series.

The men leave for the hunt, and we're brought at last to Bran's accidental discovery of the most actively treasonous secret in Westeros: Jaime and Cersei Lannister are not simply twins but lovers, and the parents of three bastard children who King Robert believes are his own.

We all know what happens next. The final scene of both versions comes down to the same dramatic moment they first outlined in the show bible: "'The things I do for love,' Jaime says, and throws Bran out the tower window."

As badly as our curiosity might burn, us regular-Joe fans will never see that first "complete piece of shit" pilot. Benioff and Weiss have pledged to keep it far from the eyes of fans, though they showed it to a bulk of the cast at a viewing party before the series finale's premiere night in New York City in April 2019. Before seeing it, actor Kit Harington used to talk about how Benioff and Weiss would threaten their stars with the footage.

"I didn't know what I was doing," Harington admitted in 2018 when asked by BBC about that first run of scenes. "And apparently it was a disaster. I still haven't seen it—they blackmail me every now and again, threatening that they'll release bits on YouTube, because apparently it was terrible and I had this awful wig."

"But sometimes the things that end up being huge successes, they start with huge failures," he continued. He does know some things, that Jon Snow.

Now that we know how *Game of Thrones* got its stumbling start, it's time to look back at how the cast (including Kit and his bad wig) wound up on that set to begin with.

CHAPTER FOUR

CASTING CALL
of a LIFETIME

Emilia. Kit. Sophie. Maisie. Lena. Peter. Nikolaj. Names that, prior to the most recent decade, had little to no meaning on their own in our catalog of screen celebrities. But with the first *Game of Thrones* season premiere, the world was introduced to what would eventually become the iconic faces of Daenerys Targaryen, Jon Snow, Tyrion Lannister, and more.

The adult cast was comprised of actors who had varying roles in successful movies. Lena Headey appeared in Zack Snyder's *300*, and Peter Dinklage's breakout role in *The Station Agent* was memorable, along with his minor part as a snippy children's book author in the 2003 Christmas movie *Elf*.

The exception spotted early on in the casting announcements was Sean Bean, a familiar face in fantasy settings who was still buoyed by his stoic (and often-memed) role as Boromir in *The Lord of the Rings: The Fellowship of the Ring*. This approach to the ensemble was a clever decision by casting director Nina Gold, and it served two main purposes.

First, it was more budget-friendly to cast relatively unknown actors. Since Benioff and Weiss were working with tight costs for their first season, it made sense not to blow that money on recognizable faces. Second, by casting Sean Bean in Ned Stark's role, Benioff and Weiss were using audience expectations to their advantage. The shock of Ned's death would be compounded by the fact that he had been the most famous face on the show up to that point.

Since the characters were aged up significantly from the books—and the actors often older than their fictional counterparts—the discrepancies between the age of the characters and the age of the actors at the start of filming season one are noted.

JON SNOW

(or, uh, Starkgaryen?)

———— ⋘ ⋙ ————

Played by: Kit Harington
Age of character in ASOIAF: 14
Age of character on Game of Thrones: 16
Actor's age at the start of filming: 21

Harington was twenty years old and just one year out of drama school when Nina Gold had him come in to audition for *Game of Thrones*. He had just finished starring in a West End production of *War Horse*, the only paid acting gig on his résumé so far.

"I remember he was quite tired because he'd been doing eight shows a week of *War Horse* for a year," Gold said in an interview with *INSIDER*. "Then he started doing the audition and playing Jon Snow, and he was completely brilliant. I do recall the emotional impact of his audition and being blown away. Kit is a phenomenal actor."

In addition to his acting prowess, Kit was showing off a black eye. According to Kit's retelling of the story in a *W* magazine feature, the night before his audition he had gone out on a date with a girl. At the end of the night, they wound up sharing a table at a crowded McDonald's with an unsavory man who began verbally harassing Kit's date.

"Then he called her something, like an ugly pig or something worse, and I got up and said, 'No, no, no you can't call her that—get up,'" Harington said. "So I called him up for a fight, which I had never done before. And of course he'd been sat down the whole time so he got up and he just kept going. I just kind of realized that I had to at that point throw the first punch otherwise I'd look like a complete wimp. And I got battered."

Though Kit says he thinks the black eye may have helped him get the job, Nina Gold said in an interview with *INSIDER* that she can't remember him having a shiner at all.

"I'm afraid I don't recall his black eye," Gold said. "All I remember is that he was really, really mind-blowingly good."

EDDARD "NED" STARK

Played by: Sean Bean
Age of character in ASOIAF: 34
Age of character on Game of Thrones: 41
Actor's age at the start of filming: 51

Sean Bean was one of the few actors who didn't even need to audition for a part on *Game of Thrones*. From the moment Benioff and Weiss first encountered A Song of Ice and Fire, they were dream-casting the roles as they read. Nina Gold told *Vanity Fair*'s Joanna Robinson they simply had a "nice lunch" with Sean Bean, and thankfully their planned leading man was onboard.

"I thought it was a very courageous move for a television company," Bean told *Entertainment Weekly*. "I know HBO has a track record of bold moves, but I thought this is pretty incredible if they can pull this off."

CATELYN "CAT" STARK
(née Tully)

Played by: Michelle Fairley
Age in ASOIAF: 33
Age on Game of Thrones: 40
Actor's age at the start of filming: 47

Michelle Fairley came to the role of Lady Catelyn after the first ill-fated pilot was filmed with Jennifer Ehle.

"It's terrible to disappoint," casting director Nina Gold also told Robinson when reflecting on the need to recast roles. "It's difficult to let down . . . that's hard. It's tough, but you've got to get it right, ultimately. Jennifer Ehle is really brilliant, but I guess things changed about the way everybody saw it."

Ehle had reportedly decided she couldn't commit to the long-term project that would be *Game of Thrones* (Catelyn may have been doomed, but four years is still a lengthy time to be holed up in Northern Ireland). Benioff was the one who found Michelle Fairley when he went to a London play, according to *Inside Game of Thrones*.

"I first saw Michelle Fairley when she played Emilia in the Donmar Warehouse's production of *Othello* in London," Benioff revealed in the book. "Emilia's not a character I generally notice in *Othello*. Iago's wife? Who cares? But Michelle was so absurdly good that I left the theater thinking, 'Who the hell was that? And is she available?'"

ROBB STARK

Played by: Richard Madden
Age of character in ASOIAF: 14
Age of character on Game of Thrones: 16
Actor's age at the start of filming: 21

Richard Madden was one of the younger actors who auditioned for multiple roles. His auburn coloring ultimately led to the perfect fit with Robb Stark, the Young Wolf and future King in the North. He changed up his natural Scottish accent to match Sean Bean's Yorkshire-based dialect (which served as the basis for the way all Northern-born characters would speak on *Game of Thrones*).

But oddly enough, it wasn't his presence in a London play or anything prestigious that first piqued Gold's or the showrunner's interest.

"At first we just liked Richard because he was the odds-on favorite for 2009's Best-Dressed Man in Scotland Award," Weiss revealed in *Inside Game of Thrones*. "He did indeed win, and in addition to his clothes, we got an amazing talent. He manages to be both period-appropriate and totally natural. . . . There's an easygoing quality to the character that comes from Richard himself, and it acts like an armor against all ponderousness."

SANSA STARK

Played by: Sophie Turner
Age of character in ASOIAF: 11
Age of character on Game of Thrones: 13
Actor's age at the start of filming: 14

Sophie Turner came to the role of Sansa Stark via a casting call put out at her local school, where she was taking acting as an elective. Turner had never performed professionally or even auditioned for a paid role before.

"They just went around normal schools, and my drama teacher just threw me in with a bunch of my other friends and we all auditioned together," Turner told *The Hollywood Reporter*'s Scott Feinberg for an episode of the *Awards Chatter* podcast. Turner says the drama teacher didn't tell the kids anything about what they were auditioning for, nor were her parents notified.

"I didn't know HBO, I didn't know *Game of Thrones*, I didn't know George R. R. Martin, I barely knew what TV was," Turner said. "[The teacher] just kind of brought a ton of us up to the front of the class at one time and said 'You guys are going to audition for this because you fit the bill.'"

Turner described the process as very lax, and since one of the drama teachers brushed it off as just "good experience" with no real prospects, Turner didn't think to tell her mom about the lunchtime audition.

"My mum only found out when she got a call from Nina Gold, the casting director, being like 'Hey, Sophie is in the final seven,'" Turner said. "And she was like 'For what? What has my child done now?'"

Once she was in the final group, Turner returned for four call-backs that included her auditioning some scenes with the prospective Arya Starks. That was where she and Maisie Williams first met and their lifelong, shimmering soul-mate friendship begun.

ARYA STARK

Played by: Maisie Williams
Age of character in ASOIAF: 9
Age of character on Game of Thrones: 11
Actor's age at the start of filming: 13

The scene Maisie Williams recorded for her audition was the same one a young Sophie Turner had filmed during her lunch break at school. It's a scene straight from the pages of *A Game of Thrones*, when Sansa tells Arya that they're supposed to spend the day traveling on the Kingsroad with Queen Cersei Lannister and Princess Myrcella Baratheon.

Though the scene was ultimately cut from the actual episode (season one, episode two, "The Kingsroad"), it's a perfect encapsulation of the ladylike Sansa butting heads with her wild, lowborn-befriending sister, Arya.

"One of the very last [kids] we saw was Maisie's face on Cast It—the name of the program we cast with—and the window is this big," Weiss said at the 2013 Emmys panel, holding his fingers up to make a minuscule square and gesturing over to Williams. "We just saw that face, this big, and we were like, 'Please be good.'"

"We were on a location scout in Morocco and we're at the hotel that had very, very dodgy internet connection," Benioff added.

"So while we clicked on the link for Maisie's audition and [while] waiting—"

"And watching the little line [load]," Weiss said.

"And all the time just seeing this tiny little thumbnail picture of a face that looked so perfect, and waiting and waiting and waiting," Benioff said. "Then it was perfect."

"It was literally ten seconds into the audition, we were like 'Yup, she's the one,'" Weiss added.

Williams, who was barely a teenager when the show began filming, was deemed by her parents too young to read the sex-and-violence-filled books. But her mom read through the books on her behalf and was the first person who told Williams that Arya was left-handed. Williams, a righty, was worried about how difficult it would be to use her left hand for the coming sword fighting with Needle. She wanted to make sure that book fans were pleased.

"When I was practicing out in the garden and things I would do left-handed just to feel that rhythm," Williams told *TV Guide* in 2011. "Unfortunately, when it came to filming, sometimes I have to do things right-handed because of the camera angle and things like that. So some people are a bit annoyed that Arya hasn't done everything left-handed. I wanted to. I really did. But sometimes it was just too tricky and we couldn't do it."

DAENERYS TARGARYEN

————— ❧❧ —————

Played by: Emilia Clarke
Age of character in ASOIAF: 13
Age of character on Game of Thrones: 15
Actor's age at the start of filming: 24

Like her future onscreen lover Kit Harington, Emilia Clarke was one year out of drama school and had very little to show for it, résumé-wise, at the time of her *Game of Thrones* audition. Ten years later, when accepting the Britannia Award at the 2018 British Academy of Film and Television Arts celebration, Clarke said her gig before *Game of Thrones* was as a kids' party caterer where she wore a Snow White costume. ("Be kind to your servers, everyone," she said. "They might be thanking you in a speech someday.")

"We knew as soon as we saw her audition video on a three-inch laptop [screen] that we had found our girl," Benioff and Weiss told *Vogue* for their feature on Clarke in 2015. "So when we went into the casting director's office to meet her, it was more a question of 'Please don't be difficult or insane.' Not only was Emilia not difficult or insane, she was adorable, grounded, relaxed, and funny."

Emilia Clarke's audition for the powerhouse role of Daenerys Targaryen is now something like a Hollywood legend.

"I was very nervous, it was a big-deal audition obviously," Clarke recalled on *The Tonight Show with Jimmy Fallon*. "I was kind of anxious and did all of the scenes and then at the end David Benioff—gorgeous David Benioff, one of the writers—I was asking them if I can do anything else . . . and David Benioff suggested I do a dance."

Clarke realized too late that Benioff was just messing around with her. She promptly began doing a robot/funky chicken combo routine, much to her later embarrassment.

"I heard some laughter going on and I thought, 'Comedy gold! This is brilliant, I'm nailing it,'" Clarke said.

THEON GREYJOY

Played by: Alfie Allen
Age of character in ASOIAF: 18
Age of character on Game of Thrones: 17
Actor's age at the start of filming: 24

Alfie Allen remains one of the most underrated actors on *Game of Thrones*, with no major award nominations honoring his phenomenal work as a supporting character. His run as Theon, a young man at once arrogant and insecure, desperate and broken, is one of the strongest side-character arcs in the series. Allen was one of the original cast members who, like Richard Madden, was actually brought in for another role.

"The odd thing is, Alfie [Allen] originally came in to read for Jon Snow," Benioff said on the season five DVD commentary. "And we thought, 'Well he's great ... he's not quite Jon Snow.' And then we thought, 'Wait a second, Theon!' And he read for Theon and he was just incredible."

We should all be grateful for this light-bulb moment, since Alfie Allen went on to gorgeously portray Theon's conflicted, damaging, and redemptive arc over the course of eight seasons.

YARA GREYJOY

―――――― ❦❧ ――――――

Played by: Gemma Whelan
Age of character in ASOIAF: 22
Age of character on Game of Thrones: 29
Actor's age at the start of filming: 30

Alfie Allen got off easy with his Jon Snow–turned–Theon Greyjoy audition, compared to Gemma Whelan, the actress who played his sister, Yara, starting in the second season. She had to audition with the cringeworthy scene from her character's introduction, where Theon and Yara engage in some very NSFW fondling before our young Iron Island prince knows it's his sister he's sharing a horse with.

But, as Whelan revealed on *The Graham Norton Show*, the audition scene was written with the roles reversed. Instead of Theon feeling up Yara, the audition version had Yara "worrying his cock" (her words!) while they rode on horseback. This meant Whelan was sitting alone in the audition room and miming the vulgar, incestuous sex act.

"I had to do that in my audition, on a chair looking straight ahead—very, very dramatically, with just one casting director in the room and a very ashamed cameraman going, 'That's not how you do it,'" Whelan said before cracking herself up and miming a pearl-clutching cameraperson.

◇◇◇◇◇◇◇◇◇◇ MAESTER'S NOTES ◇◇◇◇◇◇◇◇◇◇

Yara Greyjoy's name is Asha in the ASOIAF books. It was changed because the *Game of Thrones* showrunners were concerned people would mix up Asha with Osha, the wildling who helped Bran and Rickon escape Winterfell, played by Natalia Tena.

KHAL DROGO

Played by: Jason Momoa
Age of character in ASOIAF: 31
Age of character on Game of Thrones: 31
Actor's age at the start of filming: 30

Both intimidating in his stature and yet clearly possessing an infectious warmth that makes you want to melt into his bear hug, Jason Momoa has entered into the zeitgeist and been a welcome treasure for fans. The fearsome Khal Drogo is described to us through Daenerys's chapters in A Song of Ice and Fire, leaving him more abstract (and inappropriately older than his young bride) than the Dothraki warrior we saw Momoa bring to life onscreen starting in 2011.

"Jason Momoa came in and, of his own free will, after doing his audition he did the Haka—the Maori war dance," Weiss said at the 2013 Emmys panel. "Which was not written into the scene. It actually didn't have anything to do with the scene. But I would say he impressed us. He did the hell out of it, he really did it."

Grainy footage of this audition Haka has since made its way online, where you can see Momoa thumping his chest, tongue out, passionately performing the ceremonial dance. It's not difficult to see why Benioff and Weiss knew right away he was the perfect Khal Drogo.

Having secured the role, the next big step for Momoa was meeting his onscreen wife, Emilia Clarke. The two arrived in Belfast on the same day and happened to get to the hotel around the same time.

"I walked in, and from the other side of this enormous lobby I hear 'Wifey!'" Clarke said in a *Rolling Stone* video. "And this huge

Hawaiian man comes bounding over to me, picks me up, and genuinely gets me in a rugby tackle to the floor. It was only when he picked me back up and kind of dusted me off that I was like, 'Who are you?'"

TYRION LANNISTER

Played by: Peter Dinklage
Age of character in ASOIAF: 24
Age of character on Game of Thrones: 32
Actor's age at the start of filming: 40

Benioff and Weiss told TV critic Alan Sepinwall at *Uproxx* they had a five-hour meeting back when *Game of Thrones* was still a shoot-the-moon possibility. Before they had even written scripts, the pair agreed that Sean Bean and Peter Dinklage would be perfect as Ned Stark and Tyrion Lannister. "They were the first choices for those parts, and really the only choices," the showrunners said.

Benioff sent the actor an email even before the agreement with HBO was finalized. The two had met before, possibly at a dinner, as Benioff recalled at the 2013 *Game of Thrones* Emmys panel.

"He ignored me—talked to my wife the whole night," said Benioff, whose wife, Amanda Peet, is a well-known actress in her own right. "But I remember thinking he was really smart and he's very funny—as we've seen tonight . . . so I sent him a note and [he] had already heard about the books and the character, I think. And then we met and remember what you said? You had one demand."

Dinklage nodded as Benioff talked, smiling grimly.

"No beards," Dinklage said while miming a long beard. "I just never understood why, in fantasy, dwarves always have long beards.

No offense to Mr. Tolkien, and you know, I think I had just done the Narnia movie a couple years before."

The actor had a small role as a dwarf named Trumpkin in the 2008 film *The Chronicle of Narnia: Prince Caspian*, and clearly Dinklage was not looking to replicate the experience of wearing a bald cap and lengthy beard on set.

Though Tyrion grew a short beard later in the series, Martin's character is devoid of the stereotypes typically associated with little people in fantasy stories. Dinklage and Martin, both from New Jersey, have become great friends in the years since he signed on to the project.

CERSEI LANNISTER

Played by: Lena Headey
Age of character in ASOIAF: 33
Age of character on Game of Thrones: 38
Actor's age at the start of filming: 36

Lena Headey came to be synonymous with the golden-haired Cersei Lannister thanks to both Peter Dinklage and her uncanny ability to mine the depths of the villainous character's hubris, cruelty, and ambition. Headey costarred in a 2010 movie with Dinklage called *Pete Smalls Is Dead*. While working with Headey, Dinklage saw something in her performance that led him to think she would play his onscreen sibling wonderfully.

"During filming, her co-star Peter Dinklage mentioned 'this mad thing' he was reading for HBO, adding that 'there's this great part for his sister, who's this incestuous psychopath,' Ms. Headey recalled," *New York Times* reporter Jeremy Egner wrote in a 2017 profile of the actress.

Dinklage's instincts were spot-on. She landed the role of Cersei, and her and Dinklage's offscreen rapport helped bring a riveting dynamism to their shared scenes on *Game of Thrones*, and helped House Lannister become the most revered set of characters and performances in the whole series.

JAIME LANNISTER

Played by: Nikolaj Coster-Waldau
Age of character in ASOIAF: 33
Age of character on Game of Thrones: 38
Actor's age at the start of filming: 39

Danish actor Nikolaj Coster-Waldau was tasked with one of the most complex character journeys in the series. When Martin published a LiveJournal post announcing Coster-Waldau's casting in 2009, very little was known about the man who would play Jaime Lannister. But he did have at least one superfan out in the world.

"When he was cast, I went searching for him on the internet," Martin wrote in his blog post accompanied by an embedded video. "I found this on YouTube and couldn't resist. Watch that, and I think you'll agree, he'll make a terrific Jaime."

The video is poetically titled "2 Good 2 be true - Nikolaj" (created by a user named poetsNmadmen and uploaded on January 23, 2008). Set to Muse's cover of the 1960s song "Can't Take My Eyes Off You," the video is a mashup of scenes from nearly every role Coster-Waldau had played in both movies and on TV, including *Black Hawk Down* and the one-season Fox series *New Amsterdam*. Quite frankly, this video belongs in some sort of Museum of Prescient YouTube Oddities, and we should all be grateful for its existence.

MAESTER'S NOTES

In August 2017, *Variety* reported the estimated per-episode salaries for the five core *Game of Thrones* stars—Emilia Clarke, Kit Harington, Peter Dinklage, Lena Headey, and Nikolaj Coster-Waldau—was $500,000. But then in 2018, a contract dispute and subsequent court appearance led to Coster-Waldau's *Game of Thrones* contract entering public record via courtroom filings when the case went to arbitration. The contract revealed Coster-Waldau was paid $942,857 per episode in season seven, and that number was boosted to $1,066,667 for the six episodes of the final season. This means we can assume Emilia, Kit, Peter, and Lena were compensated the same total of approximately $6.4 million each for the eighth season of *Game of Thrones* alone.

RECASTS

Aside from earlier noted pilot episode recasts, a number of the recurring roles on *Game of Thrones* were swapped out with different actors between seasons. Some of these were subtle, but others were so blatant they became memeified parts of people's rewatches and recaps.

The first was Princess Myrcella. Sister to Joffrey and Tommen, Myrcella was originally played by then twelve-year-old Aimee Richardson for the first two seasons. Actress Nell Tiger Free, who celebrated her fifteenth birthday on the *Game of Thrones* set in 2014, took over as Myrcella for the fifth season, when Myrcella was a little more grown up and ready to get married.

When the news broke that Richardson was out as Myrcella, she shared a Vine to her followers on social media. Filmed in black-and-white, the video loop showed Richardson sitting on a sidewalk, holding a sign that said "Princess for hire." The accompanying tweet simply said, "Well this is embarrassing."

Prince Tommen was played by Callum Wharry for the first three seasons of the show (you'll notice him especially during the final moments of "Blackwater" when Cersei comes extremely close to poisoning him on the Iron Throne when she thinks Stannis Baratheon will win the battle). Dean-Charles Chapman took over as Tommen for the fourth season, likely because the showrunners needed to age up the character for his coming marriage consummation with Margaery Tyrell. Chapman stayed in the role until Tommen's suicide by self-defenestration in the sixth season finale.

Eagle-eyed *Game of Thrones* fans may have recognized Chapman as having already played another Lannister in the series. He was cast as the minor character Martyn Lannister for the third season. Martyn was held prisoner by Robb Stark in Riverrun, where Robb's wife, Talisa Maegyr, tended to the young Lannister's wounds. Rickard Karstark and other rebellious lords killed Martyn and his brother as revenge for Jaime Lannister being set free, which led to Robb executing the liege lord and losing a faction of his army.

Gregor "the Mountain" Clegane was briefly played by Conan Stevens. We saw him up-close in the Hand's tourney in season one, when he was unseated by Ser Loras Tyrell and brutally killed his horse out of anger, then fought against his brother, Sandor "the Hound" Clegane. But the Mountain was recast for the second season, when actor Ian Whyte (who looks quite similar to Stevens) took over briefly. He appeared in the council room with Tywin Lannister when Arya is serving as their cupbearer.

But then a third Mountain came along to fight in Tyrion's trial by combat, first appearing in season four, episode seven, "Mockingbird." Icelandic strongman Hafþór Júlíus Björnsson portrayed the Mountain from season four until the series' end. Since he was the version of the Mountain who fought and killed Oberyn Martell, and turned into the zombified "Ser Robert Strong" (as he's known in the books), Björnsson's version of Gregor Clegane is the most iconic of the three.

Another early season-one role that got recast was that of Beric Dondarrion, the Lightning Lord and the man Ned Stark sent to the Riverlands in order to deal with our aforementioned Gregor Clegane. David Michael Scott played Beric for that small scene in the first season, but Richard Dormer was cast in the role by the time the third season rolled around, and remained our Beric until the final episodes.

Daario Naharis, the sellsword who catches the eye of Daenerys and helps secure her victories in Yunkai, was played by Ed Skrein for the latter part of season three. His long hair and beardless face were distinctive (though nothing like the goofy way Daario is described in the books, with his beard dyed blue and shaped in three prongs underneath a dyed gold mustache and a large nose).

But on the premiere episode of the fourth season, the show had to reintroduce the character, this time with Dutch actor Michiel Huisman in the role. Now Daario had short, dark hair and a scruffy beard—still different from book-Daario, but nothing like Ed Skrein's version of the character. He stuck around until Daenerys bade Daario farewell at the end of the sixth season, leaving him in charge of Meereen.

Bran met the three-eyed raven, also known as Bloodraven, for the first time at the very end of season four. The magical tree-dweller was played by Struan Rodger for this short scene. Then Bran and Bloodraven were offscreen for the entirety of season five, and by the time the duo returned for the sixth season, the role had been recast. Max von Sydow took on the role of the three-eyed raven for three episodes until the character's death.

Leaf—one of the Children of the Forest—was also introduced on the season four finale. Back then she was played by Octavia Selena Alexandru. But when Leaf turned up on season six, Kae Alexander was in the role. Leaf died, along with the three-eyed raven (and Hodor) in the fifth episode of season six, "The Door."

In season five, actor Richard Brake wore a lot of prosthetics to transform into the Night King for the epic massacre at Hard-home. His version of the Night King is perhaps the most memed, thanks to the eerily silent way he raises his arms while staring down Jon Snow. But on season six, the same prosthetics were applied to new cast member Vladimír Furdík. The effect is the same, but you can tell there's a slightly different-shaped face under all the makeup.

Furdík is the man we see Leaf turn into the Night King during one of Bran's weirwood visions, and it's his Night King who attacks Bran in the cave in season six and takes down one of Dany's dragons in season seven. Furdík finishes the role of the Night King for the eighth and final season with his death at the Battle of Winterfell.

Lastly, Samwell Tarly's brother, Dickon, was played by Freddie Stroma when Sam and Gilly visited Horn Hill on the sixth season. But when Dickon turns up in season seven and is killed by Daenerys after the "Spoils of War" episode, a new actor was in the role. Tom Hopper and his arm muscles were an instantly more memorable take on the small role of Dickon Tarly. May he (and his arms) rest in peace.

CHAPTER FIVE

◇◇◇◇◇◇◇◇◇◇◇◇◇◇◇◇◇◇◇◇◇◇◇

WHERE *in the* WORLD IS WESTEROS?

Ten years before Martin began writing A Song of Ice and Fire, he took his first trip to the United Kingdom and visited Hadrian's Wall, a stone barrier that served as the Roman Empire's northwest frontier starting around 122 A.D.

"I stood on Hadrian's Wall and tried to imagine what it would be like to be a Roman soldier sent here from Italy or Antioch," Martin said in a 2000 interview with the digital sci-fi magazine *SFSite.* "To stand here, to gaze off into the distance, not knowing what might emerge from the forest. Of course fantasy is the stuff of bright colours and being larger than real life, so my Wall is bigger and considerably longer and more magical. And, of course, what lies beyond it has to be more than just Scots."

This visit to Hadrian's Wall, along with the idea of summer snows and a young boy witnessing an execution, was one of the first inklings of A Song of Ice and Fire to take root in Martin's mind. Later, fans would realize that the drawn maps populating the introductory pages of each Ice and Fire book were spitting images of the UK and Ireland—just flipped upside down and reversed.

If you keep the area of England where Hadrian's Wall remains today as the seven-hundred-foot-high version that towers over northern Westeros, and flip Ireland over to where the English Channel is, there are uncanny parallels between this part of our humble little planet and Westeros.

Eventually, Northern Ireland served as more than just inspiration for the shape of Westeros. When Benioff and Weiss had to decide on a home base for the production of *Game of Thrones*, the small country captured their attention for good reason. The natural landscapes of Northern Ireland were varied enough to become the perfect setting for more than two dozen *Game of Thrones* locations. Benioff and Weiss needed access to castles and lush meadows and harbors and forests and quarries—all on a tight budget.

"Northern Ireland offers a broad array of diverse locations within a short drive," Benioff wrote for *Inside Game of Thrones*. "Windswept hilltops, stony beaches, lush meadows, high cliffs, bucolic streams—we can shoot a day at any of these places and still sleep that night in Belfast."

The country is relatively small, about the size of the state of Connecticut, so having that variety all within several hours' drive is remarkable. Belfast is also home to Titanic Studios—a massive indoor filming lot where the sets for the Red Keep and throne room were built, along with interior settings like castle rooms and dungeons. Prior to the *Game of Thrones* takeover, Titanic Studios was used for the 2011 stoner-fantasy comedy *Your Highness* and

the 2008 movie adaptation of a popular YA sci-fi story called *City of Ember*.

Judith Webb is a development officer at the Tourism Northern Ireland agency in Belfast. She has spent an impressive twenty total years at the agency, but more recently her focus has been exclusively on "screen tourism"—an industry built from scratch in Northern Ireland thanks to *Game of Thrones*.

"We had no reason to have screen tourism before *Game of Thrones*," Webb said in an interview. "It's been a whole learning curve. But to work on the biggest show in the world is amazing, in terms of the spinoff for tourism."

"Screen tourism" is a sector of the agency that was built out after people realized fans were taking it upon themselves to travel to Northern Ireland and seek out various *Game of Thrones* filming locations. Nobody had anticipated just how huge the series was going to get while it was in the nascent stages. But when the locals started noticing an uptick in tourists, the opportunity to promote Northern Ireland was quickly taken up by Webb and her team.

"It's been quite a journey, and really all through that journey we're building the awareness and more and more people are coming," Webb said. "We're also building the immersive experiential offers beyond just coming and visiting. There are guided location tours, helicopter tours, treks, archery classes, and banquets—quite a lot of experiences that fans can really immerse themselves in as well as the filming locations."

As Webb explains it, *Game of Thrones* has brought a new level of excitement and pride to the locals. "A lot of people, all the extras really, are from Northern Ireland," she said. "Thousands of extras over ten years, and people have been really excited to be involved."

She talked about one man she knows who is passionate about

acting and has managed to be an extra on almost every season of *Game of Thrones*. One of the most memorable days he had on set was during an epic multiday shoot for the "Battle of the Bastards" sequence. He was playing one of the many unnamed soldiers caught up in the claustrophobic slaughter.

"He was saying he was piled up for days on end, stuck side by side with this guy, and of course they started a conversation," Webb recounted. "It turns out the guy he was lying on top of was a consulting surgeon, and this surgeon said, 'I just had to do this once, I had to be an extra once before it all went away.' And here he was rolling around [in] the muck and then the next day going and performing an amazing operation.

"So, there are all these really interesting, random stories and how it's affecting so many people's lives here," Webb continued. "And it's broken down barriers as well. It's just all the different stories are just intriguing."

Another man Webb knows was an extra on set for a battle scene in season eight. He had a full beard and "good head of hair," as Webb tells it, and went in for hair and makeup on a Friday night, expecting to be turned into a Westerosi soldier. But it turned out he had been cast as one of the bald eunuchs who make up Dany's Unsullied army.

"They said, 'Look, even though you're wearing a helmet and nobody will see your hair, we will be shaving your hair off and taking your beard, too,'" Webb recounted. He turned up for work on Monday fully bald, but with some extra cash in his bank account and a great story.

Game of Thrones did more than boost the local acting community's opportunities. From the start, Benioff and Weiss and the HBO team worked to hire local crew members whenever possible.

"People are proud," Webb said. "Somebody who maybe started [on the *Game of Thrones* crew] as a gofer or making tea or coffee or whatever is now, over the course of ten years, been trained in so many different ways and might be behind the camera now or performing a totally skill-based function."

The most noteworthy of these local crew members is Helen Sloan, the principal set photographer for *Game of Thrones*. From unit stills to promotional portraits of characters or behind-the-scenes snapshots, Sloan is responsible for nearly every *Game of Thrones*–related image you've seen.

In an interview with *Tech Insider* ahead of the season six premiere, Sloan spoke more about her role on set and how she landed the job of a lifetime.

"I can't remember a time when I wasn't the one who took photos," Sloan said. Given her first camera at age eleven, Sloan quickly settled into her "fly on the wall" personality, capturing memories of life around her. Later in life, she landed among a group of circus performers, where she says her "technical mind and non-intrusive type of photography" lent itself well to capturing juggling patterns for circus publicity shots. Sloan's ability to blend in to her surroundings and stay far enough back from the action—while still nailing the perfect shot—prepped her for a job she had no idea would land in her lap.

A series of melancholy portraits Sloan took for the circus performers caught the attention of a movie producer named Mark Huffam, who invited her to work on the set of his horror movie. This in turn led to a series of gigs on other movie sets.

"[Working in the film industry] was something I always wanted to do but I thought only people in America did that, not people from a small town in Ireland," she said. But then *Game of Thrones* came right to her doorstep. Huffam was hired as a producer for *Game of Thrones*, and he immediately turned to Sloan.

"He said 'Look, HBO is rolling into town, it's a huge production. This is the pilot that I'm gonna help produce and I think you should put in your portfolio,'" Sloan recalled, though she said neither of them were confident she would land the gig. "He said 'I don't think you'll get it because we have twenty photographers already up for the job, but I would like to put you in because I want to show them that we have people here [in Northern Ireland] who are worth considering.'"

Huffam was quickly proven wrong. HBO went for the local talent and signed Sloan on as the exclusive set photographer for the series. Sloan humbly chalks her involvement with the series up to "pure accident and luck," but her experience and style are the real factors she should credit.

"I guess my style really suited the dark, murdery, incesty, battle-y, creepy *Game of Thrones* vibe," Sloan said.

Depending on the planned shoots for the day, Sloan was on set from around 8 a.m. until 6 p.m., sometimes driving as far as an hour to get to a location in Northern Ireland. She almost never knew how low-key the scheduled scenes on any day would be, though.

"A typical day can be shooting everybody drinking wine around a table and having a nice chat, or we're setting fire to some stunt men and throwing them off the side of a boat," she said, referencing a memorable day on set for the season-two episode "Blackwater." "You just have to be prepared for anything. I've gone from being in torrential rain, a foot deep in mud somewhere around Castle Black, to going to a studio and it's Dany in Meereen and nice and dry and there's a huge light pretending to be the sun."

"So I'll walk in—soggy and muddy and a little bit sad—onto a set where everyone's in T-shirts and shorts and has like cappuccinos," Sloan said.

Sloan retro-fitted a dog trailer with all-terrain wheels so she could trek through the landscape of Northern Ireland with all her gear. Back in 2016, Sloan estimated having taken nearly 750,000 photos on set to date. HBO had recently brought on a second photographer, Macall B. Polay, for shooting on some of the locations outside of Ireland, but Sloan guessed she was still responsible for 85 percent of the series' documentation. By the final episode, her photo count was likely more than one million.

Life in Northern Ireland changed significantly for the individuals like Sloan, but things changed for the community as a whole. Belfast, the capital of Northern Ireland, was particularly transformed by the concentration of star power that came into town once a year for filming. Belfast was where the cast and crew lived for at least four months every year during the almost decade-long run of filming.

The cast and crew's children went to the local schools while their parents rented out houses around Belfast during the production-heavy months. The actors worked out in local gyms and bought toothpaste from "the local chemist," as Webb put it. Webb said Peter Dinklage was often strolling along the same streets where she would walk her dog, and they would just exchange pleasantries like "Hi, how are you?" and carry on their separate ways.

The near-decade of practice meant Northern Ireland locals knew to play it cool around the internationally famous superstars in their midst, even if it was exciting to find yourself running everyday errands next to the Mother of Dragons.

"Nobody mobbed anybody," Webb said. "They respected [the cast] and people generally asked if they could take their picture.

I think some of [the pub owners] obviously got selfies with the guys—there were a few pubs that they liked to go to frequently."

Some of the owners asked to share the pictures on Facebook, but the stars would ask if they'd wait until they had left the country and therefore wouldn't be tracked down while trying to enjoy a pint of Guinness after work.

But between pub visits and long days spent indoors at the Titanic Studios set, the cast and crew would trek out to the dozens of locations used around the countryside and coastal hubs of Northern Ireland.

Just as the terrain of New Zealand will forever be treasured by Lord of the Rings fans, Northern Ireland's screen tourism industry will extend far into the future thanks to Game of Thrones. The people who live in the small country can carry that pride with them for generations.

"People from Northern Ireland used to always joke that we're never very far from someone who knows someone because you went to school with them or they're a brother or sister of somebody," Webb said. "But now people say, 'You're never far from somebody who's been involved in Game of Thrones.' It's become a part of our world, really, and it's not going to go away."

If you've ever wanted to plan a tour of the quintessential Game of Thrones locations, look no further than the list below. For visual aid, Webb's team has put together a whole "Discover Northern Ireland" mobile app you can download, which guides fans through the various recognizable locations seen on the show.

WINTERFELL AND THE NORTH

Castle Ward is a real-life castle built in the eighteenth century near the village of Strangford, in County Down, Northern Ireland. It serves as the skeleton for many of the early Winterfell scenes in season one. You can see the walls and towers of Castle Ward when Jon, Bran, Robb, and Rickon are laughing during shooting practice in the pilot.

For the more somber scene of Will's execution outside of Winterfell in that same episode, the crew traveled to Cairncastle, a grassy plateau to the north of Belfast. Later that location would be used for the scene where Littlefinger tells Sansa they're headed to meet the Boltons in season five, episode three, "High Sparrow."

For Jon Snow's scenes at the Wall, the crew built the whole Castle Black set inside a real Northern Ireland quarry called Magheramorne. The natural wall behind the set is dusted with fake snow, and then CGI is used to create the surrounding view of the icy Wall.

Having the full Castle Black set came in handy for the ninth episode of season four, "The Watchers on the Wall," which is when the major battle between the Night's Watch and the wildling army takes place. Director David Nutter was able to film the memorable single-take shot that swept through the entire courtyard because the whole castle was actually there.

THE KINGSROAD AND THE RIVERLANDS

On the first season finale, we watched as Arya left King's Landing with some trepidation, hitching a ride north with Yoren and the Night's Watch recruits. Northern Ireland's famous Dark Hedges are a well-known attraction located in Stranocum, Northern Ireland. The beech trees there were planted by an eighteenth-century family, and with *Game of Thrones* they became synonymous with the Kingsroad.

Farther south in real life, the River Quoile in County Down, Northern Ireland, is a scenic woodland area. *Game of Thrones* used it as the backdrop for Riverrun, Catelyn Stark's childhood home featured in season three. Most notably they filmed the outdoor scene of Lord Hoster Tully's funeral at the banks of the Quoile.

PYKE AND THE IRON ISLANDS

Heading farther up north and onto the coast, Northern Ireland's Ballintoy Harbour is a small fishing haven. You know it best as the Iron Islands, home to House Greyjoy and the rough 'n' tumble Ironborn. Ballintoy was first seen in season two when Theon returned home, and again in season six when Euron Greyjoy was submerged in the surf by a Drowned Priest.

Near Ballintoy is Larrybane Quarry, another coastal landmark with limestone cliffs that served as the backdrop for Renly Baratheon's camp in the Stormlands on season two. Later it was repurposed for another Ironborn scene: the season six Kingsmoot.

DRAGONSTONE

Dragonstone was introduced as a new location for the premiere of season two. Melisandre and Davos burned effigies of the gods worshipped by the Faith of the Seven at the real-life Downhill Beach, located at the northern coast of Northern Ireland.

Fair Head is a cliff that sits about six hundred feet above sea level overlooking the ocean. The *Game of Thrones* team used this location for a few key Dragonstone scenes on the seventh season. The first time we saw Fair Head was when Varys and Melisandre have a little tête-à-tête about Jon Snow. Coincidentally, Conleth Hill (who plays Varys) lives nearby that very cliff.

"Do you know what? I'm standing at my front door now talking to you and I can see Fair Head, where that was filmed," Hill said in an *INSIDER* interview. "And so it's yet another travelogue for the beautiful place where I live, and I'm very proud of that."

Fair Head was used again in the fifth episode of season seven for Jon's big moment with Drogon and Daenerys. That particular day the wind was so gnarly that the crew had to tie Kit Harington to the ground for fear he would blow off the ledge.

"There was such a howling gale blowing, and it was blowing towards the ocean off the land," Robert McLachlan, the episode's cinematographer, said in an *INSIDER* interview. "In fact, it was blowing so hard that we had to put a safety cable on Kit Harington when he was meeting the dragon because his cape, which is very heavy fabric, was about to turn him into a kite."

MAESTER'S NOTES

One of the funniest behind-the-scenes *Game of Thrones* videos came by way of Emilia Clarke's Instagram. While the seventh season was airing, Clarke shared a video from that day of filming at Fair Head, and the very same cable McLachlan had talked about can be seen attached to Kit Harington. Kit clearly wasn't fearing for his life—in the video he's too busy goofing off by pretending his cape is a set of dragon wings.

DORNE

The sand dunes of Portstewart Strand, located on the north coast of Northern Ireland, serve as the series' southernmost fictional location in Westeros: Dorne. Jaime and Bronn encountered several Dornish horseback riders on these dunes in season five.

ESSOS

The cliffs of Murlough Bay were a perfect backdrop for Tyrion and Jorah's season five, episode six scene when they get captured by slavers. This spot also doubled as the Stormlands for Renly and Stannis's parlay in season two, episode four.

West of the town of Antrim in Northern Ireland, the Toome Canal is a small waterway where the crew filmed Jorah and Tyrion's dangerous venture through Old Valyria. They placed a real boat in the canal for Jorah and Tyrion's scenes, including the attack from the Stone Men, but relied on visual effects for the Valyrian ruins in the background.

The Shillanavogy Valley, near Slemish Mountain in Northern Ireland, was the perfect choice for the Dothraki grasslands of Essos. Daenerys's season-one journey was filmed among the grass here, with plenty of extras and horses.

Binevenagh, located in the county of Londonderry, is a large plateau in Northern Ireland, and it's where Drogon lands Daenerys at the end of season five. Daenerys wanders below the sharp cliffs in the season five finale, and is eventually found by an enormous horde of Dothraki. The same location was used in the sixth season premiere when Jorah and Daario track down Dany's location.

SPAIN, ICELAND, AND CROATIA

Aside from Northern Ireland, *Game of Thrones* had filming units stationed in Spain, Iceland, and Croatia. The bustling city of Dubrovnik in Croatia has become a hot destination in the years since *Game of Thrones* premiered. Many King's Landing scenes are filmed there, and the producers even kept the signature Croatian red-tiled roofs as a feature of the Westeros capital.

The Vatnajökull National Park in Iceland contains stunning mountaintops and glaciers. This is where Jon Snow and the wildlings trekked in season two. Another Icelandic location used was Svínafellsjökull, with more snowy ridges and icy ground that made up the Fist of the First Men.

Though coastal Dorne scenes were filmed in Northern Ireland, HBO went to Spain in order to bring the iconic Water Gardens to life. The Alcázar of Seville is a historic royal palace featuring lush gardens and detailed architecture. The royal grounds were the idyllic location where Princess Myrcella and Prince Trystane

Martell were seen walking and canoodling in the fifth season. The interior of the Alcázar of Seville is just as stunning as the exterior, with elaborate mosaics and tiled floors. Prince Doran greeted Jaime Lannister inside the colorful palace after his failed mission was discovered.

Now that we know more about the visualization of *Game of Thrones*, it's time to dive into the luscious soundtrack of Westeros.

CHAPTER SIX

The LITERAL SONGS of ICE and FIRE

Ramin Djawadi is the forty-five-year-old composer making his mark in the world of film and television scores thanks in large part to his work on *Game of Thrones*. Since the show's inception, Djawadi has been the man behind every musical note heard by fans around the world.

By the time HBO, Benioff, and Weiss reached out to Djawadi about scoring their new show, the young composer was making small waves in Hollywood. Djawadi worked under composing legend Hans Zimmer at Remote Control Productions, and scored the first *Iron Man* movie in 2008.

He's since composed music for blockbuster films like *Pacific Rim* and *A Wrinkle in Time* and worked on CBS's *Person of Interest* and now HBO's *Westworld*. Just as acclaimed writer-director

Christopher Nolan has harmoniously worked with Djawadi's mentor Hans Zimmer to great effect, Djawadi's collaboration with Jonathan Nolan and Lisa Joy on *Westworld* has been some of the most thrilling musical work in modern television. But the real core of his fame began when Benioff and Weiss found him.

"[Benioff and Weiss] showed me the first two episodes, which of course blew my mind," Djawadi said in an interview with *INSIDER*. "Then a meeting was set up, and we sat down and talked about the show and concepts and it was off from there."

The creative team behind *Game of Thrones* is stacked with some of the most brilliant minds in television, but Djawadi's job is unique in that he is responsible for so much heavy lifting when it comes to the emotional intensity of the series. In a show overflowing with drama, tension, grief, and action, that's a large weight to carry—and to carry so gracefully.

Sure, Hodor's death and sacrifice happening at the same time we learn the reason why he became "Hodor" in the first place was gutting—but when the Stark music kicks in, Djawadi clenches his fist over our already aching hearts. Did you wonder why "Light of the Seven" felt so hauntingly profound in those opening moments of the sixth season finale? It was because Djawadi had purposely never used piano in the score up until that scene, so he was able to instantly signal something unprecedented was happening.

Watching Daenerys finally (finally!) set sail for Westeros would have been a satisfying moment regardless, but the scene was imbued with a new sense of ambition and achievement thanks to the way Djawadi blended both House Greyjoy's and House Targaryen's music. If you listen closely to "The Winds of Winter" track, you can hear how the opening notes of the song match the melody of the Greyjoy theme, but it's overlaid with a vocal chorus singing

Daenerys's theme. Djawadi said getting those two pieces of independent music to blend together was no easy feat.

"The themes are made and written to stand completely on their own, but every season I try to come up with something new, and to expand on the themes," he said in an *INSIDER* interview. "I thought, 'Well, we have [Daenerys and the Greyjoys] together so let's just put their themes together as well and combine the power.' That was tricky to figure out, but it was a really amazing finale."

Djawadi's approach to using vocals, primarily only heard in Daenerys's theme music, is fascinating. He pulls syllables and words from Valyrian, a fictional *Game of Thrones* language, and organizes them into a sort of music-only dialect. The lines aren't translatable, though.

"[The lyrics are] what I call 'Valyrian-inspired,'" Djawadi explains. "I treat it like another instrument, so they're not singing actual full sentences because I didn't want it to distract the audience too much."

Unlike most of the production team, Djawadi often had no idea what was coming in a season until the episodes were all shot and edited together. He was typically sent the nearly completed episodes, sometimes one at a time, other times in sets of up to five. This way he could see how the character arcs develop and where he might need to create a new theme or a variation on an existing one. Only for a few key storylines did Benioff and Weiss decide to clue Djawadi in ahead of time—like when they needed him to write the music for "The Rains of Castamere" a full season before the Red Wedding would take place.

Benioff and Weiss knew they needed to start laying the musical groundwork for the shocking Red Wedding well in advance; otherwise the television audience would miss out on a memorable turning point in the narrative. In both the books and the show, Catelyn Stark first realizes something is terribly wrong when she hears the Freys' band begin to play "The Rains of Castamere," a song that details the Lannisters' brutal quashing of a lesser house who foolishly thought they could rival the lions of Casterly Rock.

In order to pull off this revelatory moment, Martin sprinkled references to "The Rains of Castamere" throughout his first two novels and leading up to the Red Wedding in *A Storm of Swords*. But Benioff and Weiss wouldn't have the advantage of being able to tell the audience directly, as Martin did in the book, that "Catelyn knew 'The Rains of Castamere' when she heard it." They needed viewers at home to recognize the song at the same time Catelyn does.

Thankfully the team had years to prepare. Before filming for season two started, Benioff and Weiss went to Djawadi and asked him to compose a melody for "The Rains of Castamere." Djawadi was able to work from Martin's written lyrics, but the choice of notes and composition was all down to him.

"It needed to be haunting but beautiful, and all these other criteria because the theme had to be really flexible," Djawadi said in an *INSIDER* interview.

Flexibility was key so people unfamiliar with the books wouldn't immediately connect "The Rains of Castamere" with total dread, though the song is meant to carry a warning within its lyrics. Once Djawadi wrote the melody for the tune, Benioff and Weiss had him teach it to Peter Dinklage, who in turn whistles the song a couple times in season two of *Game of Thrones*.

The next spotlight moment of "The Rains of Castamere" came with season two's epic penultimate episode: "Blackwater." Bronn sings the ballad in a tavern as the soldiers await Stannis Baratheon's attack, and one man directly asks how Tyrion's hired sellsword came to learn "the Lannister song."

Thanks to Djawadi's early efforts working the song into the language of the score, those who hadn't read the books were still able to realize things were about to go horribly, horribly wrong before the first dagger was unsheathed in the feasting hall of the Twins.

That wasn't the first time Djawadi had planted an early musical clue at Benioff and Weiss's direction. In the pilot episode, after Cersei and Jaime discuss Jon Arryn's death in King's Landing, the scene transitions to show a raven carrying the news to Winterfell. In that moment, the music playing is Littlefinger's theme, providing us with our first clue as to the real culprit behind Jon Arryn's murder.

We wouldn't learn until the fourth season that Littlefinger had convinced Lysa Arryn to poison her husband and write a note to her sister blaming the Lannisters, which in turn led to Ned Stark going to King's Landing. Littlefinger's theme music plays once more during the unforgettable "chaos is a ladder" speech in season three, episode six, "The Climb."

Another example of a time Djawadi gave us a heads-up on a character's story came in the sixth season, in the buildup to Jon Snow's return from the dead.

"I have to admit—I knew he was coming back all along," Djawadi said. "It was so hard to stay quiet when everybody asked me, but of course I always said 'I have no idea what you're talking about.'"

Djawadi had to know ahead of time so he could begin composing a new theme for Jon once he left the Night's Watch. Many characters, as well as their families and followers, have separate theme music. As we've already established, the Lannisters have "The Rains of Castamere." If you rewatch the cold open of season four, you'll hear the Stark theme play as Tywin Lannister unsheathes Ned's greatsword, Ice. As the blade is melted down and turned into two new Valyrian steel weapons, Djawadi blended the music and transitioned into the Lannister theme—a direct signal of the way Tywin has co-opted power over the Starks (for now).

The other characters have their own musical cues, too. Stannis and Melisandre's scenes often had the same music, as heard on the season-six track "The Red Woman." And Daenerys has her instantly recognizable theme in "Fire and Blood" from the first season's score. Her music blares every time she rides her dragons into a battle or when her armies emerge victorious in Essos.

The Stark theme was first heard in season one, episode two, "The Kingsroad," when Jon and Robb say goodbye for the final time. Djawadi aptly named that track "Goodbye Brother" on the released score. Up until the sixth season, the House Stark theme was played during most of Jon Snow's onscreen moments, with the exception of his and Ygritte's romantic musical cues.

"When we first started meeting for season six, we decided Jon Snow will definitely have his own theme this season," Djawadi said. "For example, at the Battle of the Bastards, we used Jon's theme a lot because that was so personal and it was all about him and his mistakes and thinking it was over. That was not really an overall Stark moment—it was really personal [to Jon]."

The first time viewers heard the new Jon Snow theme was in the third episode of season six when he ended his duty as Lord Commander of the Night's Watch after executing Alliser Thorne, Olly, and the other betrayers.

"At the end of episode three, when he walks away and says, 'My watch has ended,' that was a good spot too where it was just a Jon Snow moment rather than a Stark moment," Djawadi said.

The new music was a signal to viewers that Jon's character had shifted—something in him was moving away from his old self. His melody sounds similar to the Stark theme, but with a heavier focus on cello and less violin.

"The Stark theme, like with 'Goodbye Brother,' is associated with a lot of goodbyes—it's a very emotional theme," Djawadi says. "But with [Jon's] theme, he's brought back to life and you can see he's wondering why and how did this all happen. Plus, with the internal struggle he's facing in the battle . . . it's definitely a little bit dark."

Though Djawadi was speaking of an emotional darkness, there is a relationship between color hues and the music you hear on *Game of Thrones*. Djawadi is afflicted by synesthesia; in other words, he can hear color.

"The phenomenon—its name derives from the Greek, meaning 'to perceive together'—comes in many varieties," an American Psychological Association article on synesthesia explains. "Some synesthetes hear, smell, taste or feel pain in color. Others taste shapes, and still others perceive written digits, letters and words in color."

For Djawadi, certain colors are inextricably connected with musical notes and tones. This visualization of music was something Djawadi experienced his whole life without thinking twice about it. He didn't realize it was peculiar until his wife asked him about his writing process.

"My wife asked me questions like, 'When you write, what do you think or what do you feel?'" he recalls. "I thought, 'Well it's blue so it should be X or it's green so it should be Y, just like painting.' Talking it through with her made me aware of my process."

Synesthesia is a very mysterious sensory condition, one that psychologists and synesthetes both sometimes have trouble explaining.

"Even if you tried to—and I don't want to get too technical—but if you tried to say well the color blue is A and the color green is

G or something, it gets much more complicated because obviously you never just have one color," he explained. "So sometimes it triggers me to write in a certain key or certain notes or instruments. Really it's very complex and I don't totally understand it myself."

The show's tendency to indicate geographic changes with different color palettes helps Djawadi immensely. For example, King's Landing has a distinct reddish glow that differentiates it from the Riverlands or the Vale.

"What's great about *Game of Thrones* is how the different locations [change color]—like how north of the Wall has this great blue tone and Daenerys in the desert has more of a yellow," Djawadi said. "So it triggers certain things for me, which is super inspiring."

Another sense-based association Djawadi has with music is warmth versus cold. The theme music used for the White Walkers is meant to evoke a chilliness in the atmosphere. Just as the White Walkers bring cold with them, so does Djawadi's score. In a 2013 interview with *The Hollywood Reporter*, journalist Victoria Ellison asked Djawadi about the way his music for the inhuman beings sounds like "walking in the ice."

"Yes, [Benioff and Weiss] will say, 'This needs to be really a cold sound, what can we do?'" Djawadi said. "So sometimes I use these glass bowls for when we're north of the Wall, so it really gives you this weird mood. The White Walkers are the same thing, it's eerie when they talk. We have this eerie glassy sound—even though you don't see them, you know, 'OK, that's the White Walkers again.'"

Glass and ice are of course linked to the White Walkers in several ways. By the end of the series, we're shown how the first White Walker, the Night King, was both made and destroyed with dragonglass buried in his heart (though his death involved the key ingredient of Valyrian steel). The way White Walkers die invokes the visual of a glass figurine shattering into thousands of pieces. In the books, the White Walkers' voices are described as sounding "like the cracking of ice on a winter lake." Their theme song isn't immediately recognizable as any one instrument, but that chilly effect works all the same.

This subconscious manipulation came again with "The Light of the Seven," used in the opening scene of the sixth season finale as Cersei carries out her deadly wildfire plot. As mentioned earlier, his use of piano (which he played himself, as is the case with many of the individual instruments on the score) was emblematic of the surprise element of the scene itself. Not only had he never used piano before, but pianos are an anachronism within the medieval-inspired setting of Westeros.

"What's so cool about 'Light of Seven' and what's so great about *Game of Thrones* is how you never know what's going to happen, right?" Djawadi told me. "You never know who's going to die, you never know who's going to turn on who and all that. So the piano was such a surprise to people because it's just not in the language of the score at all."

As revealed in an *INSIDER* interview, the idea to deploy piano for this scene was the result of a big meeting between himself, Benioff and Weiss, and the episode's director, Miguel Sapochnik.

"We discussed this very early on, because it's such a significant scene . . . there's not a lot of dialogue [and] it's very long," Djawadi said. "Miguel brought up [the piano] and we all discussed it. We went back and forth about it and experimented quite a bit. But we ended up just going for it and I'm so happy we did."

The key direction given to Djawadi was that it had to be "a completely new piece of music."

"'We don't want to use the Lannister theme for Cersei, we don't want to tip the audience in any direction,'" Djawadi recalled being told by the showrunners and Sapochnik. "'It has to be a new piece of music and it has to start minimal and then just develop.'"

The track begins with piano and eventually escalates into an intense organ melody. Djawadi had used organ during Cersei's walk of atonement in the fifth season finale, so it was already baked into the DNA of the soundtrack. "The organ also made sense because of the religious aspect and all that, so it was a great instrument to add," Djawadi said. "The organ is so powerful, so it just had this great build to it."

The result was a nearly ten-minute-long composition that almost instantly jumped to the top of Spotify's Global Viral 50 chart. Fans were clamoring for Djawadi to be awarded an Emmy at long last.

Much to their disappointment, "The Light of the Seven" wasn't eligible for an Emmy because the composition includes the *Game of Thrones* opening credits melody. Compositions are only nominated if they are wholly new, created for the show's most recent season "with no prior usage through any other media." By repurposing the intro music into "The Light of the Seven," Djawadi had inadvertently disqualified himself from the Emmys that year.

But justice came during the next *Game of Thrones* award season, when he was awarded his first-ever Emmy for the music on season seven's finale, "The Dragon and the Wolf." Now Djawadi has gone from spiking on Spotify charts to touring the world with the *Game of Thrones* Live Concert Experience, where fans dressed up in cosplay can collectively cheer for their favorite characters as Djawadi conducts a live orchestra playing the soundtrack's greatest hits.

Djawadi's talents for enhancing different characters' journeys with music and bringing people to tears reached new heights with the eighth and final season of *Game of Thrones*. First he kicked off the opening episode, "Winterfell," with a theme we hadn't heard since the pilot episode. The piece is titled "Arrival at Winterfell" on the officially released soundtrack, and it's nearly identical to the season-one track called "The King's Arrival." Daenerys coming to Winterfell is intentionally mirrored with King Robert and Queen Cersei's royal visit, and Djawadi's matching musical themes were only the start.

This time a little Winter Town boy scurries up to higher ground to watch the army approach, just as Bran had done all those years ago. Arya watches the Hound trot into her family's castle, as she had done in episode one. Even Jon's greeting kiss to Bran's forehead mirrors the exact way he had kissed his little brother goodbye before leaving for the Wall.

Another highlight of the final season music came when Djawadi composed a melody for a song sung by Podrick Payne (played by Daniel Portman) in "A Knight of the Seven Kingdoms." The tune was inspired by a song mentioned in Martin's book series called "Jenny's Song." In one of Arya's chapters in *A Storm of Swords*, the third book in A Song of Ice and Fire, she's traveling with the Brotherhood Without Banners when they visit a mystical place called High Heart.

High Heart is a hill where dozens of weirwood tree stumps still exist, signaling the connection of the location to the Children of the Forest and old gods of Westeros. While there, a small woman called the ghost of High Heart approaches Arya's party. She says she'll tell them about her "dreams" in exchange for some wine and a song.

The song she requests is simply referred to as "Jenny's song," and we never get the lyrics in Martin's book. Instead, Arya notices that the ghost of High Heart cries as she sings along to the tune. The "Jenny" in the song refers to a character in Martin's books from decades past named Jenny of Oldstones. Some fans have theorized that Jenny and the ghost of High Heart are the same person, but the relationship between the two remains mysterious.

As for the dreams the ghost of High Heart speaks of, they all seem to be prophetic. She describes one as "a maid at a feast with purple serpents in her hair, venom dripping from their fangs," representing Sansa Stark wearing the purple poison crystals at King Joffrey's wedding. But that deadly event wouldn't happen until much later in the book, showing readers that the ghost of High Heart was sensing the future.

So "Jenny's Song" is linked to Martin's books at a point where much of the lore and fantasy intersect with Arya's storyline. This makes it a fitting choice for season eight, episode two, when so many of our beloved characters are contemplating their mortality as the great war approaches Winterfell's gates.

Weiss wrote lyrics for the song, which he renamed "Jenny of Oldstones," and handed those over to Djawadi so he could write the music to go with them. They had pop band Florence and the Machine record a version of "Jenny of Oldstones" for the closing credits of the episode.

Even before Podrick overwhelms audiences with the sweet and sad beauty of "Jenny of Oldstones," this episode was marked by another meaningful moment when Brienne of Tarth kneels in front of Jaime Lannister and arises a knight. Just a few episodes later, Ser Brienne, the Lord Commander of the Kingsguard, writes down Jaime's deeds in *The Book of Brothers* following his death. The tenderness and emotion in both of these scenes is palpable, but what you might not have noticed was that Djawadi seemingly hinted at their great love story in the music for both moments.

As fans on Twitter and Reddit pointed out, the tracks on season eight's score titled "A Knight of the Seven Kingdoms" and "The White Book" both carry a similar melody to a key song Djawadi used back on season two: "I Am Hers, She Is Mine," which plays when Robb Stark and Talisa say their marriage vows. Even though *Game of Thrones* ripped away Jaime and Brienne's happily ever after, Djawadi made sure we felt the permanent impact of their vows of knighthood, and those fleeting moments of love.

We also heard a new, haunting piece of piano-based music in season eight, "The Night King," which builds in terror as the army of the living are nearly eradicated by the undead forces attacking Winterfell. That almost nine-minute-long track plays toward the end of "The Long Night," and it's the closest Djawadi comes to surpassing the genius of "The Light of the Seven." You are supposed to sense a kinship between the two pieces, as if the piano was harkening a particular dread.

"['The Night King'] starts at a different key and a different tempo," Djawadi said in an interview with *The Hollywood Reporter*. "And I even went as far as ending up in the same tempo and key as 'The Light of the Seven,' to even give you the subconscious sense that this is over, and this is the end of everybody. I really hope everyone was holding their breath. That was certainly the intention."

For Daenerys's death scene, Djawadi turned to her and Jon's love theme from season seven, titled "The Truth." The familiar melody begins when Jon kisses Daenerys, leading us to believe this is another moment of unity for them, as the Mother of Dragons believes she is safe in his embrace. But with the slip of his dagger, the song is brought up short on purpose.

"We really made sure it's written in a way that ends just during the phrase," Djawadi told *The Hollywood Reporter*. "It comes out of nowhere. You don't expect it at all. When they kiss, you want to feel their love is stronger than anything else. You don't want to anticipate that he's going to kill her. That's why I actively wrote it the way it is now. It stops mid-phrase."

Finally, in the closing moments of the series, when we see the last remaining Starks setting off down their own paths, Djawadi keenly repurposes the melody from his season-four-finale track, titled "The Children." Just as the montage moves from showing Arya on her ship (itself a direct parallel to the fourth season finale when she set sail for Braavos) to Jon Snow leaving the Wall, the Stark theme of "Goodbye Brother" kicks in and harmonizes with "The Children."

The surviving Stark children are the focal point of the series finale, and Djawadi's score works its magic to crack our hearts open in those closing minutes. The mournful theme of the Starks is somber no more, and instead we're left with that sweet ache as we say goodbye to *Game of Thrones*.

CHAPTER SEVEN

◇◇◇◇◇◇◇◇◇◇◇◇◇◇◇◇◇◇◇◇◇

WORDS
ARE WIND:
GREATEST
MOMENTS *in the*
SERIES' HISTORY

O ver the course of its seventy-three episodes, *Game of Thrones* gifted us with indelible one-liners, rousing monologues, and some of the best hours of television ever created. On a series packed to the gills with brilliant writing (no, this is *not* the time to talk about the "bad pussy" line), it's hard to narrow down the best of the best when it comes to the verbal jabs and shrewd philosophical observations that make up the most iconic moments in *Game of Thrones* history.

Even more challenging is the additional task of highlighting just a single episode from each season to serve as the defining, essential set piece for every annual installment of the show. It seems appropriate to start, as Martin did all those years ago, with a boy witnessing an execution amid the summer snows of Westeros.

"The man who passes the sentence should swing the sword."
—Ned Stark (season 1, episode 1: "Winter Is Coming")

————— ❧❧ —————

Ned may have been short-lived within the series, but the children he raised carry his legacy with them until the very end of *Game of Thrones.* The Starks are of the North, and take more solemn responsibility for duty and for those they commit to death. It's an act of respect for life, and for the burden of leadership.

We see this lesson put into practice for three key moments later in the series. The first occurs when Theon Greyjoy takes Winterfell and is goaded into executing Ser Rodrik Cassel. He carries out the beheading himself, but his lack of conviction leads to a butchering of the task. The second comes when Robb Stark executes Lord Karstark and is anguished by the decision, but firm in his path forward.

Lastly it comes into play when Jon Snow is elected to be Lord Commander of the Night's Watch and Janos Slynt refuses to obey his new Lord Commander's order. With only the slightest hesitation, Jon beheads Slynt. The young leader takes no pleasure in the task, but by following Ned's philosophy he earns the respect of his fellow brothers.

"Let me give you some advice, bastard. Never forget what you are. The rest of the world will not. Wear it like armor, and it can never be used to hurt you."

—Tyrion Lannister (season 1, episode 1: "Winter Is Coming")

———— ❧❧ ————

Tyrion and Jon's first meeting stands out as one of the better pairings of two characters who are otherwise kept apart for most of the series. The two outcasts in their family would go on to become great players in the game of thrones, but first they get to know each other under much humbler circumstances.

The line comes after Tyrion asks Jon if he's Ned Stark's bastard. The sullen and eager-to-prove boy simply gives Tyrion a hardened look and turns away to mope. Tyrion could have taken that slight for what it was and ended the conversation then and there. But the ever-clever Tyrion Lannister instead uses the moment to prod deeper into Jon, sensing a potential kinship with the young man. He does have a soft spot for cripples, bastards, and broken things, after all.

"There is only one god, and his name is Death. And there is only one thing we say to Death: 'Not today.'"

—Syrio Forel (season 1, episode 6: "A Golden Crown")

———— ❧❧ ————

Syrio Forel, the First Sword of Braavos, is a beloved minor character for good reason. Arya's compelling arc of vengeance wouldn't exist without those critical moments when her water dancing instructor taught her how to be focused and deadly before she was forced into the horrible underbelly of Westerosi society.

The quote is told to Arya the day after Jaime Lannister attacks Ned Stark and his men in the streets of King's Landing. Arya is shaken and scared, and unable to focus on her sword fighting. She fights back tears as Syrio teaches her that bravery and mindfulness, particularly in the face of terror, is the only way to survive. Arya's embrace of the god of Death would eventually lead her to an unexpected destiny when she kills the Night King in the godswood of Winterfell, bringing Syrio's lesson full circle.

"When you play the game of thrones, you win or you die."
—Cersei Lannister (season 1, episode 7: "You Win or You Die")

———— ❧❧ ————

You can't say Cersei didn't warn him. In this conversation, which takes place right before King Robert dies, Cersei sends a clear message to Ned Stark as he does his best to be both honorable and merciful when facing the conniving Lannister matriarch.

Cersei is so rarely given the chance to drop the façade she learned to create when she was a young girl, the mask of ladylike deference and minimal ambitions. This makes it all the more powerful to see her laid bare, with no more secrets to keep, speaking of her own wrath and position of power.

SEASON ONE, EPISODE NINE
"BAELOR"

Coming into the show's rookie season, Sean Bean was the most well-known actor cast in *Game of Thrones*. He stood out among the group of largely unknown names, especially to an American audience, where Bean was widely known for his role as Boromir

in the Lord of the Rings films. The promotional materials for the first season all centered around Ned Stark, Lord of Winterfell and Warden of the North.

"Ned Stark is the center of the series," Martin said in HBO's first behind-the-scenes video for *Game of Thrones*, released a few months ahead of the first season premiere. Ned was the audience's conduit into the confusing political landscape of Westeros. Following him to King's Landing made it easier for people to grasp the rules and hierarchies of the medieval-fantasy world while also rooting the story of the show in a morally admirable character.

Benioff and Weiss knew Sean Bean was a smart face to attach to early press buzz about a new HBO drama series. "Traditionally in a book, whether it's fantasy or any other genre, you might do a terrible thing to a side character," Benioff said in HBO's *Inside the Episode* segment after Ned's execution. "You might murder a minor character, but you're not going to kill Tony Soprano."

First-time fans of Martin's story might have failed to grasp the heartbreaking detail of Ned being beheaded by his own Valyrian steel greatsword, Ice, but those details—along with many other significant storytelling choices—were baked into the nearly perfect episode of television. Not only are the events throughout this episode some of the most consequential for the rest of the series, but themes of valor, victory, and sacrifice are coursing throughout the beautifully crafted scenes.

"Baelor" opens with one of the most riveting scenes in the series, when Varys comes to Lord Eddard Stark in the cells of the Red Keep. By 2019, the world would think of *Game of Thrones* more or less as the "tits and dragons" show (thanks to an oft-quoted Ian McShane interview). But the show was built on a foundation of these small, quiet, character-driven scenes. Just two men and a flickering torch, hashing out the weight of honor and honesty against a life and legacy.

Game of Thrones is crafted with the intent of forcing the audience to shoulder the burdens of shock and grief alongside the characters who lose loved one after loved one. The lives of the many characters do feel precious to fans. The impact of "Baelor" rings throughout the entire series, like a note of grief on a frequency we cannot pinpoint, reminding us constantly of the things we'll do for love.

Ned only wants to save the children. His children. Cersei's children. The children for whom it's too late, like little Aegon and Rhaenys Targaryen. The child for whom Ned risked everything, his (secret) nephew and his greatest unintended shame, Jon Snow. With this in the core of his character, Varys asks Ned if his daughter's life is worth anything to him. The question is left unanswered throughout the rest of the episode as the weight of family versus honor comes into play for nearly every other scene in "Baelor."

For Robb and Catelyn, the most Tully-ish of all the Starks, the House Tully words of "family, duty, honor" (in that order) serve as their ethos as they treat with Walder Frey, knowing it's the fastest path to Ned. Jon Snow is forced to confront his loyalty to the Night's Watch vows while he stands among the ravens of Castle Black. Those dark, winged creatures are often linked to prophecy or the messengers of gods. They bear witness as Aemon Targaryen unknowingly counsels his great-great-great nephew, telling him "love is the death of duty."

We finally get an answer to Varys's proposal when Ned falsely confesses to treason, saving Sansa in the process. The episode's climax comes not with a scream or a stampede of hoofs or the soaring flame of dragon's breath. Instead, the jeers and boos fade into the stunned silence of Ned's perspective. We are left with the sound of his final breaths, the Sept of Baelor pushed to a blurred background. Ned's eyes dart around, searching in their final moments for his youngest daughter. She is no longer crouched on the statue of Baelor the Blessed where he had seen her. Is she safe? Ned will never know.

In the books, Ned doesn't speak to anyone when he's brought out and, since we're contained to Arya's point of view, there's no way for us to know if Ned even noticed she was there. But Benioff and Weiss changed the scene so Ned not only notices Arya, but leads Yoren to her so she will be safe. Martin himself later told *BuzzFeed* he thought the idea was a "beautiful" change to his chapter. "That little touch is not in the books, but I wish it had been in the books because it was a great addition," he said.

By this point in the story, audiences had watched multiple attempted child murders, incestuous sex, undead corpses rising to attack, and dozens of other brutal, bloody deaths. But the execution of Ned Stark surpassed them all when it came to shock. We follow Arya into the mob with mounting anxiety, wondering who is going to swoop in or how Arya will manage to get onto that platform in time to rescue her father. But *Game of Thrones* is a show with no tidy victories. Ned's mercy was his defeat. His honor is his legacy. The lone wolf dies, but his pack (well, most of them) survives.

> *"I'm not questioning your honor, Lord Janos.*
> *I'm denying its existence."*
> —Tyrion Lannister (season 2, episode 2: "The Night Lands")

———— ❦❦ ————

Janos Slynt is a real slimeball, and watching Tyrion make him squirm is one of the most satisfying scenes of the second season.

During his time as Hand of the King, Tyrion expertly weeded dishonest people out of King's Landing. Slynt was the captain of the City Watch and betrayed Ned Stark when Ned asked for their help in removing Joffrey from the Iron Throne.

Justice isn't often doled out in *Game of Thrones*, so it's particularly satisfying that we get a double dose of it for Janos. First Tyrion sends him to the Wall in this scene, and then later down the line Jon Snow executes him. That the one-two punch comes from our beloved outcasts, Tyrion and Jon, is all the more sweet.

"Power resides where men believe it resides. It's a trick, a shadow on the wall. And a very small man can cast a very large shadow."

—Lord Varys (season 2, episode 3: "What Is Dead May Never Die")

———— ❧❧ ————

As Tyrion makes his moves in the capital, Lord Varys becomes his unexpected ally. Varys sees the power Tyrion possesses—not through physical brutality, but through his knack for manipulation and wit.

Varys posits a riddle to Tyrion about the perceived power of kings, priests, and sellswords. Varys is both talking circles around Tyrion and complimenting him, while also calling into question the power of the respective "kings" in Westeros at the time. Gods, kings, soldiers—who truly controls the events unfolding in Westeros? It's a minispeech that summarizes all of the power struggles contained in *Game of Thrones*, which is no easy feat. Bravo, Spider.

"Anyone can be killed."

—Arya Stark (season 2, episode 5: "The Ghost of Harrenhal")

———— ❧❧ ————

There are a few character pairings invented for the show that occupy a special, magical place. Tywin Lannister and Arya Stark's shared Harrenhal scenes are one such example. During one of their conversations, Lord Tywin asks Arya to tell him everything the Northerners say about Robb Stark, the King in the North. Arya tells Tywin that people say Robb can't be killed. When the Lannister lord asks her if she believes them, she tells him in a cold, vaguely threatening tone that "anyone can be killed."

There's also a meta message in this line. Viewers at home may have been rattled by Ned Stark's death, but we fell prey to the trap of hoping Robb Stark and our other beloved characters would survive. As the coming third season would prove, no one is truly safe.

This line was also retroactively given new meaning when Arya killed the Night King halfway through the final season of *Game of Thrones*, a move that took the fandom by surprise. She did say *anyone*, which means even the man-turned-physical-embodiment-of-death counts.

"Gods help you, Theon Greyjoy. Now you are truly lost."

—Rodrik Cassel (season 2, episode 6: "The Old Gods and the New")

———— ❧❧ ————

Rodrik is a minor character, but his last words before Theon beheaded him clang like a bell throughout the remainder of Theon's storyline. This scene happens almost right after Theon decides to take Winterfell for his own—a decision that eventually leads to his capture and horrific torture at the hands of Ramsay. Many people try to talk him out of this, including his sister, Yara, and Maester Luwin, but Rodrik is the one who tells it like it is. Theon is lost, and no one can help him now.

That Rodrik says this with Theon Greyjoy's full name is even more powerful. Down the line, Theon loses his sense of self as Ramsay torments him and transforms him into "Reek." Though Theon acts foolishly and even cruelly, he does so at the behest of others and out of a desperate wish to feel a sense of belonging to one family or the other. It isn't until later that Theon is able to reconcile his sense of belonging to both the Starks and Greyjoys.

> *"We've had vicious kings and we've had idiot kings,*
> *but I don't know if we've ever been cursed*
> *with a vicious-idiot-boy king."*
> —Tyrion Lannister (season 2, episode 6: "The Old Gods and the New")

Tyrion's tirade at the insufferable King Joffrey is a particularly satisfying moment in the series. Watching the verbal sparring is cathartic thanks to both the palpable anger and energy given off by Jack Gleeson (Joffrey) and Peter Dinklage (Tyrion) in the scene. During the Q&A portion of his featured New York Comic Con panel in 2016, *INSIDER* asked Gleeson about the experience of filming that scene.

"We were filming in basically the epicenter of old Dubrovnik, which I absolutely love," Gleeson said. "And it was really cool to act with Peter in that scene. I remember really going for it, really screaming at him and just really trying to get into the moment."

In the scene, Joffrey stalks angrily into the safety of the castle walls after the lowborn mob attacked them, screeching until Tyrion snaps and slaps him across the face.

"We called cut and we were hanging out and I just remember Peter looking [at me] like, 'Nice . . . nice,'" Gleeson said while imitating his costar, his mouth setting into an impressed frown. "I feel like I got some fist-bump kudos from Peter in that moment."

The mutual respect the two actors clearly had for each other shines through the scene, and it remains one of the best moments for both Joffrey and Tyrion in the series.

SEASON TWO, EPISODE NINE
"BLACKWATER"

Something we might take for granted now is the way *Game of Thrones* reworked audience's expectations about the pacing of a TV season. Ned Stark's death, the Battle of Blackwater, the Red Wedding, the Battle of Castle Black, Hardhome, the Battle of the Bastards—all of these were major events that any other series might save for its season finale. But the *Game of Thrones* showrunners took a literal page from Martin's books and sprinkled in huge, upending plot points earlier in the seasons.

If "Baelor" was an achievement in narrative twists we'd come to associate with the series, "Blackwater" was the first episode to really showcase what *Game of Thrones* could do when money wasn't an object. The Battle of the Blackwater was a milestone for Benioff and Weiss, who talked HBO into shelling out nearly $2 million more than any other *Game of Thrones* episode up to that point. At the time, the budget averaged $6 million per episode. But in order to pull off this confluence of major characters and naval-battle-meets-nuclear-wildfire-bomb, Benioff and Weiss upped the ante.

They also tapped Martin to pen his second script for the series (the first had been season one, episode seven's "The Pointy End"). He was able to distill his characters down to their cores for the brilliantly paced hour of television as King Stannis descends upon King's Landing. Everyone is reduced to their flight or fight instincts, revealing the true selves of our beloved (and hated) characters.

Tyrion takes up the mantle of House Lannister, proving himself a worthy successor to his father in both cunning and leadership. Though both Tywin and the people of King's Landing will squander Tyrion's efforts, in this moment he is at the peak of his power. And unlike King Joffrey or Cersei or the pyromancers, who delight in exacting violence against their enemies, basking in the brutality like pigs in mud, Tyrion is clearly unnerved by his knack for slaughter when he sees the damage unleashed by the wildfire plot.

Tyrion's attitude toward the battle of "kill or be killed but don't revel in it" lands somewhere between Bronn's casual bloodlust and the Hound's intense distaste for the dog and pony show of knighthood. Bronn and Sandor are juxtaposed in a pre-battle scene, neither one of them knowing this will be the night that pushes the Hound to desertion and Bronn into knighthood.

Where Tyrion surprises himself and his soldiers with an impassioned speech, Stannis contrasts him with cold, pragmatic leadership. He charges into the city with calculated determination, the simple truth of his right to the Iron Throne coursing through his veins. Stannis is not the charismatic or inspiring king we may think of in traditional tales of valor, but his unflinching storming of the walls is an arresting sight nonetheless.

Meanwhile, inside those city walls, Cersei and Sansa square

off in a dance of ladylike and unladylike behaviors. Cersei may counsel fear and brutality as a queen's best weapons, but Sansa is learning how to manipulate men around her by leaning into her "little dove" persona, slinging barbs of a much deadlier variety at Joffrey and Tyrion and all but explicitly threatening their lives.

As Cersei gulps down her wine, her measured facade drops. She is unable to contain her spite for the ladies of court around her, and her annoyance at being treated different than Jaime simply because she is a woman is all-consuming. The only thing able to overshadow it is her love for her children. When Cersei stalks away from Maegor's Holdfast, it is Sansa who rises to the task at hand.

Sansa's reaction in this moment will be a through line to the final seasons and her ennobled fight for the North, while Cersei's flight to the cold Iron Throne foreshadows her journey. Cersei sits upon that steely seat of power, not hers by right, with Tommen in her lap. She tells him a tale about all the beasts in the realm, promising to keep him safe even as she guides poison to his lips.

Cersei will have the Iron Throne in time, and Tommen will die as a result of her smothering manipulations and simultaneous negligence. Tywin only delays the inevitable as he charges into the throne room, declaring a victory he will not hold in the long run. We fade to black with the soft baritone of The National crooning "The Rains of Castamere," warning us of the perils of hubris and foreshadowing the Lannisters' own doom even in this moment of triumph.

"All men must die, but we are not men."

—Daenerys Targaryen (season 3, episode 3: "Walk of Punishment")

———— ❧❧ ————

Daenerys's rejection of the saying "Valar morghulis" (translated to "all men must die" in the Common Tongue) comes at a time in the series when she is building momentum. The Mother of Dragons is about to acquire the army of Unsullied in Astapor, and it feels as though nothing can prevent her from getting what she wants. Not even the promise of inevitable death.

Though this line is *just* on the verge of cheeseball, it does enough to invoke the iconic Lord of the Rings moment when Éowyn declares "I am no man!" before slaying the Witch King. For that, and for the surprised smirk Missandei gives Dany, it's a moment we will always bask in.

Unfortunately both Daenerys and Missandei will die in the closing episodes of the series, making this line much more bittersweet upon rewatch.

"Rhaegar fought valiantly.
Rhaegar fought nobly. And Rhaegar died."

—Jorah Mormont (season 3, episode 3: "Walk of Punishment")

———— ❧❧ ————

While speaking with Daenerys about the Unsullied and the nature of war, Jorah warns her of the inevitable violence involved. Dany experienced a taste of this when Khal Drogo began slaying and enslaving people in order to get his Khaleesi to Westeros, but the young queen still hopes to find a pathway to the Iron Throne that doesn't include butchery of the innocent.

When the topic turns to Prince Rhaegar, Jorah points out that even if a man does everything in as noble a fashion as possible, it doesn't guarantee a happy ending. Dany will eventually be unable to reconcile her desire to rule Westeros with her wish to protect all innocent lives, and the citizens of King's Landing pay the price. There is no happy ending for Daenerys as she fails to thread the needle between benevolent conquerer and ruthless ruler.

> *"He would see this country burn*
> *if he could be King of the Ashes."*
>
> —Lord Varys (season 3, episode 4: "And Now His Watch Is Ended")

———— ❧❧ ————

Here Varys once again manages to suss out the realm's real issue: The various would-be kings are (for the most part) too obsessed with winning the throne and not with protecting the realm. The notion of a king—or queen—of the ashes comes up later when Daenerys finally arrives in Westeros with her dragons. Sure, she could rule the Seven Kingdoms in a snap if she lets Drogon, Viserion, and Rhaegal lay waste to cities. But at what cost? Would the ends justify the fiery means?

Many fans also spend a lot of time trying to guess which side Varys is truly on, but within the show's universe he makes it pretty clear that the common folk and the realm are his charges.

"If you look at him talking to Ned in the first season, Ned's going 'Who do you work for?' and he says 'The realm,'" the actor behind Varys, Conleth Hill, said in an *INSIDER* interview. "So I think if he's a liar then he's been a consistently good liar. But to me it makes sense."

As Hill sees the character, Varys is not interested in sitting on the Iron Throne himself, but he does want to prevent people like Littlefinger from getting there. "I genuinely believe that he's not interested in that," Hill said. "He's just making a better world for everybody else."

"A dragon is not a slave."

—Daenerys Targaryen (season 3, episode 4: "And Now His Watch Is Ended")

———— ❧ ☙ ————

This is the epic moment when Daenerys unveils her secret plan to acquire the Unsullied and kill the slave masters of Astapor. The man she's been dealing with doesn't realize she speaks Valyrian, and so has been referring to her as a "bitch" and "whore" in front of her during their dealings. She kills him by ordering Drogon to breathe fire with the command she taught her dragons: *dracarys*.

This gloriously brutal power move is the first time we see the dragons, now more grown, in action, and the wait was well worth it. Forget the season-two trickery of keeping the dragons in medieval cages, conspicuously where we could hear but not see them. *This* is what fans were waiting for: the roast of a lifetime, delivered to the misogynistic and cruel slave traders.

This important stepping-stone in Daenerys's pathway to queendom is marked by fire and blood. Those are not merely the words of House Targaryen but also her rallying cry whenever it is time for the Mother of Dragons to reclaim power and exact justice on her abusers and oppressors.

"By what right does the wolf judge the lion?"

—Jaime Lannister (season 3, episode 5: "Kissed by Fire")

———— ❦ ❦ ————

Jaime's character arc is among the most nuanced in the series, especially his journey throughout the second and third seasons. In this season-three scene, he sits with Brienne in a hot bath and tells her the story of how he earned the nickname "Kingslayer." Until now, the story was a reason for viewers to judge Jaime harshly for oathbreaking.

But his explanation makes you see that he had little choice but to kill the king he was sworn to protect. His final line of the speech—"By what right does the wolf judge the lion?"—drives home the point that Ned Stark and his honor may not be the only moral way of living.

Nikolaj Coster-Waldau is also one of the most skillful actors on the series, and his delivery of this entire monologue remains among the best of the series.

"Chaos isn't a pit. Chaos is a ladder."

—Petyr "Littlefinger" Baelish (season 3, episode 6: "The Climb")

———— ❦ ❦ ————

For most of the first two seasons, Littlefinger's motivations are veiled in secrecy. Viewers know he's up to something, but his ambitions aren't made fully clear until this pivotal moment. Littlefinger's retort to Varys reveals his penchant for chaos and violence, even if it means destruction for the realm (just as Varys predicted earlier in the season). His power resides in his ability to create chaos and come out on top. "I did what I did for the good of the realm," Littlefinger tells Varys.

Though Littlefinger would eventually climb too far and up the wrong ladder (hello, Sansa) he dominates the power struggle for an impressive amount of time after this little speech. Hate him as you may, you gotta give Littlefinger some props for this one.

SEASON THREE, EPISODE NINE
"THE RAINS OF CASTAMERE"

"The Rains of Castamere" is a mini archetype of *Game of Thrones* as a whole. It's punishment for an audience daring to hope, and another lesson in the mortality of our heroes. The episode starts with Robb and Catelyn operating from a position of strength, surely about to succeed as they press forward on a heroic path of vengeance. The literal game of thrones is laid on the table in Robb's war room, daring us to think he might just pull this off.

Unlike other episodes on our highlight list, the pacing of "The Rains of Castamere" is more muted. For a majority of the episode, Benioff and Weiss smartly lulled everyone into a false sense of confidence. Small victories are peppered into the hour as Jon finally breaks away from his double life as a wildling and a man of the Night's Watch. Daenerys successfully sacks Yunkai, her campaign to end slavery succeeding more with each passing episode. Edmure realizes his bride is more lovely than he could have imagined. Arya, as much as she loathes the Hound, has grown used to his presence. In turn, he's taken over a protective role for the girl, though he can't admit it yet. Arya is our proxy in this episode, feet away from the family she's yearned for and fearful it will all disappear. She lets her guard down and smiles with optimism as she nears the gates of the Twins. All seems okay on the Westerosi front.

But it's too late. The dread creeps in with only sixteen minutes to go, as Catelyn hears the introductory notes to "The Rains of Castamere" and we feel the episode shift. While moments before, Robb and Talisa were joyfully talking about teaching their child (a little Ned Stark, perhaps?) how to ride horses, suddenly a shadow is cast over the celebration. Few *Game of Thrones* moments feel as haunted upon rewatch as the slow turn Catelyn makes toward the sole man playing cello.

Lady Stark is our catalyst once more, as she realizes Roose Bolton is dressed for a fight. But before anyone can make a defensive move, Lothar Frey unsheaths a small dagger and plunges it, repeatedly, into Talisa's belly, killing both her and poor dead Ned all over again.

From then on, the blood and horror feels endless. It's not a glorified fight. It's not sanitized. People are dying, screaming, bleeding, and we get no reprieve. No hope. No sign of an end to the pain. The disorientation is overwhelming. Robb, already pricked with arrows like a morbid pincushion, cradles his dead wife's head.

Even as Catelyn screams and begs for his life, voice hoarse and face swollen with tears, Robb can't bring himself to fight anymore. He rises one final time, our King in the North, his spirit deadened much like our own, before Roose Bolton slides into frame and delivers a final twist of the knife. Robb fought. He lost. Now he rests.

"Show them how it feels to lose what they love," Catelyn had said to Robb at the episode's start. We can't have possibly realized she was speaking about us. Nothing will ever top this moment in television history.

"Any man who must say 'I am the king' is no true king."
—Tywin Lannister (season 3, episode 10: "Mhysa")

———————— ❧❧ ————————

Aside from Tyrion, Tywin is the one character who has no issue putting Joffrey in his place. This line was a sharp lesson to the boy-king: Simply screaming your title at your enemies is not going to make them believe you have power. Tywin's cool, calm demeanor is striking in the face of Joffrey's unhinged immaturity.

This is also a line that comes back to haunt House Lannister. After Joffrey's death, Tommen finds himself having to yell "I am the king!" at the High Sparrow, and Cersei screams about her queenhood when the Faith Militant arrest her.

"If any more words come pouring out your cunt mouth, I'm going to have to eat every fucking chicken in this room."
—Sandor "The Hound" Clegane (season 4, episode 1: "Two Swords")

———————— ❧❧ ————————

In this scene, the Hound and Arya have been traveling without food for days, and all they want is a hot meal and some peace. But when they run into a band of Lannister soldiers, the Hound is forced to kill nearly every man in the room before he can actually eat his precious chicken.

He didn't have to cause a ruckus, but something about the way Arya seems determined to kill the Lannister scum triggers Sandor's protective instincts to kick in. This is the true moment when Arya and the Hound are bonded, marking the slow erosion of him from her little list. The scene concludes with Arya and the Hound riding horses into the sunset, gloriously eating chicken.

SEASON FOUR, EPISODE TWO

"THE LION AND THE ROSE"

King Joffrey's death is almost a relief—the key word being *almost*. Given the trauma we'd all experienced during the climactic moments of "The Rains of Castamere," it was only fair we see the Lannisters get their comeuppance. But in this episode, the last of Martin's penned scripts for the series, the final moment delivers the much-needed catharsis wrapped up in a bittersweet pill.

The episode plays like a fantastic whodunit when you rewatch it. The masterful staging and editing of the scene obfuscates Olenna Tyrell's role in Joffrey's death the first time around, but when you know what to look for, the truth unfolds clearly. Joffrey's crown, seen clearly during the ceremony in the sept, now has silver roses wrapping around its prongs. The Tyrells are throttling Joffrey in more ways than one.

"Cursed be he who would seek to tear them asunder," the septon says as the camera focuses on Olenna Tyrell, framed just over Margaery's shoulder.

Later Olenna fusses with Sansa's hair just at her neckline as she laments about the awfulness of killing a man at his own wedding. When the camera angle changes, we can see a jewel missing from Sansa's necklace. The episode is cleverly staged to show Tyrion's innocence. After Joffrey humiliates his uncle, Joffrey takes a sip of wine from the goblet handed to him by Tyrion. Then Margaery takes it from his hands and places it on the table behind them.

We don't have eyes on the goblet again—though Olenna is clearly standing near the spot Margaery left it—until Tyrion is ordered to retrieve the cup once more and hand it to Joffrey. Olenna stares hard at him as he lifts the glass, but Tyrion doesn't add any wine, or poison (obviously), to the cup before Joffrey takes a swig.

Aside from the murder-mystery dinner party aspect of it

all, Sansa and Tyrion have a particularly tender set of scenes together. When the dwarves are trotted out for entertainment, mocking both Tyrion and Robb Stark's murder, Sansa sits looking shell-shocked. This is a torment the newlyweds share, leaving us thinking the odd couple could survive with each other as support. In the smallest of scene cuts, we see Tyrion reach gently for his wife's hand, a small gesture of kindness, and evidence of their nascent trust in each other. They had begun working together as a team, a partnership found in an unwanted marriage, just moments before they are separated.

"The Lion and the Rose" delivers up more lighthearted dynamic duos than a smorgasbord of amuse-bouches at a feast. Jaime and Bronn training together, Tyrion and Varys whispering in the gardens, Stannis and Selyse (okay, this one is like the antiduo but their dinner scene sings nonetheless). Olenna and Tywin trade barbs, Brienne and Cersei discuss Jaime, Jaime and Loras discuss Cersei, and Oberyn continues having sexual tension with every human on Planetos. The whole episode is an embarrassment of riches when it comes to one-liners and loaded glances.

Joffrey in particular is perfectly petulant, setting us up to loathe him entirely before he chokes and dies in his mother's arms, eyes bleeding and face purpled from the poisoned wine. In the end, the death we wanted to happen most is satisfying, but not quite triumphant. Martin wants us to feel a tinge of empathy in this moment, once again surprising our emotional instincts and keeping us on our toes.

"I did not kill Joffrey but I wish that I had.
Watching your vicious bastard die gave me more
relief than a thousand lying whores."
—Tyrion Lannister (season 4, episode 6: "The Laws of Gods and Men")

———————— ✤✤ ————————

The trial for Joffrey's murder was brutally unfair to watch unfold, especially as a viewer who knew Tyrion had no part in the king's death. Finally hearing Tyrion defend himself, and lash out at all the betrayers and liars in the room, was a gleeful, fist-pumping moment. Tyrion's anger is palpable, and no one can fault him for cracking at last.

"Nothing isn't better or worse than anything.
Nothing is just nothing."
—Arya Stark (season 4, episode 7: "Mockingbird")

———————— ✤✤ ————————

As Arya finds herself surrounded by death and destruction, she begins taking a rather nihilistic view of the world. Her family is dead, and everywhere she turns only betrayal and dishonor are found. So when she meets a strange man who is slowly dying, Arya's words to him are not meant to be comfort. She is cluing him in on the reality of death, and the nothingness that lies ahead for everyone.

Though Arya will never truly be No One (her Stark identity is too much a part of her), there does come a point when her self-preservation kicks in and begins to stamp out any sentimentality or optimism. Watching *Game of Thrones*, it's hard not to agree with her. Anyone can be killed. Nothing is just nothing. All men must die, and all men must serve.

> *"A ruler who kills those devoted to her is
> not a ruler who inspires devotion."*

—Tyrion Lannister (season 5, episode 8: "Hardhome")

———— 🦑🦑 ————

More infinite wisdom from Tyrion. This line comes during Tyrion and Dany's first meeting, when she asks him to advise her on what to do with Jorah. Tyrion partially owes his life to Jorah, since he saved him from the Stone Men. But Tyrion needs to win favor with Daenerys if he wishes to continue living. With this advice (banish Jorah instead of killing or forgiving him) Tyrion placates both Daenerys and Jorah in one fell swoop.

SEASON FIVE, EPISODE EIGHT
"HARDHOME"

The reason "Hardhome" is so effective lies entirely in the element of surprise. The comically underwhelming episode description ("Arya makes progress in her travels. Sansa confronts an old friend. Cersei struggles. Jon travels.") left casual audiences with tempered expectations. Book-readers knew from the title alone that *something* would happen here, but what exactly was a mystery.

In A Song of Ice and Fire, we only hear about Hardhome secondhand when a Night's Watch brother sent there to make peace with the wildlings sends Jon an ominous letter mentioning "dead things in the woods" and "dead things in the water" while asking for the Lord Commander to send help.

Book-readers never learned what happened at Hardhome, but they knew it wasn't good news for the living. In this way, "Hardhome" managed what no previous *Game of Thrones*

episode had been able to pull off—thrilling new storytelling for show-watchers only, and a bounty of ASOIAF references tucked into a plot that would be fresh and satisfying for book-readers, too. "Hardhome" showed what Benioff and Weiss were capable of without the strict guidance of a George R. R. Martin chapter.

After the show had made a string of horrible story choices, starting with the introduction of Dorne and leading to Ramsay's assault of Sansa, fans needed something to cling to, something that would prove this beloved program wasn't heading irreversibly down a path of thin character arcs and nonstop doom. Yes, "Hardhome" was more massacre than battle, and the eerie silence of its final moments as bone-chillingly dismal. But it was a gloriously compiled episode of television, and could not have come at a more welcome time in the series' history. This was fan service at its finest.

The first of these moments came with Tyrion and Dany's first conversation, a milestone Martin's novels hadn't yet reached. This is a nexus of many different character paths, and the scene serves as a brilliant mini-recap of the paths Tyrion and Dany have taken to get to this moment. The death of Joanna Lannister in childbirth, and Tyrion's more recent murder of his father. Dany's tumultuous birth at Dragonstone that gave her the title of Stormborn, and her rise to power with nothing but a name, willpower, and strong invocation of the House Targaryen words: fire and blood.

Their first conversation is a master class in Tyrion's learned talents of negotiation and political strategy. He wisely advises Dany, and Ser Jorah is banished once more. As the two troubled people discuss their terrible fathers, we get yet another glimpse into the brilliant reasons why Martin was intent on getting these two family outcasts into the same room.

But then we get to those glorious twenty-nine minutes, an

isolated battle sequence that starts with a shot of Jon Snow looking like George Washington crossing the Delaware. Jon shoulders his role as Lord Commander well, even if he can't help being a melodramatic sad boy by telling a room full of murderous wildlings that he put an arrow through Mance Rayder's heart without giving the proper context. Thankfully Tormund steps in and explains why Jon's arrow was a mercy.

Before Jon can complete his mission, all hell breaks loose. The episode's direction works in harmony with Ramin Djawadi's score, alternating between increasingly terrifying ticking and horror that lapses into stunned silence. With a ramping tension and the impeccably CGI'd wight zombies, "Hardhome" plays out more like a horror film than an episode of television.

The crowning moment of the episode comes when Jon (and the rest of us at home) learned that his Valyrian steel sword, Longclaw, can hold its own against a White Walker's icy blade.

A high-pitched ringing is suddenly the only sound you can hear, a precursor to the coming destruction. Jon cries out and looks at the White Walker. The White Walker stares back, hesitating one millisecond too long before pulling back for a final swipe at the man before him. Jon blocks him easily and Longclaw comes down with a quiet swoosh that ends with the sound of shattered glass.

Though book-readers had long theorized that Valyrian steel (sometimes called dragonsteel) possessed the same zombie-killing function as dragonglass, this epic moment was the first sign of confirmation. Jon was already a thriving hero, but for him to be the first character on the series to kill a White Walker with a Valyrian blade put him at the next level.

We also must acknowledge Birgitte Hjort Sørensen, aka Karsi the wildling, for having the best mini-arc of any side character in *Game of Thrones* history. Karsi's no-nonsense introduction at the gathering of elders shows us how savvy and pragmatic she is compared to the stubborn male leaders of other wildling tribes. Her compassion turns on her partway through the battle, when a band of child-wights descend upon her and she can barely bring herself to raise her arms in defense. When her corpse sits up at the episode's end, the pang we felt for Karsi's loss is a testament to how well written her character was for just a thirty-minute sequence in a TV show comprised of hundreds and hundreds of named roles.

Truthfully, the entire episode brought the whole season up to the next level. "Hardhome" didn't just save the fifth season, it also was our first experience of the genius that is Miguel Sapochnik. The thinnest of lines separate the greatest *Game of Thrones* episodes, and nearly all of those top contenders were directed by the same man: Miguel Sapochnik. "Hardhome" introduced Sapochnik's brilliant perspective on the *Game of Thrones* universe. He would go on to direct the sixth season's final two episodes, "Battle of the Bastards" and "The Winds of Winter," as well as the two most action-packed episodes of the final season "The Long Night" and "The Bells."

> *"And meat and mead at my table."*
> —Podrick Payne and Sansa Stark
> (season 6, episode 1: "The Red Woman")

———— ❧❧ ————

The further along in the series we got, the fewer scenes of honor and custom were included. People simply didn't have time for such formalities. But on the sixth season premiere, Sansa is rescued by Theon, Podrick, and Brienne of Tarth. When Brienne kneels and places Oathkeeper at Sansa's feet, the scene transports us back to season two, when Brienne made the same oath to Lady Catelyn Stark.

Sansa recognizes the moment for its solemn importance, but she's freezing, terrified, and tired. When it's her turn to speak, Sansa starts confidently but stumbles over the words. Her mother taught them to her at some point, surely, but time and tragedy have sapped them away.

And so Podrick, sweet and brave Podrick, gently recites the next line for her. It's a small gesture, but one so simple and kind that it has an added weight. The emotion running through this ritual is tangible, and never more so than when the simple promise of meat and mead is made.

> *"It's yours, it will always be yours."*
> —Jaime Lannister (season 6, episode 8: "No One")

———— 🦑 🦑 ————

Seeing Brienne and Jaime reunite during the siege of Riverrun was a bitter pill to swallow. Jaime is fully back on Team Cersei (at least at this point) and Brienne realizes how far backward he's slid into Lannister loyalty. But for the many fans who believed Jaime and Brienne's relationship is among the most understated and deeply romantic connections in the whole series, it was easy to melt a little bit when Jaime refuses to take Oathkeeper back.

"It's yours," he says, in a voice that sounds like he's talking about his heart and not a Valyrian blade. "It will always be yours."

SEASON SIX, EPISODE TEN
"THE WINDS OF WINTER"

The sixth season struggles with pacing and its internal storytelling logic, but "The Winds of Winter" is an absolutely flawless episode of television, and the best in all of *Game of Thrones*. The chilling "Light of the Seven" opening is the first sign of greatness. Djawadi's slow-building piano tune immediately signaled change. Once again, director Miguel Sapochnik works masterfully to build the episode up to a heart-pounding explosion.

Though "The Winds of Winter" manages to kill off more major, named characters than the Red Wedding, the death here is more elegant. Horrible? Of course. But there's a graceful quality to the assassination. The stage is set, populated, and incinerated. The audience isn't overcome in an instant by the violence, but instead it builds more subtly. We're trapped in the room as Margaery, the better queen in every sense, the one who came closest to unseating Cersei, tries and fails to make the inept men around her see the obvious: They are all about to die.

Djawadi's score kicks into gear with the eerie vocals as Qyburn's little birds extract daggers from their sleeves. By the time the green flames bloom, we are mesmerized. The Red Wedding was all shock, but the explosion at the Sept of Baelor is pure awe.

Somehow, the episode improves from there, sinking into quieter, more meaningful scenes. Jaime's disgust with Walder Frey moves forward his personal push for reclaiming honor. The introduction of Oldtown and the Citadel alone could command an essay on set design, the score, and John Bradley West's ever-endearing performance as Sam.

When Ser Davos confronts Melisandre about the burning of Shireen, the exchange is so purifying that, ironically, the Lord of Light would love it. Afterward, Jon and Sansa stand on the battlements of Winterfell and share an honest, loving moment as "siblings." You can practically feel Ned there, smiling sadly as Sansa tells Jon that winter is here.

Another tearjerker comes when our resident cynic Tyrion confesses he's become an idealist thanks to Daenerys. When she produces a silver Hand of the Queen badge, the emotion of the gesture is overwhelming to both Tyrion and us at home. Two of our three favorite outcasts have found each other at the edge of one world and are about to embark on the trip west that Martin's longtime fans had been hoping for since 1996.

The real mastery of "The Winds of Winter" is shown through the back-to-back-to-back scenes of the Tower of Joy, Jon's crowning, Cersei's coronation, and Dany's armada setting sail.

Benioff and Weiss at long last showed fans who Jon Snow's real mother was, with the gutting flashback to Ned Stark finding Lyanna in her bed of blood. Again (and this cannot be emphasized enough) Djawadi's score works its incredible magic as the camera zooms in on the innocent baby's face, crescendoing into the Stark theme as the scene transitions to Jon Snow's scarred and battle-worn face.

Jon went from being literally dead at the end of season five to standing before the Northern lords (and lady) as the leader he was reborn to be. Young Lyanna Mormont stands, chastising the men around her and declaring Jon her King in the North. The men follow suit, rallying one by one until the crowd chants in unison for their true leader.

As Jon gets his triumphant crowning, Cersei ascends the Iron Throne in her more, well, Cersei way. She went from sobbing through the humiliation of her walk of atonement in the fifth season finale to literally burning down the house of worship responsible for her shame. She made that walk to get to Tommen, only to lose him thanks to her nearsighted need for revenge. This poignancy is lost on Cersei, who is crowned in the dark, cold throne room. There is no cheer, no resounding sense of support from her subjects. Only fear. Even from Jaime, the only one left in the world who may love her.

The score once again makes a masterful transition to Dany's full-circle moment. She ended the fifth season by fleeing from her queendom in Meereen on Drogon's back, heading into a wasteland where captivity awaited her. Now she is setting sail with an armada of ships at her back and all three of her dragons soaring proudly overhead. Daenerys Stormborn of House Targaryen, the First of Her Name, the Unburnt, Queen of the Andals and the First Men, Khaleesi of the Great Grass Sea, Breaker of Chains, and Mother of Dragons, is finally going home.

> *"Tell Cersei. I want her to know it was me."*
>
> —Olenna Tyrell (season 7, episode 3: "The Queen's Justice")

———— ❧ ❧ ————

Virtually no one gets a clean death on *Game of Thrones*. Maester Aemon dying of old age was about as close as we saw. But Olenna motherfucking Tyrell, still raw with grief over Cersei's murder of her family, gulped down the poisoned wine handed to her by Jaime like it was the elixir of life. Dame Diana Rigg does a beautiful job in this moment—you can feel the adrenaline coursing through the Queen of Thorns as she launches into her final verbal spar.

"I'd hate to die like your son," she says, her voice somehow stronger and louder after the poison has gone down her throat.

Olenna then proceeds to reveal to Jaime that it was her who poisoned Joffrey, Jaime's firstborn son and then King of the Seven Kingdoms. While Jaime was poised and respectful of Olenna before, his face becomes a mask of shock and loathing. Then Olenna speaks her one final wish. The Queen of Thorns will die in peace, knowing she has been able to inflict one final, festering wound on the Lannisters.

SEASON SEVEN, EPISODE FOUR

"THE SPOILS OF WAR"

Despite being a record-short runtime of just fifty minutes, "Spoils of War" is an unparalleled feat in *Game of Thrones* history. As you may have realized at this point, the best episodes of this show follow a certain recipe. There needs to be balance between epic scale and intimate human tragedy. You need a dash of sexual tension (if not outright sex) and a sprinkling of humor. Most important, the best *Game of Thrones* episodes are the ones where you find yourself rooting for an unexpected character.

"Spoils of War" had it all. Arya's return to Winterfell is a peak Stark moment for the season. Her training session with Brienne is the first time we see Arya's skills put to a proper test. Arya cheekily tells Brienne that "no one" taught her how to fight, which is technically true.

On Dragonstone, Jon and Daenerys work on their alliance with a cozy cave scene (a not-so-subtle nod to Jon's first foray into love with Ygritte—in a cave). Davos throws around some great quips and grammar lessons he learned from Stannis, and Jon confronts Theon about his past grievances.

This is when the best part of the episode kicks off and the tension is immediately palpable. Even after Jon tried to talk Daenerys out of using her dragons on King's Landing, we hear that she's left Dragonstone. To where? The scene stops short of having Jon explain, but the immediate cut to Jaime and the Lannister army says it all.

The ensuing showdown between Daenerys's Dothraki army and Drogon against the Lannister forces is arguably one of the best battle sequences *Game of Thrones* has ever delivered. And that's a very high bar. The episode is reminiscent of "Hardhome." The element of surprise cannot be underestimated when it comes to *Game of Thrones*. Whenever epic, game-changing episodes were placed in earlier slots rather than the expected penultimate spot, hype levels among fans always went through the roof.

Just as in "Hardhome," the madness onscreen in "Spoils of War" was a feat of CGI magic, incredible stunt work, fantastic directing, and seamless writing. All done without the support of Martin's book material (that we know of).

The "Spoils of War" battle triggered surprising sympathy for the Lannister soldiers. We had all cheered after the season seven premiere when Arya slaughtered the Frey men, right? We'd have expected a Lannister massacre to bring about similar feelings of vengeance and righteousness.

"The first thing I decided was that I wanted it to be mostly from Jaime and Bronn's point of view," the episode's director, Matt Shakman, said in an interview with *INSIDER*. "I wanted to tell the story of what it was like to be on the ground and in the middle of a dragon attack and what it was like when war changes forever and a truly horrific weapon like napalm or an atom bomb is suddenly unleashed and what that does to the men on the ground."

Shakman took care to show you the young Lannister soldiers literally shaking as they face the Dothraki. Men shriek as they are burned alive inside their own armor, turning into piles of ash within seconds. The bleakness is only made worse when we see Tyrion standing on a nearby cliff, watching as the men sworn to defend his family name are wiped out without a second thought from Daenerys.

"Because we've seen dragon battles before and they're very exciting," Shakman continued. "You're with Daenerys as she kills the slavers in Meereen and that's all very heroic and you're rooting for her, but this is suddenly the first battle where you've got two opposing people who you're really rooting for and you like and you're not sure how you feel about them going up against each other, so I wanted to make sure we felt that humanity."

Jaime, who had been a rather boring character of late, was the star of this episode. His first sighting of a dragon along with seeing Daenerys Targaryen—the last remaining daughter of the Mad King, Aerys II—is breathtaking. Jaime has spent his whole life dealing with the fallout of his decision to break his Kingsguard oath and kill Aerys, a difficult choice he made when faced with the prospect of allowing Aerys to burn King's Landing, and everyone in it, to the ground.

Watching Jaime see that Daenerys was just "more of the same" (as Jon put it), was extremely powerful. *Game of Thrones* excels when Martin's characters, whom you might have been separately cheering for, come together and force the viewer to realize that picking sides isn't nearly as black-and-white as you might have thought.

This story is more than just Lannister versus Targaryen or good versus evil. It's not about dragons or direwolves or magical ice zombies. *Game of Thrones* is a story about the cycles of war, vengeance, and justice, and how those larger-than-life purposes affect change at a human level. "Spoils of War" homed in on this theme with the perfect amount of nuance as well as the grandiose production quality often seen in feature films, all in just fifty minutes of screen time.

"But you never lost him. He's a part of you, just like he's a part of me."

—Jon Snow (season 7, episode 7: "The Dragon and the Wolf")

———— ❧❧ ————

Theon's torn loyalties to both House Greyjoy and House Stark make for one of the best subplots and character journeys in the entire series. In this moment, when Theon is desperately bereft over failing Yara, he seeks out Jon's advice and validation. Jon could easily dismiss Theon, the person who betrayed his family and caused irrevocable damage.

But instead of furthering the divide between them, Jon chooses magnanimity. He gives Theon a small bit of absolution by letting him know that Ned Stark will always be a part of him. This permission to identify with the rest of the Starks is an act of compassion so deeply foreign to Theon at this point that he almost can't take it in at once. While he was once so traumatized and abused and only knew himself as Reek, both Sansa and Jon helped bring Theon back from the brink. Jon's gesture to Theon is also a poignant foreshadowing of his own looming identity crisis. Jon is a Stark . . . and a Targaryen. But he doesn't have to choose. He will eventually live out his days far removed from the realm where it matters whose blood runs in his veins. But Jon will always hold his family in his heart.

SEASON EIGHT, EPISODE TWO

"A KNIGHT OF THE SEVEN KINGDOMS"

Heading into the final six episodes of *Game of Thrones*, fans who had fallen in love with the show's early balance of high fantasy elements with grounded character work were concerned about the ramped-up pacing. Remember how Benioff and Weiss were forced to write those little two-hander scenes in which just a few characters would talk, digging into the themes of power and honor and duty? Those early scenes may have originated as a way to simply fill minutes cheaply, but they became the bedrock of what drew people into the show and made us care more deeply about each of the many characters.

Unfortunately the final season of the series had less time for quieter, emotionally impactful character payoff moments. But "A

Knight of the Seven Kingdoms" gave us a true embarrassment of riches when it came to these character-driven, soul-stirring scenes. The episode was penned by Bryan Cogman, a man who started out working as the personal assistant to Benioff and Weiss but was eventually invited to write for the show. He scripted several memorable episodes, including season four's "The Laws of Gods and Men" (with Tyrion's trial), season three's "Kissed by Fire" (with Jaime's bathtub monologue and Jon and Ygritte's passionate cave scene), and season five's infamous "Unbowed, Unbent, Unbroken" (with Sansa's upsetting wedding to Ramsay Bolton).

Cogman's episodes were the ones that usually reworked the best of Martin's dialogue or followed the themes closest to the heart of A Song of Ice and Fire, and "A Knight of the Seven Kingdoms" was no exception. "What I really wanted that episode to be was a love letter to the characters, because I love them so much," Cogman said in HBO's "The Game Revealed" video for the episode. His voice breaks just at the end, and it's impossible to watch him speak about this episode and not feel just how thoughtfully he approached this key moment in the final season.

"A Knight of the Seven Kingdoms" is a slow wave of heartache, building masterfully as the prelude to a coming doom. Happy tears begin building when Jaime and Brienne are first reunited, bringing together the twin swords made from Ice, the ancestral Valyrian steel greatsword of House Stark, in Winterfell for the first time since Ned Stark's death. The sword was taken by the Lannisters when Ned was arrested, and later melted into two new blades by Tywin Lannister.

He gave one of these swords to Jaime, who in turn gifted it to Brienne. She named it Oathkeeper, and vowed to protect Ned Stark's daughters in fulfillment of Jaime's promise to their mother, Catelyn. The second sword was given to King Joffrey, who named it Widow's Wail. After Joffrey's death, Jaime took the blade for himself.

And then Theon Greyjoy arrives, and his loving embrace with Sansa Stark chips one more hole in the dam holding back a flood of feelings. Those heartaches are compounded when Davos and Gilly see a young girl with a facial scar, reminding them of the sweet and kind young princess who was tragically killed on her own parents' orders.

Grey Worm and Missandei have their final meaningful conversation in the series, caving to wishful thinking that they might someday share a peaceful life together on the far shores of the Isle of Naath. Arya reexamines what it means to be something more than a hardened killing machine. She goes to Gendry and reclaims an important piece of her humanity, allowing herself to be vulnerable and desired and *feel* something in a way the trauma of her childhood had blocked her from before.

The last twelve minutes of "A Knight of the Seven Kingdoms" are sheer perfection. Like all the best *Game of Thrones* moments, the simplicity of Brienne being knighted by Jaime is executed with some of the most thoughtful and heartfelt direction, acting, and writing the show has ever produced.

After watching Brienne operate within Westeros as the most noble and honorable fighter for years, fans had hardly dared to hope she would actually become a knight one day. As she says within the episode, women in Westeros are not allowed to be knights. But customs are easily changed, and traditions go by the wayside when death is knocking at your door.

Brienne and Jaime find themselves sitting around the fire with Tormund Giantsbane, Tyrion Lannister, Ser Davos Seaworth, and Podrick Payne. With wine flowing and war stories being traded, the scene feels like watching a small, intimate house party. But the light atmosphere shifts when Tormund shows disbelief that Brienne isn't a "ser" like her male peers. He boasts that he would make her a knight if he were a king, and Jaime chimes in to point out that it doesn't take a king to make someone a knight. He says he'll prove it, and offers to knight Brienne on the spot.

She laughs it off at first, but Podrick watches her carefully. As Jaime presses Brienne to come and kneel, Podrick gives her a quiet nod. He's been at her side for years, learning from her and witnessing her chivalry. Podrick knows what this would mean to her, and how serious this moment is about to be. He encourages her to take that risk and allow herself to be vulnerable in this moment.

And so Brienne goes to Jaime.

"In the name of the Warrior, I charge you to be brave," Jaime says, placing his sword upon her shoulder. "In the name of the Father, I charge you to be just. In the name of the Mother, I charge you to defend the innocent. Arise, Brienne of Tarth, a knight of the Seven Kingdoms."

Brienne stands, tears in her eyes, as Tormund begins to clap excitedly. Jaime looks around, almost surprised to realize there are other people in the room. And we at home cheered, seeing the truest knight of the Seven Kingdoms standing in her rightful place.

"A Knight of the Seven Kingdoms" ends with Daenerys seeking out Jon in the crypts of Winterfell as the final notes of "Jenny of Oldstones" fade into sweet nothing. The entire episode, and especially these closing moments, has been built around scenes that highlight both Dany and Jon's loneliness and isolation. As everyone around her gets tender parting moments with loved ones, Dany tries and fails to find that same comfort in Jon.

Instead, he reveals the devastating truth of his parentage. This is the truth that will lead neither of them to the throne as some fans may have expected, but instead will be a driving force behind Dany's increasing bitterness and paranoia as her time in Westeros unfolds in a way antithetical to her dreams. She spent her whole life wishing for a home, a place of comfort and love. When she finally set sail, leaving behind Essos and heading into the "great game" (as Tyrion called it), Daenerys believed she was charting a course for her true home. But here, her entangled desires for both the Iron Throne and loving relationships begin working against each other, and the cost will be her life.

MAESTER'S NOTES

The episode title of "A Knight of the Seven Kingdoms" has a double meaning. First, it refers to Jaime himself. The episode begins with Ser Jaime standing trial for his crimes against the houses Stark and Targaryen, his honor and motives under question. The second meaning comes from Brienne's knighting and Martin's ASOIAF universe of characters outside of *Game of Thrones*. In 2016, Martin attended a Baltimore fan convention and hinted at a connection between Brienne and a famous Westerosi knight called Ser Duncan the Tall.

Ser Duncan, or "Dunk," was name-dropped in the first season when Old Nan is talking to little Bran about stories, and again on the fourth season as King Joffrey reads through the White Book of the Kingsguard.

Martin wrote three novellas about Dunk and little Aegon V Targaryen, who was known simply as "Egg." Remember in the fifth season when Maester Aemon cries out on his deathbed for "Egg"? He was remembering his younger brother, the one who became king after Aemon himself refused the crown.

Martin packaged the Dunk and Egg novellas into one book titled *A Knight of the Seven Kingdoms*, published in 2015. The Dunk and Egg stories take place about one hundred years before the events of *A Song of Ice and Fire* and *Game of Thrones* itself. Thanks to similar descriptors used for both Brienne and Dunk, fans had long guessed that the two might be connected. Many believe she is Dunk's descendant, and (in the show's canon, anyway) now they are both knights of the Seven Kingdoms who served on the Kingsguard.

"All right, then. Let it be fear."

—Daenerys Targaryen (season 8, episode 5: "The Bells")

———— ❧❧ ————

Dany's downward spiral in the final hours of *Game of Thrones* was difficult to digest, given how heroically positioned the Mother of Dragons had been for so many years. The few moments of tension and desperation afforded to Dany in these episodes were burdened with carrying most of her fast-paced final arc. The most crucial of these small scenes comes when Daenerys laments to Jon about how the people of Westeros have not come to love her the way thousands had done in Essos. Her loneliness and heartache are palpable as she makes one last plea to Jon, hoping his love for her can transcend his qualms about their shared blood. But he denies her that reassurance.

When Jon breaks off their kiss, Daenerys shakes her head and steps back as she speaks with a whisper. Fear it is. She believes the people of Westeros could have lived in peace under their rightful queen, but mistake after mistake (by both herself and those around her) has led to this parting of ways. One of the lessons Syrio teaches Arya in A Song of Ice and Fire is how "fear cuts deeper than swords." Dany's tragic arc reaches a tipping point in this moment. She chooses fear, and with it cuts away the last of her advisers' goodwill.

"Ask me again in ten years."
—Tyrion Lannister (season 8, episode 6: "The Iron Throne")

———— ❧❧ ————

The series finale is written and directed by Benioff and Weiss, and their penchant for inserting meta-commentary about storytelling in *Game of Thrones* was displayed prominently throughout the episode. Whether it was a literal book titled *A Song of Ice and Fire* being slammed down on the small council table or Tyrion making a speech about the connective power of storytelling, there were many small, extra-textual lines of dialogue in "The Iron Throne."

The most successful of these comes when Jon Snow achingly asks Tyrion if he did the right thing by killing Daenerys. Tyrion deflects, clearly uneasy with confronting the choice they both made. "Ask me again in ten years," he says gently. The same answer should be in fans' minds when attempting to parse exactly what *Game of Thrones* achieved (and what it didn't) in its eight-year run on television. Just a day, a week, a month—heck, even a year—is too soon when it comes to fully understanding how this behemoth series fits into our cultural history. Just as the ripple effects of the dagger lodged in Dany's chest were felt around the universe within *Game of Thrones*, so too is the real world going to feel the impact of this show for decades to come.

CHAPTER EIGHT

DRAGONS *or* DIREWOLVES?

The closing weeks of *Game of Thrones* were dotted with vociferous debates about the importance of the Stark direwolves. People were clamoring online about the amount of screen time and pets given (or not given) to our favorite good boy, Ghost. Though more direwolves wound up surviving the entire series than dragons, the Starks' wolf companions were short-changed in the critical hours leading up to the series finale.

Nearly each of the final six installments featured an epic dragon moment: Jon Snow's first ride on Rhaegal, the midair dragon-on-dragon battle resulting in Viserion's mangled jaw spouting blue flames, the horrible death of Rhaegal, and lastly Drogon's decimation of King's Landing and subsequent melting of the Iron Throne. But Ghost was relegated to the side until the very last minute, while Nymeria, Arya's direwolf, was never seen again.

Thankfully the closing minutes of *Game of Thrones* made one thing abundantly clear: The hour of the wolf was upon the world.

Not only did the optimistic montage of Arya, Sansa, and Jon lean into the metaphorical resilience of House Stark's wolves, but we were gifted with Ghost getting one last meaningful scratch under the chin and a pat on the head.

When Martin first conceived of the A Song of Ice and Fire series in the early 1990s, the plan was to write a trilogy. Now that's blossomed into seven total planned books, the final two of which Martin intends to call *The Winds of Winter* and *A Dream of Spring*. But back in 2012, Martin told *Adria's News* that one working title for the last book of the series was *A Time for Wolves*. He's since changed his mind, though he did use that title for a 2014 blog post about literal wolves.

The phrase "a time for wolves" is also connected to Martin's 2018 history book, *Fire and Blood*, a history of House Targaryen charting everything from Aegon's Conquest to the regency of King Aegon III. One section of the book details "The Dance of the Dragons," a horrific civil war that broke out between different Targaryens and resulted in the deaths of many royals and many more dragons. The chapter immediately following this saga is titled "Aftermath—The Hour of the Wolf," which is awfully similar to "A Time for Wolves."

How poignant, then, for HBO's adaptation to close that loop with a beautiful scene of Jon Snow, the bastard of Winterfell, finding a semblance of peace with his direwolf after experiencing the horrors of war. There are parallels between Dany's struggles with the line of Targaryen succession and The Dance of the Dragons saga. In "The Hour of the Wolf," the twenty-year-old Lord of Winterfell, Cregan Stark, comes to King's Landing and helps restore order after the devastation of the Targaryen war. He temporarily serves as Hand of the King, but eventually returns to the North.

This is not unlike the way Bran, Arya, and Sansa are left to deal with the aftermath of Daenerys Targaryen's and Cersei Lannister's final fight for the throne. Not to mention the fallout from Jon Snow (himself part Targaryen) killing Queen Daenerys so shortly after she claimed the Iron Throne. But the game of thrones is over, and now it's the time for wolves. So why, if the ASOIAF story of was always building toward this Stark-centric ending, were the direwolves not featured more prominently in the final seasons of *Game of Thrones*?

The answer lies with visual effects, and the simple truth of pri-oritized storytelling. Remember how George R. R. Martin readily admitted that A Song of Ice and Fire was a completely "unfilmable" series? This assertion isn't thanks to just the epic battles and gigantic wall of ice or sweeping castle towers. One of the core aspects of the series, magical beasts, proved to be one of the most consequential book storylines that was immensely difficult to pull off onscreen.

The long direwolf saga started in the pilot episode of *Game of Thrones*, when we learn about the threat of the White Walkers and then cut to the introduction of House Stark. After witnessing the execution of the Night's Watch deserter, Robb, Bran, and Jon Snow discover the litter of direwolf pups. This was the first time the mys-tical beasts had been seen south of the Wall in more than two hun-dred years. But their auspicious presence was seen as a warning. The pups' mother lay dead in the snow with a stag's antler piercing her throat. She had killed the beast and given birth to exactly six little direwolf puppies before succumbing to her own wounds and dying in a snowbank.

When Ned Stark and the men of his household saw the direwolf, the sigil of House Stark, lying there dead thanks to a stag, the sigil of House Baratheon, they didn't yet know of Jon Arryn's death and the king's pending visit north. But they understood the gravity of the sign nonetheless, even as the children focused on the endearing pups.

Benioff and Weiss adapted this scene straight from the pages of Martin's first chapter in A Song of Ice and Fire, which is told from Bran's point of view. Bran is fretting after Ned's men say the direwolf puppies will have to be killed. Bran protests, but it's Jon Snow whose voice cuts through the bickering.

Thanks to Jon's fast thinking and plea to the superstitious side of Lord Eddard Stark, the pups are saved, and the group starts back to Winterfell. But then Jon hears something and turns around. Jon "hearing" Ghost when no one else can, and especially given that the direwolf never makes a sound again for the rest of the series, indicates that the bastard boy was likely warg-connecting with Ghost before any of the Stark kids even realized that was possible. He shared a mind with Ghost from the beginning, and though the show doesn't make this explicit, fans of the book series have long theorized about the importance of Jon's warging.

The show's version of the direwolf discovery was faithfully adapted, albeit with some changes—like Theon taunting Jon about getting the "runt of the litter" instead of pointing out his albinism. Jon's direwolf, Ghost, is pale white with red eyes, a unique coloring that serves as an early hint of the young man's blended Targaryen (red) and Stark (white) traits.

The Targaryen sigil is a red three-headed dragon on a black field, while the Stark sigil is a gray direwolf on a white field. Though the show never makes this clear, we know from Martin's novels that highborn bastard children invert the colors of their house sigil for an insignia. This would mean Jon's herald should be a white wolf on a gray field.

In the seventh season, Jon stands in the great hall of his Stark family home as the young Lady Mormont chastises her elders for forgetting their allegiance to House Stark and Jon Snow. Jon Snow is the White Wolf, the King in the North, and his faithful Ghost is not only immortalized in the pommel of Jon's Valyrian steel blade, Longclaw, but he's the physical embodiment of the newest King in the North. Ghost simultaneously represents Jon's bastard status and his unique link between House Stark and Targaryen. Ghost is Jon's royal blood and his Northern sensibility all packaged into one creature.

Each of the wolves has a spiritual and narrative connection to the Stark kids. Even their names reflect their importance. In the books, little Bran Stark struggles with choosing a name for his pup. It's only after he wakes up from his coma and his very first greenseeing dream that the perfect moniker comes to him: Summer. Both Bran and his direwolf represent the antithesis of winter. Their mere existence is diametric to that of the White Walkers. But the young king-to-be loses his direwolf in the show, a blow that is emotionally overshadowed by the subsequent death of Hodor.

Arya's, Sansa's, and Rickon's direwolves have their own narrative importance, too. Lady, Sansa's wolf, falls victim to the Lannisters' scheming and cruelty after Arya attacks Joffrey on the Kingsroad.

The death of Sansa's wolf was an early sign of how awful things would become for Sansa in King's Landing and within the manipulative grip of Cersei. As for Arya, she becomes untethered from her family following the betrayal of Ned, and as Nymeria grows more wild in Westeros, so too does Arya undergo dramatic and dark changes.

MAESTER'S NOTES

Sophie Turner (Sansa Stark) wound up adopting the Northern Inuit dog who played Lady in the first season of *Game of Thrones*. The wolflike dog, named Zunni, lived with Turner and her family until she reportedly died in 2017. "Growing up I always wanted a dog, but my parents never wanted one," Turner told the *Coventry Telegraph* in 2013. "We kind of fell in love with my character's direwolf, Lady, on set. We knew Lady died and they wanted to re-home her. My mum persuaded them to let us adopt her."

Turner's early Instagram posts include photos of Zunni (or "Zoonz," as Turner calls her) celebrating Christmas with the Turners and romping around in a grassy yard.

Martin has hinted at the forthcoming importance of Nymeria's wolf pack currently ravaging the Riverlands. In an interview with Mashable, Martin compared the wolf pack to the literary principle known as "Chekhov's gun." The principle is named after its creator, who famously said: "If in the first act you have hung a pistol on the wall, then in the following one it should be fired." The idea is that every big detail contained in your literary narrative should serve a greater purpose down the line. "You know, I don't like to give things away," Martin told *Mashable* with a reported grin on his face. "But you don't hang a giant wolf pack on the wall unless you intend to use it."

By the seventh season, Arya sees Nymeria again during a chance encounter in the woods. But the two part after Arya realizes her once loyal wolf pup is now untamed and unfit for a human-centric life. Indeed, Arya's parting words to her direwolf are "That's not you." This is a callback to a scene between Ned and Arya in the first season, when Ned tells his youngest daughter she will one day marry a lord and run his castle.

Fans who knew about Martin hinting about the wolf pack being a Chekhov's gun were mystified by this scene, and remained convinced we hadn't seen the last of Arya's wolf pack. Surely they'd partake in the great battle against the White Walkers, right? But we had been cheated once more of a satisfying end to a Stark's relationship with their direwolf.

Rickon's wolf is aptly named Shaggydog—a term defined by *Merriam-Webster* as "a long-drawn-out circumstantial story concerning an inconsequential happening"—and the beast mirrors his own wild behavior as a young orphaned boy outside the control of any would-be parental figures. The show killed Shaggydog off-camera, cruelly tossing his head around a couple times on the sixth season for good measure. Rickon dies shortly afterward when Ramsay uses him as live bait for Jon Snow at the Battle of the Bastards. And Grey Wind, Robb Stark's wolf—the fiercest and most battle-experienced of all the direwolves—also comes to an untimely end at the hands of the Starks' enemies.

Regardless of all the significance Martin placed upon the direwolves and the Stark children, their roles in the show are reduced to a few fan-service shots in the final two seasons. The reason for this is twofold. First, there's a problem with realism. You're probably thinking that is a bananas thing to say about a fantasy-based show that features reanimated corpses and shadow-babies and dragons, but let me explain.

Everyone knows what a wolf looks like. Close your eyes and imagine a giant wolf—one that comes up to the shoulders of a young man. You probably don't have any trouble with that visual.

And in fact, the way you imagine that giant wolf and how it moves is probably going to be exactly the same as a thousand other people.

But now close your eyes and imagine a dragon. What dragon are you thinking of? Daenerys's Drogon, with two hind legs, enormous wings, and a thick, hulking neck? Or do you think about the fluffy titular creature from *Pete's Dragon*, with a big pear-shaped body, four legs, and confoundingly small wings? Is it spiked and beaky, like the Hungarian Horntail in *Harry Potter and the Goblet of Fire*?

Now that you've picked a dragon design, how does it move? Is your dragon more like a T. rex with wings? Or is it basically a reptilian cat, like in the How to Train Your Dragon movies? (Sidenote: The How to Train Your Dragon movies are basically required viewing for any fan of *Game of Thrones*. Trust me, you'll love them.)

The point is—there is no one way a dragon looks or moves or sounds. Because it is wholly fictional, there is more wiggle room when it comes to creating a convincing CGI dragon. The *Game of Thrones* creative team did not have that luxury when it came to the direwolves. They had to stop using real wolves on the set altogether, which added complications to the process of having them in the show.

The bigger the wolves got, the more risky it was to put them in scenes with people.

"At the beginning of season two, we discussed how the wolves would be filmed," visual effects (VFX) producer Steve Kullback said in HBO's *Inside Game of Thrones* book. "By then, we had some experience filming live animals, and that had not been pleasant. Everyone on the production and at the studio was keen on exploring the possibility of CG wolves."

The first season had been easy enough. Real trained wolves and dogs were brought on set for scenes with the Starks. But by the second season, as dictated by the books, the wolves were supposed to have grown far beyond the size of regular dogs.

"We worked through what the direwolves were and what they needed to be—they were essentially just very large wolves," Kullback continued. "They didn't need to speak languages; they didn't need to perform judo or dance. And the best solution should solve the two most pressing needs: to get the most realistic and threatening possible creature that looks like a wolf, and to have it be as least burdensome on production as possible."

The resulting plan called for removing the wolves from the shooting set altogether. Instead, Kullback and his team came up with the plan to use a separate green-screen set for any direwolf scene. This would protect the actors, since, as Kullback said, "wolves remain dangerous even after training. The reality is, wolves can be trained to do only so much, and that has introduced a challenge in its own right, which the writers sometimes have to work around."

The direwolves were meant to be growing larger, about "30 to 40 percent bigger than a standard wolf," VFX supervisor Joe Bauer explained. And the risk of having the actors continue working with real wolves on set was becoming an issue, so the second season was the start of a new direwolf filming method. Stuffed versions of the direwolves were crafted and brought to set as stand-ins for what would become Ghost and Summer. An on-set supervisor with the actors would use rigs to show where the wolves would be looking or how they'd move. "Sometimes it's a stick with a piece of tape on it; sometimes it's a tennis ball on a stick," Bauer said.

The core filming crews for *Game of Thrones* were stationed in Northern Ireland, Iceland, and Croatia. But the wolf actors and the green-screen stage were actually all the way across the ocean, in Canada. Bauer and the VFX team would re-create the filmed scenes with real wolves, scaling everything down on the green-screen set so that the wolves would look larger once they were added into the scene during post-production.

"We also shoot at a slightly faster frame rate, say thirty frames per second rather than twenty-four frames per second, just to slow them down ever so much to accommodate their size, but not so much that they are moving in slow motion," Bauer explained. "Then integrate or 'marry in' the image of the wolf on the shot, matching the light of the original day to keep it consistent."

Though Bauer said the goal was not to make the wolves look like they're walking in slo-mo, you can definitely see how the wolves' movements were altered if you pay close attention. For example, in an early season-two episode set beyond the Wall, Ghost intimidates Gilly as she holds a dead rabbit. The wolf is adjusting its weight on its paws, and you can tell that it's ever-so-slightly slowed down. This technique worked for the second season, as we saw Summer, Ghost, and even Robb's direwolf, Grey Wind, in numerous scenes with people. But as the third season approached, and the wolves were supposed to be even bigger, the creators began to see a problem.

"We did some testing, and at a certain point they look unreal," D. B. Weiss told *Entertainment Weekly* ahead of the third season. "We reached a nice balance with them. And frankly, no matter how much money you spend on CG wolves—and we've seen the best that's out there, state of the art, and some of it looks great—it still doesn't look [and] move and feel like a real animal."

"With dragons, you get some leeway," Benioff added. "You can't say, 'Well, that doesn't look like a real dragon.'"

"With a wolf, you have a million years of evolution telling you what they're supposed to act like," Weiss concluded.

Martin's direwolves may be fictional, but there is record of a real animal called the dire wolf, which existed tens of thousands of years ago in both North and South America.

"Their fossils are scattered across North and South America, from the mountains of Virginia to the Las Vegas strip, through Mexico and as far south as Bolivia," according to a *National Geographic* article on the ancient animals that inspired the *Game of Thrones* beasts. "Known scientifically as *Canis dirus*, dire wolves were actually not that much larger than modern gray wolves, but they boasted a larger skull and jaws, and a stronger bite."

Not only are the direwolves of A Song of Ice and Fire based on a real creature, but again, it required a lot more time and effort (and therefore money) to make these extinct creatures live again on your TV screen.

But does some of the blame simply lay with prioritized story-telling on the part of Benioff and Weiss? The second reason for the lack of direwolves in later seasons may simply be that Benioff and Weiss didn't believe them essential enough to the story for a consistent (and expensive) presence. But other seemingly impossible feats of VFX were made possible. An undead polar bear wight attacks Jon Snow and his companions who travel north in season six's "Beyond the Wall." In that episode's behind-the-scenes video, Weiss said they'd been writing a "zombie polar bear" into every season for four years only to be told by executive producer Bernie Caulfield and the VFX team "in the nicest possible way, 'Fuck you, we cannot afford a zombie polar bear.'"

"We thought they'd be so excited to do a zombie bear," Benioff said. "And uh, it was kind of like, 'Oh my god, they're serious about doing this fucking zombie bear.'"

"This year . . . we really put our four feet down and we said, 'Goddammit, we want a zombie polar bear,'" Weiss recounted.

As the seasons progressed, the issue of creating a believably gigantic wolf began clashing with the growing budget and (apparently) the crew's priorities of other CGI'd creatures. It wasn't all zombie polar bears, thankfully. Clearly Dany's dragons made up the bulk of the VFX budget.

So let's sidebar our direwolf gripes for a moment and revel in the magic and might of Drogon, Viserion, and Rhaegal. Just as the early season-one scenes establish the Starks' supernatural link to the direwolves, their house sigil, the final episode of the season concludes with Daenerys's magical birth of her own house sigil: dragons. The birth of dragons in the world again is nothing short of a miracle and is central to Dany's own sense of destiny and purpose.

Ned Stark's death was the character-based climactic moment that helped put *Game of Thrones* on the map. But Daenerys Targaryen stepping into a funeral pyre and emerging naked with three baby dragons was the pivotal moment when the high-fantasy threads of the story really kicked in.

Though the very first scene of the show displayed the truth about White Walkers and magical creatures long thought extinct, the rest of the season serves up character after character insisting these stories are nothing more than myth. *"The dragons are dead, Khaleesi." "There's no such thing as grumpkins and snarks, Tyrion." "Do the dead frighten you?"* Up until that first season finale, folks at home were getting a much heavier dose of *The Sopranos* than Middle Earth from this new HBO series. Thanks to the daring nerve of a young girl, magic reentered the world of *Game of Thrones* and brought high fantasy to mainstream television.

Before Dany decides to invoke the House Targaryen words "fire and blood" (which coincidentally doubles as the two-part recipe for hatching a dragon) she loses her child, Rhaego, as a result of blood magic performed by the "witch" Mirri Maz Duur. While unconscious, Daenerys has a series of dreamlike visions that help guide her toward the birth of her dragons. Her "fever dreams," as they're called in *A Game of Thrones*, feature the threatening line Viserys would often spit at her when she displeased him: *"You don't want to wake the dragon, do you?"*

Dany sees a series of scenes, including the red door she associates with her sense of home, and Drogo on the Dothraki sea, and her unborn son. Viserys's quote is repeated and reduced one word at a time until Dany hears simply "wake the dragon." Her back splits open and wings emerge from the burning blood, and Daenerys flies within her dream. "All that lived and breathed fled in terror from the shadow of her wings," Martin writes. When Daenerys finally breaks through the door in her dream, she sees her brother Rhaegar sitting on a black horse that matches his armor, and hears Ser Jorah whisper, "The last dragon." But when she lifts the visor of the mounted figure, Daenerys sees her own face.

"After that for a long time, there was only the pain," her chapter reads. "The fire inside her and the whispering of stars. She woke to the taste of ashes."

Once Dany is finally able to open her eyes and move, she is drawn to her dragon eggs. Her handmaids tell her about Rhaego's cursed birth and death, but Daenerys is barely able to grieve for him. She is consumed by the memories of her dream, and with each passing moment is more resolute in her path forward. While the show was unable to mimic this dream sequence, Dany's resolution is clear by the time she steps into the burning flames of Drogo's funeral pyre.

When Daenerys Stormborn rises from the ashes as the Mother of Dragons, her path of conquest begins. The destructive force of her children will not be unleashed until they grow older and stronger, like their mother, but it is with those dragons that Daenerys will both save the world and seek to control it. They are her children and her scourges, sentient tools of destruction that will embolden her dreams of reclaiming her home and complicate her desire to rule with both love *and* fear.

Unlike the Starks' direwolves, Dany's dragons are as pivotal to every step of her journey in the show as they are within the five published books. The dragons are a large basis for Dany's ascension to power and ability to topple cities. To leave out or diminish the role of the dragons in *Game of Thrones* would have been antithetical to the story's approach to magic and high fantasy.

Speaking with TV critic Mo Ryan and NPR's Peter Sagal at Chicon7, a World Science Fiction Convention in Chicago in 2012, Martin revealed that early in his writing process for A Song of Ice and Fire he was considering leaving "overt magic" (and therefore dragons) out of the books entirely.

"My friend Phyllis Eisenstein, a wonderful fantasy writer who lives here in Chicago, I happened to be talking to her at a very early stage in the process," Martin said. "Phyllis has written some great fantasies herself. She said, 'Nah, you have to have dragons. It's a fantasy, you know.' And so I dedicated *A Storm of Swords* to Phyllis, who made me put the dragons in,' and I think that was the right thing to do.

"The dragons work on all sorts of symbolic and metaphorical levels," he continued. "But also they're just kinda cool. And it's nice to have cool elements in your fantasy."

You know what else is cool? A gigantic, oversized wolf who is linked to your soul and spirit and will protect you at any cost. Oh, and bonus! You can take over its mind and live a second life after you die.

Humans, wolves, and domesticated dogs share thousands of years of history on our planet. There's good reason why wolves and pups are featured in so many classic and iconic works of fiction. There's the wolf-pack leader Akela, who takes in Mowgli in Rudyard Kipling's *The Jungle Book* (1894). American novelist Jack London's seminal works, *The Call of the Wild* (1903) and *White Fang* (1906), explore the thin instinctual wall between domesticated dogs and feral wolves, and how we humble humans fit into that natural order.

Dodie Smith's novel *The Hundred and One Dalmatians* (1956), later adapted into the endearing Disney animated movie, is an adventure story about anthropomorphized dogs who believe humans to be their pet companions. There's Hayao Miyazaki's *Princess Mononoke* (1997), featuring the wolf god Moro who adopts and protects a young girl.

Balto. Clifford the Big Red Dog. Beethoven. You get the idea.

And mythical companion creatures are not limited to wolves in fantasy storytelling. Whether it's the guiding, nurturing beasts of The Chronicles of Narnia or the symbolic choosing of a pet animal in Harry Potter, the concept of bonding a protagonist to a hyperintelligent animal is in the DNA of fantasy literature.

Phillip Pullman's His Dark Materials trilogy takes the idea even further, giving all people in Lyra's universe a special being called a dæmon. Far beyond the idea of a "pet," dæmons are a physical manifestation of your very inner self, living externally in the world alongside you and taking the form of an animal. Pullman smartly notes within his books that every person, in every universe, has a dæmon—the problem is that not everyone can *see* theirs. This allows his readers to envision their own dæmon, and yearn for the ability to see it and interact with it.

The loss of direwolves as a prominent narrative part of *Game of Thrones* upset legions of fans for good reason. Unlike Dany's dragons, the Stark direwolves were more easily removed from the narrative, which therefore saved money and headaches for the VFX teams. But without knowing the reason behind the choices, it was simply frustrating for fans.

Take, for instance, Ghost's disappearance from virtually all of seasons six and seven. He was around during Jon Snow's dramatic death and resurrection, but then slipped offscreen. Fans noticed his omission more sharply than ever during the Battle of the Bastards. Surely Ghost, a gigantic man-eating wolf, would have been some help against the Bolton army? Director Miguel Sapochnik said in an interview with *Business Insider* that Ghost was originally meant to partake in the battle for Winterfell.

"He was in there in spades originally, but it's also an incredibly time-consuming and expensive character to bring to life," Sapochnik said. "Ultimately we had to choose between Wun Wun [the giant] and the direwolf, so the dog bit the dust."

Earlier in the same season the writers had chosen to simply kill off Bran's direwolf, Summer. In the waking-nightmare episode of "The Door," director Jack Bender worked in a steady frenzy up to the wrenching reveal of Hodor's death and name origin (all wrapped up in a mind-twisting time travel/warg combo). As Bran, Hodor, and Meera are attacked by the Night King and his White Walker henchmen, Summer sacrifices himself to a group of wights. The death was quick, practically just a blur of wolfish fur and then the high-pitched yelping that's unmistakably a dog in pain.

"My objective [with Summer] was not to take anything away either rhythmically or dramatically from what Hodor was about to do," Bender told *Vanity Fair*'s Joanna Robinson after the episode aired. "As much as the direwolf sacrifice was upsetting, I didn't want to spend too much time on it. I felt like we were building toward and literally racing toward Hodor. I felt it was very important to spend the time to tell that part of the story but not dwell on it."

"Did you and Dan and David talk at all about what it means when a direwolf dies?" Robinson replied. "It feels like it means something more than just a beloved pet dying. They're spiritually connected to the Starks."

"We had to deal with so many things creating that sequence in terms of what the set would be, what the sequence would be, what we would see, what we wouldn't see, what would be off camera, what would be on camera," Bender said. "Most of the time, I think, was spent on that as opposed to the emotional or mythological ramifications."

By the eighth season premiere, all hope in seeing meaningful, extended interactions with the Stark direwolves had practically vanished. Then salt was sprinkled into the wound when the opening episode showed Jon's return to Winterfell with no Ghost *and* Jon riding a dragon for the first time. Jon quipped to Daenerys that she had "ruined horses" for him by letting him hop on Rhaegal's back—but what about his direwolf? Sure, Ghost wasn't taking Jon on joyrides, but he was a protector and one of Jon's strongest physical manifestations of his Northern blood. Ghost was the weirwood of the old gods, the premonition of Jon's own slip into the arms of death, the warmth he turned to during the cold nights.

Imagine for a moment that the Northern lords proclaimed Jon Snow "The King in the North!" and "The White Wolf" while Ghost sat by his side, nearly coming up to Jon's shoulder and silently observing the raucous cheers. Imagine Daenerys having to reach out her bare hand, slowly, gingerly, taking an intimate step into Jon's life by winning the trust of his faithful direwolf.

The Stark direwolves were more than just pets. They were the ancient Stark sigil come to life after centuries, beings of the North and protectors of Ned Stark's children long after his death. If Jon and Daenerys were always the endgame union, then their respective familial animals, their guardians and source of power and magic, were also meant to play a role in the story. Sure, it was easier for Benioff and Weiss to write out the direwolves from a majority of their final seasons, but this choice also shows their priorities when it came to characterizing the Starks, and deemphasizing the high-fantasy aspects of their narratives.

Martin has long said the inspiration for A Song of Ice and Fire came to him out of seemingly nowhere, while he was working on a science fiction novel called *Avalon*. "Suddenly it just came to me, this scene," he told *Rolling Stone*. "It's from Bran's viewpoint; they see a man beheaded and they find some direwolf pups in the snow. It just came to me so strongly and vividly that I knew I had to write it." That this scene, and specifically the wolves in the snow, was the seedling for the entirety of Martin's lush garden of A Song of Ice and Fire, is incredibly powerful.

But what is the ultimate purpose of the direwolves? Perhaps we need to lay a bit of blame at Martin's feet for their lacking presence in the show. In the books, both Jon's and Arya's warging abilities with their direwolves is strongly hinted at, but no major twists have come of it thus far. Rickon is currently separated from the rest of the pack, and Bran and Summer are still in that cave beneath a weirwood tree. Maybe Benioff and Weiss allowed the direwolves to fall by the wayside because Martin wasn't able to map out exactly why Nymeria's wolf pack was going to be important down the line. It's worth noting that book-readers have a strong suspicion that Jon being a warg will play an essential role in his resurrection, but that fan theory is for a later chapter.

One piece of Martin's puzzling plan for the direwolves can be found in the script notes for season four's "The Lion and the Rose." This is the last episode Martin penned for the series. He abstained from contributing for the final four seasons because, as he said in a 2015 blog post, his "energies are best devoted to [*The Winds of Winter*]." But his fourth-season script included an interesting note about the Stark children's direwolves. It comes after the scene that opens the episode, when Ramsay Bolton and his masochistic lover

Myranda are hunting a young woman with the help of their blood-thirsty hounds.

As reported by *Vanity Fair*'s Joanna Robinson, the script contains a piece of bracketed text: a note communicating to Benioff and Weiss. Martin writes that "a season or two down the line Ramsay's pack of wolfhounds are going to be sent against the Stark direwolves, so we should build up the dogs as much as possible in this and subsequent episodes."

Say what now? The whats are going to be sent against the... hmm. Nothing about this scenario is happening in Martin's published works thus far. The most recent installment, *A Dance with Dragons*, ends with Ramsay Bolton under siege in Winterfell and Jon Snow getting stabbed at Castle Black by the Night's Watch mutineers. When and how are Ramsay's hounds going to be ordered to attack the *direwolves*—plural! And which wolves? Ghost and Summer? Shaggydog and Summer? Nymeria and Ghost?

Based on this single note alone, it seems as if Martin would have been able to map *some* narrative pathways for Benioff and Weiss to lead the direwolves down. But they, for whatever reasons monetary or otherwise, snuffed out the importance of the pups.

Both dragons and direwolves were not seen for hundreds of years before the events of *Game of Thrones*. Both creatures serve as the sigils for two of the main seats of power in Westeros. Both are resurrected or rediscovered by the children of those great houses. Dragons are fire made flesh, the most fearsome and indestructible forces of mythological creature we know. Direwolves are the ancient companions of the Northerners, the people born from the descendants of the First Men who dwelled in the icy tundra beyond the Wall.

Game of Thrones concluded with two landmark moments for the dragons and direwolves of Westeros. Drogon destroyed the Iron Throne, melting the corruptive seat of power into a pool of Valyrian steel after Daenerys was murdered. Her killer, Jon Snow, returned to the true North to live out his days with his direwolf and the Free Folk beyond the Wall. The time for wolves was upon us at last.

CHAPTER NINE

FAN THEORIES *and a* DIVISIVE FATE

Ages before Arya killed the Night King, or Sandor Clegane plummeted to his death with his brother, or Daenerys burned thousands of innocents, or Jon Snow stabbed his love in the heart, or Bran the Broken was crowned King of the Six Kingdoms, the most dedicated readers of A Song of Ice and Fire spent decades analyzing Martin's works and coming up with well-crafted predictions for where his story was headed. This culture of fan theorizing mutated and evolved as *Game of Thrones* progressed beyond Martin's books. Some theories were confirmed by the show, while others were muddled with new revelations we couldn't be sure were part of Martin's plans.

By the time the eighth season came about, the extra-long wait between seasons meant that more casual viewers had had time to catch up with all the various predictions and loose threads expected to be addressed in the final episodes. The market for *Game of Thrones* theories had no limit.

While these predictions and frame-by-frame analyses of trailers all made for a much more exciting and attentive level of discussion, the expectations or beliefs in some of these theories or assessments wound up causing people more strife. In particular, the choice to have Arya sneak up on the Night King at the end of the Battle of Winterfell was the first of many moments in the final season that led to a major reckoning. The way "The Long Night" was written was emblematic of how Benioff and Weiss's adaptation moved away from Martin's carefully plotted narratives and closer to their invented storylines.

The moment Arya's Valyrian steel dagger made contact with the Night King, a whole universe of theories came crashing down. People had been certain Jon Snow or Daenerys or at least Bran would be instrumental in the Night King's demise and the end of the White Walkers. The wave of confusion and annoyance and heated debate that sprang from that episode was an inevitable tipping point in the fandom.

When you start scratching the surface of how Arya came to that moment in the godswood, and how *Game of Thrones* as a whole has come to its end, it's clear why the backlash was inevitable, no matter what choices the show made in its final six episodes. The eighth season had been doomed to divisiveness the moment Benioff and Weiss overtook Martin's story.

By 2013, the third season of *Game of Thrones* was close to airing on HBO and Benioff and Weiss realized they were catching up faster than expected. Martin hadn't yet finished his sixth book, *The Winds of Winter*, and the HBO showrunners had begun thinking about cutting some storylines and characters from the books.

"Last year we went out to Santa Fe for a week to sit down with him and just talk through where things are going, because we don't know if we are going to catch up and where exactly that would be," Benioff told *Vanity Fair* in 2014. "If you know the ending, then you can lay the groundwork for it. And so we want to know how everything ends. We want to be able to set things up. So we just sat down with him and literally went through every character."

This meeting happened before scripts for the fourth season were written. "They know certain things. I've told them certain things," Martin said in his own 2014 *Vanity Fair* feature. "So they have some knowledge, but the devil is in the details. I can give them the broad strokes of what I intend to write, but the details aren't there yet.

"Ultimately, it'll be different," Martin said. "You have to recognize that there are going to be some differences. I'm very pleased with how faithful the show is to the books, but it's never gonna be exactly the same. You can't include all the characters. You're not going to include their real lines of dialogue or subplot, and hopefully each will stand on its own."

Arya killing the Night King was very likely not one of the things Martin told Benioff and Weiss, because the Night King doesn't even exist as a character in his book series. Martin has scarcely shown the White Walkers in his published chapters, let alone a White Walker leader. In HBO's "The Game Revealed" segment for "The Long Night," Benioff said they decided a few years ago that Arya would kill the Night King.

"For, oh God, I think it's probably three years now or something we've known that it was going to be Arya who delivers that fatal blow," Benioff said.

That decision was likely made around 2016, when the sixth season of *Game of Thrones* was in production. The sixth season also happened to be where the series truly started striking out on a narrative that diverged from Martin's book series. The climactic moment of "The Winds of Winter," for example, shows Cersei blowing up the Sept of Baelor and wiping out a handful of major characters, namely almost all of House Tyrell. After that episode aired, Weiss seemed to indicate that Cersei's storyline was born from a need to both push her character forward and use plot devices they had already worked into the show from earlier seasons.

"At this point in the story, we're trying to kind of play with the pieces that we've got on the board," Weiss said on HBO's "Inside the Episode" video. "The wildfire was something we had on the board."

The wildfire was a key part of seasons two and three, first for the Battle of the Blackwater and then again when Jaime mentions it during his memorable bathtub monologue to Brienne of Tarth. Fans knew Martin had told Benioff and Weiss broad-stroke ideas of where the main cast of characters ends up, but he didn't tell them how they got there. Cersei concocting a plan to blow up the Sept of Baelor was again not something Martin had laid out, but instead a way Benioff and Weiss had decided to trim down their cast ahead of the last two seasons and position Cersei against Daenerys with the same blow.

We can see now how Benioff and Weiss used this same strategy to find the way forward for Arya Stark. In Martin's books, Arya is still in Braavos with the Faceless Men. Many book-readers believe the story will lead her back to Westeros at some point, but the how and why are unclear. But the sixth season of *Game of Thrones* was all about Arya breaking from the Faceless Men and deciding to head back to Westeros.

Again, by this stage of production, Benioff and Weiss had decided they wanted Arya to kill the Night King, so they clearly needed to start positioning her to do so. Arya left Braavos and arrived in Westeros to assassinate Walder Frey. Her arc on the seventh season then focused on getting her to Winterfell, reuniting her with the remaining Starks, and giving her the Valyrian steel dagger (more on that in a bit).

Following the Battle of Winterfell episode, the two showrunners provided more details about why they picked Arya as the character to vanquish the Night King. "We hoped to kind of avoid the expected," Benioff said in "Inside the Episode." "Jon Snow has always been the hero and the one who's been the savior, but it just didn't seem right to us for this moment.

"We knew it had to be Valyrian steel, to the exact spot where the Child of the Forest put the dragonglass blade to create the Night King," Benioff continued. "And he's uncreated by the Valyrian steel."

In HBO's other behind-the-scenes video, The Game Revealed," Benioff said they had known "for a long, long time" that that particular Valyrian dagger would "end the Night King." By the time the seventh season rolled around, they had started planting clues about both Arya and the Valyrian dagger's destiny with the Night King.

"When Samwell's reading the book about dragonglass, there is a picture of the dagger," Weiss said in the "Game Revealed" video. "It is very possible that the same thing that created the Night King is the thing that was necessary to destroy the Night King. Or maybe it's Valyrian steel. Figure it out for yourself; I'm not going to say."

When Sam is reading the book showing the dagger, he notes that the Targaryens "used dragonglass to decorate their weapons." Based on Weiss's cryptic hint and the line they wrote for Sam during that important page-turning moment, it's possible the dagger Arya used worked on the Night King only because it was made from both Valyrian steel *and* dragonglass.

Isaac Hempstead Wright, who plays Bran Stark, also said in an

INSIDER interview after the seventh season that he was directed to play the moment when Bran hands Arya the dagger as having a loaded significance for the future.

Entertainment Weekly's James Hibberd interviewed Benioff and Weiss while on the set for season six. In his report of the visit, Hibberd wrote that Benioff and Weiss already knew the planned ending for the show at that point, even though the cast had no idea what was coming. "Sometimes they gave actors cryptic suggestions when filming certain scenes, with those final episodes in mind," Hibberd said. "The actor didn't know why they were doing something a certain way, only that it was somehow important."

A scene between Arya and Bran on the seventh season was very likely one of these moments, especially given what we know now about the Valyrian steel dagger. When Arya and Bran reunited in the seventh season of *Game of Thrones*, he had just been given the Valyrian dagger by Littlefinger. Bran in turn handed it over to Arya, telling her he had no use for it. But he has a strange expression on his face as she takes it, almost as if he's puzzling over a somber thought. *INSIDER* spoke with Isaac Hempstead Wright about this scene after the seventh season finale, and he said that moment was supposed to be played for a greater importance. Hempstead Wright said Bran was able to get "an idea of destiny" or "fate."

The secondary strategic choice Benioff and Weiss made for "The Long Night" was to look backward at scenes they could use to bolster the link between the Night King and Arya. It's telling that they picked two scenes they invented early on in the show, both referenced within "The Long Night" battle by Melisandre, the red priestess and believer in the Lord of Light.

Melisandre was one of those "pieces" Benioff and Weiss knew they had on the board, and it helped that she has a bit of prophetic power already baked into her character as written by Martin. Melisandre was able to give Arya (and therefore the audience) a reminder of two important moments from earlier in the series. First, Melisandre repeats the premonition she told Arya in season three. "I see a darkness in you," Melisandre said. "And in that darkness, eyes staring back at me. Brown eyes, blue eyes, green eyes, eyes you'll shut forever. We will meet again."

Melisandre and Arya never meet in the books, so this scene stood out to fans of Martin's novels when it aired in 2013. People believed it was an adaptation of a creepy scene from the books when Arya meets a character called the ghost of High Heart, but replacing that character with the red priestess was puzzling. The added mention by Melisandre that she'd meet Arya again left people curious, but the comment about her shutting eyes forever seemed to simply be a nod to her future deadly endeavors as a Faceless Man.

Benioff and Weiss changed up the order of the eye color when Melisandre repeats this line to Arya in "The Long Night," putting "blue eyes" at the end so Melisandre can more pointedly be seen referencing the Night King.

Then, to really hammer in the point, Benioff and Weiss pulled another piece from the board, much like they did in season five, when they brought one of Martin's book moments to life— Melisandre spooks Jon Snow by saying Ygritte's iconic words to him: "You know nothing, Jon Snow." Just as Melisandre uses that line on Jon Snow to display her powers, Melisandre reminds Arya of the question posed by Syrio Forel: "What do we say to the God of Death?"

"Not today," Arya replies, just as she had in season one.

Why does any of this matter, you might be asking yourself? These choices and the circumstances that brought Benioff and

Weiss here matter because they uncovered the core reality of their new adaptation process. Both Syrio's piece of wisdom given to Arya and the premonition told by Melisandre are not examples of true foreshadowing, because Benioff and Weiss had no idea Arya would kill the Night King when they wrote them into seasons one and three. Instead, they're examples of retcons. A retcon, or "retroactive continuity," is when writers introduce a new piece of information that gives past events new context.

The way Benioff and Weiss retconned Arya's storyline to fit in with the Night King's death was successful in a way many retcons often aren't. But—and this is an important but—retcons can feel like a cheaper version of storytelling, especially when clunkily executed.

In Martin's books, Arya is indeed steeped in death and destruction. More than most of the other Stark children, Arya is the one who experiences the brutalities of war and torture and death firsthand while she's traveling in Westeros. And she does indeed go to Braavos and begin her training in the arts of effective assassination. Pivoting her established narrative of death and vengeance into a mini arc that led her to kill the Night King was a crafty move pulled by Benioff and Weiss when the original structure of the adaptation process had crumbled around them.

This move also showed their interest in highlighting pieces of the story they most had a hand in writing. In the first edition of *Inside HBO's Game of Thrones* by writer and executive producer Bryan Cogman, he interviewed Benioff and Weiss and asked them about which scenes or lines of dialogue they were "most proud of writing."

"The bit where Syrio tells Arya about his beliefs: 'There is only one god. His name is Death. And there is only one thing to say to

Death. Not today,'" Benioff replied. Martin's books include many teaching moments between Arya and Syrio, but the scene as it appears in season one of *Game of Thrones* was a mix of Martin's characterization of Syrio and newly invented dialogue. Benioff said the scene "perfectly showcases the collaborative process on *Game of Thrones.*"

He added: "George, of course, invented both Arya and Syrio. We originally didn't plan to have this particular Arya-Syrio scene in the episode, but [episode 106 cowriter] Jane Espenson convinced us it was a good idea. Dan took Jane's original scene and reconfigured it. I came up with those lines about Death."

Benioff and Weiss choosing this scene as the groundwork for the death of the Night King makes sense because it was a distillation of their entire experience adapting Martin's work. They had chosen to adapt an intricate, dense, foreshadow-laden book series that wasn't yet finished. Part of that adaptation process was always going to include a culling of characters and scenes and narrative development in order to tell the complicated story to a television audience.

A major part of the backlash to "The Long Night" stems from a faction of the fandom that has been heavily invested in Martin's book series for at least ten years. The chosen ending of the "Great War," as characters on the show have called it, was baffling to people who have pored over Martin's texts and followed the bread crumbs of prophecy pointing to Jon Snow or Daenerys Targaryen.

Benioff and Weiss wrote "The Long Night," which contains very little dialogue and is much more of an action- and horror-driven episode. But it also closed the door on many, many storylines that began in Martin's books. Which is precisely the problem. We don't know where Martin was heading with the prophecy because he hasn't finished his story yet. For two earlier-season twists that hadn't happened yet in the books, the burning of Shireen Baratheon and Hodor's death, Benioff and Weiss spoke openly about how Martin had told them these events were planned. But for the final season, the showrunners are keeping their lips sealed about which parts of the ending came from Martin and which they crafted on their own.

This means that fans were left to devour one another, debating the narrative arcs on *Game of Thrones* and whether they were as true to Martin's story as they were for the first several seasons, when the show was closely adapting his novels. Benioff and Weiss were cornered into finding solutions for character arcs once the show overtook Martin's books, a scenario nobody wanted to happen or ever thought would—until it did.

Fans searching for answers among the shattered piles of glass that were once the White Walkers only found misery. Benioff and Weiss looked at the pieces they had on the board and made their choice to "avoid the expected." Fans who had expectations rooted in decades of theory crafting and analysis of Martin's work feel as if all those layers of true foreshadowing were tossed out the window in favor of retconning new meaning into Arya's story.

Arya Stark, the once servant of Death and student of killers, defeating the personification of Death is poetic. Of all the players left in the game, she had the most skill and training for a one-on-one fight against the inhuman Night King. Benioff and Weiss telegraphed her ability for a silent attack both during the episode itself with the library scene, and earlier in the season when she snuck up on Jon Snow in the godswood. They also repeated her dagger-flip move from the training session she had with Brienne in season seven.

Regardless of how incredible this moment is for Arya's arc and for the story as a whole, fans, especially book-readers, were inevitably going to tear into the choice because Benioff and Weiss admitted it wasn't part of the foundations of the story from the beginning. Benioff and Weiss couldn't have truly foreshadowed an ending they didn't know at the time.

That didn't stop people from being pissed, though.

This was not how *Game of Thrones* was supposed to end. It's not what Martin wanted, HBO wanted, Benioff and Weiss wanted, or fans wanted. People thought they'd read the final book of A Song of Ice and Fire and then tune in to see the awe and emotion and spectacle brought to life in a TV adaptation. There was no dodging the divisiveness or fervor once the former ceased to be an option.

Another reason Benioff and Weiss found themselves in a pickle by the eighth season was because they seemed to engage with wish-fulfillment or fan service for certain theories. There were times throughout the later seasons when it clearly seemed as if the showrunners were bringing a fan theory to life simply because it would be great or cool, not because it was well-laid out in Martin's books.

This happened in a major way with Benjen's return in the sixth season. In A Song of Ice and Fire, Coldhands is a mysterious figure who helps guide Bran and his companions to the three-eyed raven's cave. Coldhands is described as a sort of hybrid human/wight; he is both dead and undead at the same time. He wears all black just like the men of the Night's Watch, and his hands are blackened as if the blood in them has congealed.

Benjen is never heard from again in the books after his disappearance beyond the Wall, so when this curious character of Coldhands was introduced, some readers immediately wondered if this was really Benjen. Then in 2015 a copy of the manuscript for *A Dance with Dragons* was put on display at a library. Fans were able to see the handwritten notations and questions Martin's editor, Anne Groell, had made on the pages along with Martin's replies. On one page (a photo of which was uploaded to the ASOIAF subreddit by a Redditor named u/_honeybird), Groell specifically asked if Coldhands was Benjen, and Martin wrote back "NO" in red pen.

But in the show, Benioff and Weiss chose to turn Benjen into Coldhands anyway. He is referred to as Coldhands in the episode's script, as seen in the Writers Guild Foundation Shavelson-Webb Library, even if that name is never used in the show's dialogue itself. Fans took to calling him "Benhands" as a compromise. But this was just one of several ways the showrunners began indulging in fan service as a way to expedite the story. It was easier to have a recognizable character like Benjen swoop in to save both Bran and Meera, and later Jon Snow.

Cleganebowl—the epic fight to the death between Sandor and Gregor Clegane—was arguably the biggest act of fan service ever done on the show. There is no *hard* evidence in A Song of Ice and Fire to bolster the idea that Sandor Clegane was still alive and out in Westeros somewhere and would one day return to the fold of the story and fight his brother to the death. Instead, there is some evidence that Sandor hadn't died when Arya left him to succumb to his seemingly mortal wounds, and then there was also evidence that Gregor had been gruesomely transformed by Qyburn and would serve as Cersei's champion in a trial by combat.

Everything changed in 2013 when "Cleganebowl" was popularized after someone on 4chan combined two separate fan theories about the Hound and the Mountain and slapped a catchy title on it. The title for the theory likely was inspired by that year's Super Bowl, when the two coaches of the opposing teams were brothers Jim and John Harbaugh. Football fans and sports announcers nicknamed the game "The Harbowl." Since the Hound and the Mountain are brothers, and the theory assumed they will have an epic fight, Cleganebowl became the best-fitting title. This trial by combat would basically be the equivalent of a Westerosi Super Bowl.

Let's take a quick detour down the valonqar path. The original 4chan post about Cleganebowl references the "valonqar" prophecy, which is yet another theory Benioff and Weiss played cat and mouse with. In A Song of Ice and Fire, Cersei Lannister is told by a woods witch that she will die at the hands of the "valonqar," which means "little brother" in Valyrian (as far as it's been explained, this is not a case where the Valyrian word is gender neutral the way "The Prince (or Princess That Was Promised)" prophecy wound up being).

Benioff and Weiss cut the line about the valonqar from their prophecy-focused scene in the opening of the fifth season. That season began with a flashback to young Cersei seeking out a fortune teller named Maggy the Frog. In both the books and show, Cersei is told she can ask three questions of the witch.

The first question and answer were almost word for word from Martin's fourth ASOIAF book, A Feast for Crows. Cersei says she was promised to the prince (who happens to be Rhaegar Targaryen, Jon Snow's father) and asks Maggy when they would marry. Maggy tells her she'll never wed a prince, but she will marry "the king." Little Cersei is unperturbed by this, and asks if she is destined to be a queen.

"Oh yes," Maggy says. "You will be queen, for a time . . . until there comes another, younger and more beautiful, to cast you down and take all that you hold dear."

Cersei will come to believe that the "younger and more beautiful" person is Margaery Tyrell, though Maggy's fortune is actually referring to Daenerys Targaryen. In the flashback, young Cersei moves on from this disconcerting answer and asks her second question: "Will the king and I have children?"

"The king will have twenty, you will have three," Maggy says. Cersei tries to interrupt, clearly confused. Readers and viewers alike now understand that she and the former king, Robert Baratheon, never conceived together; all of his children are bastards and all of hers are born from the incestuous relationship she has with her brother Jaime. "Gold will be their crowns, and gold their shrouds," Maggy says before devolving into hysterical laughter.

This line can be interpreted in a few different ways. The gold crowns could be literal crowns, since Joffrey and Tommen are both crowned king. Plus, in the books, there is a plot centered around the women in Dorne crowning Myrcella queen. But it probably simply refers to their hair color: blond, like their parents. "Gold their shrouds" is more direct. Maggy is warning that all of Cersei's children will die before her, and indeed they do. Joffrey and Myrcella are both murdered, and each is shown in golden funeral garb. Tommen dies by suicide while wearing a golden jacket.

Readers of Martin's book series thought they knew exactly what Maggy was going to say next in that tent. Instead, the scene quickly ends, cutting to present-day Cersei on her way to her father's funeral. The book text has a third, and crucial, line in Maggy's answer: "And when your tears have drowned you, the valonqar shall wrap his hands about your pale white throat and choke the life from you."

Putting stock in this prophecy seemed like a sure bet, since all of Maggy's other predictions for Cersei's life had come true. But how would it happen? Who was this "valonqar"? Valonqar means "little brother," so Cersei spent most of her life assuming Tyrion Lannister, her youngest brother, would one day kill her. In the books, Cersei devolves into a terrifying state of paranoia following Tyrion's murder of their father and escape from King's Landing. She believes the prophecy foretold her death at the hands of Tyrion and imagines him creeping up in the dead of night to strangle her.

Since Martin loves to subvert prophetic expectations, the very fact that Cersei believes Tyrion is the valonqar meant it is extremely unlikely he would be. So who else was plausible?

That's where Cleganebowl comes back into play. Some people believed Sandor Clegane was the little brother Maggy referred to. At the time of Cleganebowl's origins, people thought Cersei would demand a trial by combat against the Faith of the Seven, and the Hound would possibly serve as the Faith's fighter while Cersei chose the Mountain. If the Hound beat the Mountain, and Cersei was executed as a result, then in a backward way the "little" Clegane brother would be responsible for Cersei's death.

Believers in the Cleganebowl were a unique brand of fans who embraced the tagline "GET HYPE." There was an entire subreddit dedicated to the converted believers in Cleganebowl. Fans made YouTube videos about the theory, combining footage from the show with glaring strobe-light text and an intense hip-hop/dub-step/electronic music soundtrack, all in the name of building hype for the coming fight.

Benioff and Weiss leaned in to this hype over the course of the last three seasons, starting when Cersei first plots her revenge against the High Sparrow. In the third episode of season six, "Oathbreaker," Cersei tells Jaime of the plan to position the undead Mountain as her champion in a trial by combat. He remarks that it is "one trial by combat [he] looked forward to watching." That scene, penned by Benioff and Weiss themselves, feels like a direct nod to Cleganebowl truthers.

But then Benioff and Weiss dashed the very hype they had stirred when King Tommen declares trial by combat unlawful in the Seven Kingdoms. As quickly as it seemed like we were getting Cleganebowl, the theorized circumstances for the fight are suddenly impossible. The sixth season ended, and the believers turned their gaze toward the seventh season in the hopes of spotting more clues about the coming fight.

Their optimism was rewarded when Benioff and Weiss once again dropped several major teases about Cleganebowl in season seven. First came the scene of Sandor Clegane literally digging a grave. Before we knew he would return, the "Gravedigger" theory was the shorthand for people's guess about Sandor's survival after Arya left him for dead. And in the seventh season finale, "The Dragon and the Wolf," Sandor confronts his brother and gives him a warning. "You know who's coming for you," Sandor says. "You've always known."

Benioff and Weiss cashed in fully on the Cleganebowl hype by the penultimate episode, "The Bells," regardless of Martin's unknown plan for the two deadly brothers. "We've always wanted to see these two face off again," Benioff said in HBO's "Inside the Episode" segment after the episode. "And they finally did."

Cleganebowl unfolds in the chaos of Daenerys destroying King's Landing. The scenes cut between Arya desperately trying to escape the city, choosing life over revenge at the same moment when Sandor is struggling to finally destroy his lifelong nemesis. The fight ends when Sandor launches them both out of the castle tower and into the blazing rubble of the city, but not before stabbing Gregor through the eye.

Back in the third season, just before the deadly Red Wedding, Arya turned to her then captor. "Someday, I'm gonna put a sword through your eye, and out the back of your skull," she told Sandor. All these years later, Sandor turns this threat into a reality against his brother, and then throws himself headfirst into the fire he feared for so long. Perhaps, in that final moment, he is thinking of Arya Stark, the young girl who helped him grow the most.

In this same episode, Benioff and Weiss revive the valonqar prophecy in an imperfect manner. In addition to the Hound, Jaime Lannister was another dark horse candidate for the valonqar. He is also technically Cersei's younger brother, born just minutes after her. Throughout Martin's book series, Jaime and Cersei speak about how their bond as twins and lovers means neither of them can live without the other—literally.

"Jaime and I are more than brother and sister," Cersei tells Ned Stark in the first book, when he confronts her about sleeping with Jaime. "We are one person in two bodies."

"I cannot die while Cersei lives," Jaime thinks in the third book. "We will die together as we were born together."

Then, in the fourth book, Cersei says she and Jaime "will leave this world together, as we once came into it." Martin's last-published book, *A Dance with Dragons*, ends with Cersei's walk of atonement and Jaime still in the Riverlands, tangled up with Brienne of Tarth's storyline. But with two more planned books, many fans believe Martin will somehow bring Jaime and Cersei back together with devastating consequences.

The version of Jaime's and Cersei's deaths we saw on *Game of Thrones* is likely different than Martin's plan. Cersei lived far longer on the show than most expect her to in Martin's books. And who can blame Benioff and Weiss for wanting to keep one of the show's best actresses, Lena Headey, around for more phenomenal performances? Plus, Jaime didn't technically wrap his hands around

Cersei's throat and kill her. But he was the person with her in her final moments. Cersei's tearful sobs are only quelled when Jaime embraces her, holding her close as they meet their end together, just as they'd always wanted.

This means the manner of both her's and Jaime's deaths is likely different from the path their characters are taking in Martin's books. Perhaps that's why Benioff and Weiss left out the valonqar prophecy altogether. Maybe Martin wasn't able to convey to them exactly how this would play out in A Song of Ice and Fire, or maybe once again Benioff and Weiss just decided to mess with fans a bit. Choices which lean into fan service, like Cleganebowl, aren't inherently bad. In the same way retcons can be handled successfully, it's possible to write fan service–y scenes without cheapening the story.

But, based on their comments about Arya and Jon Snow and the Night King, Benioff and Weiss seem to have chosen a path made to specifically go against "the expected." But if the reason why fans are "expecting" something to happen is that they've had years and years to sit with the existing material and draw logical conclusions, then falling short of those expectations for the sake of "surprise" is going to result in anger—not appreciative shock. By planting subtext in the show that seemed to show Benioff and Weiss were aware of theories like Cleganebowl or the valonqar, they stoked the possibility for people to be right about their theories, or to think Benioff and Weiss would do more wish fulfillment in the final season. Instead, it felt to some as if they opted for anti–fan service when it came to axing plot threads.

A whole other entanglement of the fan-theory cultures is the way media sites covered fan theories. Theory posts had always existed on Reddit or Tumblr or Westeros.org, and media sites and reporters (including yours truly) began writing up articles about some of the most compelling of these predictions. Soon this theory-aggregation strategy got out of hand, though. Outlets would run sensationalized headlines about poorly thought-out theories with little to no basis, but some fans would latch on to the ideas anyway because of the catchy headline.

If a lot of people became convinced of a theory, and then wound up being wrong, it could lead to a deeper sense of disappointment about how the final season was unfolding. All of these expectations, hopes, subversions, and surprises were met with a level of unmatched intensity. *Game of Thrones* started with humble beginnings and a few popular online forums in which predictions and guesses were swapped by people with a genuine curiosity and passion for analysis. But the show finished in an era of unprecedented information sharing and social networking and Twitter trends and viral hot takes and media sites that would get carried away with any and every fan theory regardless of realistic evidence for it.

Thankfully the most ludicrous predictions, such as "Bran is the Night King" or "Arya Stark is really the Waif now," were left by the wayside. And at least the best, most popular fan theory in ASOIAF history was at the heart of Jon Snow's and Daenerys Targaryen's storylines until the bitter end.

CHAPTER TEN

The DRAGON and the SHE-WOLF

R + L = J (Rhaegar + Lyanna = Jon) is shorthand for the most famous fan theory in perhaps any book or TV show community. The math equation solves for the consequential truth buried in between the lines of Martin's novels: That Jon Snow is the son of Rhaegar Targaryen and Lyanna Stark. Just as the first book in A Song of Ice and Fire dates back to 1996, the R + L = J theory has been documented in online discussions for more than twenty years.

By the time *Game of Thrones* was set to air in 2011, a large swath of Martin's fans believed this theory to the point that it was practically accepted as fact. This meant extra attention was on the early episodes of *Game of Thrones*. People wanted to see if the show could add more context, clues, or nods to the theory as Ned, Jon, and the rest of the characters were introduced. People rightfully assumed Benioff and Weiss would know the truth about Jon's mother, so they waited to see if her identity would permeate the script.

Rhaegar Targaryen and Lyanna Stark are two of the most enigmatic characters in *Game of Thrones*. Before we can get into the slow-building confirmation of R + L = J, it's important first to explore the historical context of Jon's parentage and all the clues Martin planted along the way. The show might have shied away from flashbacks or heavy exposition about the long-dead characters, but we can turn to A Song of Ice and Fire to better explain how and why the two lovers risked decimating Westeros for the sake of their union.

First, let's explore how the Targaryen prince wound up sparking Robert's Rebellion thanks to a secret love, a prophecy, and his father's failing sanity.

PRINCE RHAEGAR'S EARLY YEARS AND THE MAD KING

Rhaegar was the firstborn child of King Aerys II and Rhaella Targaryen (who themselves were brother and sister, wed in traditional Targaryen fashion to keep their bloodlines more pure). In A Song of Ice and Fire, Barristan Selmy tells Dany that her oldest brother, Rhaegar, was "bookish to a fault" as a child and disinterested in fighting.

But one day Rhaegar discovered something in his readings, something that upended his habits and made him eager to begin training with his master-at-arms. "It seems I must be a warrior," the young Rhaegar said.

Some fans believe Rhaegar uncovered a prophecy in those ancient scrolls, and that this prophecy motivated most of his life choices from then on. By the time he was seventeen, Prince Rhaegar was already knighted and winning tournaments, besting legendary warriors like Barristan Selmy. He played the harp and sang beautifully at feasts and gatherings as noblewomen around Westeros swooned for his silver hair and dark indigo eyes. In the books, Cersei remembers how excited she was when she thought Rhaegar would marry her one day. "Next to Rhaegar, even her beautiful Jaime had seemed no more than a callow boy," Martin wrote.

Meanwhile, the already insecure King Aerys grew more paranoid and resentful by the day.

During a skirmish in which a rebelling lord held King Aerys hostage, Tywin Lannister (who was Hand of the King) seemed unconcerned about his potential death, saying they had "a better king right here," as he gestured toward Rhaegar. Once the rebellion was put to an end and he returned to his seat of power, King Aerys was more distrustful than ever. He believed Rhaegar and Tywin had plotted together to have him slain so the young prince could sit on the Iron Throne with Cersei at his side as queen.

So King Aerys refused Tywin's offer of marrying Rhaegar to Cersei Lannister. Instead, Rhaegar was married to Princess Elia Martell of Dorne, the younger sister of Oberyn and Doran Martell. They had two children together, Rhaenys and Aegon. Rhaegar and Elia chose to live on Dragonstone instead of in King's Landing, which only fueled Aerys's suspicions of Rhaegar's every move.

LYANNA STARK AND THE UNWANTED BETROTHAL

Now we turn to Lyanna Stark, the only daughter of Lord Rickard and Lyarra Stark. She was one of four children—Brandon was the oldest, then came Eddard (Ned), next Lyanna, and finally Benjen. In the books, this generation of Stark children are described as having different wolfish personalities. Lyanna was the "she-wolf," Brandon was the "wild wolf," Ned was the "quiet wolf," and Benjen was the "pup."

Lyanna is often compared to Arya Stark in the books. In one chapter from *A Game of Thrones*, Ned tells Arya that she is similar to Lyanna after he discovers her sword, Needle. He calls it a "wildness," and once again that willful spirit is connected to "wolf blood," which brought both Lyanna's and Brandon's lives to an early end.

Lyanna was also known for being a talented horseback rider. Again in the books, Arya is told she resembles Lyanna by a man named Harwin. He was the son of Winterfell's master-of-horse, and so knew both Lyanna and Arya well.

In the sixth season of *Game of Thrones*, Benioff and Weiss used Bran Stark's greensight as a vehicle for showing young Lyanna and her siblings. Bran sees Lyanna ride a horse into the Winterfell courtyard as her brothers chastise her for showing off. Lyanna, again just like Arya, is described as tomboyish but still beautiful. Arya is said to have a long face with brown hair and gray eyes, so it's possible Lyanna had similar qualities. It's also no coincidence that Arya and Jon Snow are said to look the most similar out of all the next generation of Stark children.

Ned and Robert Baratheon were raised in the Vale by Jon Arryn during their formative years. By the time they were teenagers, Ned and Lyanna's father, Lord Rickard, agreed to marry his daughter to Robert Baratheon. In the books, Ned thinks back to the night Lyanna was told the news and remembers his sister expressing doubt that Robert would be a faithful husband. He had already sired a bastard in the Vale.

In Ned's memory, Lyanna was neither excited nor hopeful about the prospect of her marriage to Robert. But as we see on the first season of *Game of Thrones*, Robert has fond memories of Lyanna and his passionate love for her.

In the show, Robert and Cersei discuss Lyanna and how she was the reason their marriage could never have worked. On their wedding night, Robert came to bed stinking of wine and whispered "Lyanna" into Cersei's ear. He mourns and rages about Lyanna's death nearly two decades later.

All of this points to Robert being out of touch with the real Lyanna, and instead fixating on an idealization of his once future bride. Ned calls out Robert on this misunderstanding of Lyanna in the books. "You never knew Lyanna as I did, Robert," Ned tells him. "You saw her beauty, but not the iron underneath."

THE FATEFUL TOURNEY AT HARRENHAL

Rhaegar and Lyanna met for the first time during the legendary Tourney at Harrenhal. This tournament, hosted by Lord Whent, was like the Westerosi equivalent of an epic house party where people swapped tales of the night over breakfast the next morning. Who hooked up with who, which guys got into fights, the new factions of friends and bonds made over numerous cups of beer.

Rumors turned into presumed facts, while other secrets were taken to graves.

One such rumor is that the tournament was secretly funded and organized by Prince Rhaegar himself, who was using Lord Whent as a decoy. People believed the tournament was a way to cover up the mass gathering of every important lord "in order to discuss ways and means of dealing with the madness of his father, possibly by means of a regency or a forced abdication."

But when it comes to the rumored story of Rhaegar and Lyanna, the biggest hint Martin gave us was a story Meera and Jojen Reed tell Bran in A Song of Ice and Fire as they're traveling north. The scene was cut for *Game of Thrones*, but HBO created a mini-animation of the story for the season six Blu-ray extras.

The story Meera and Jojen tell is about their father, Howland Reed, and a mysterious figure called the Knight of the Laughing Tree. While on his way to the Tourney at Harrenhal, Howland was attacked by three squires who thought a crannogman (a person from the swampy area of the Neck where the Reeds live) had no place at a great tournament.

Lyanna Stark intervened and brought Howland back to the Stark tent with Benjen, Ned, and Brandon. The Starks convinced Howland to stay and enjoy the festivities and feasts, saying he should enter the tournament and beat the knights whom the hateful squires served. Howland watched as Rhaegar Targaryen sang a ballad so beautiful it made Lyanna cry, and her brothers teased her.

The next day, a mysterious contender entered the tournament wearing ill-fitted armor and bearing a shield with a laughing weirwood tree painted on it. This so-called Knight of the Laughing Tree challenged the knights whose squires had attacked Howland and won. Though Meera and Jojen's retelling leaves open the possibility for the mystery knight to have been their father, it's far more likely that Lyanna was underneath the armor. She was known for her prodigious horse-riding skills (a necessary talent for anyone jousting) and would have needed to disguise her appearance since she was a woman.

King Aerys was furious when he saw the Knight of the Laughing Tree's victory, because he believed it was one of his enemies making a mockery of him. When the mystery knight seemed to vanish overnight, King Aerys sent Rhaegar to look for him. Rhaegar returned from his mission and said he only found the knight's shield—but the theory goes that he might have actually found Lyanna and chose to protect her from his father. Was this the beginning of their fated relationship?

Prince Rhaegar won the Tourney at Harrenhal and was given a crown of blue winter roses so he could name one of the attending highborn ladies as the "Queen of Love and Beauty." Instead of choosing his wife, Elia, Rhaegar gave the winter roses to Lyanna. On the fifth season of *Game of Thrones*, Littlefinger remembers being there that day, and seeing how "all the smiles died" in the crowd at the sight of this slight.

According to Martin's retelling in *The World of Ice and Fire*, Lyanna's brothers were furious at Rhaegar's decision, considering it a mark on Lyanna's honor as a noblewoman. Some months later, Rhaegar and a dozen of his closest companions journeyed out into the Riverlands, where he met Lyanna once again. We don't know how or why, but Lyanna ran off with Rhaegar in that moment and abandoned her promise to Robert while Rhaegar left behind his wife and children. As revealed on the seventh season of *Game of Thrones*, Rhaegar had his marriage to Elia annulled and he wed Lyanna in a secret ceremony.

THE TOWER OF JOY
AND RHAEGAR'S DEATH

The rest of Westeros assumed the young Stark lady had been kidnapped. Neither Rhaegar or Lyanna explained themselves, and so Brandon Stark went to King's Landing to demand Aerys address Rhaegar's "crime." King Aerys summoned Lord Rickard to King's Landing and had both Stark men executed. He then ordered Lord Jon Arryn of the Vale to send him the heads of Ned Stark and Robert Baratheon for good measure. Jon Arryn refused, and called his own banners to prepare for the fight ahead.

Robert was furious over the disappearance of his betrothed, and believed Rhaegar had stolen her and raped her. With Ned, who was now the heir to Winterfell, the young lordling led a rebellion against King Aerys and Prince Rhaegar.

Brandon Stark had been promised to Catelyn Tully, but now Ned took his elder brother's place and cemented the Riverlands alliance. Ned and Catelyn consummated their marriage before he left for war, and the new Lady of Winterfell was pregnant with Robb while the war waged in Westeros.

As the battles continued, no one knew for certain where Lyanna had been taken. Prince Rhaegar led the Targaryen forces in battle, and Elia Martell and her children remained in King's Landing. King Aerys wanted his son's heir close, as he grew more paranoid with each passing day.

The war came to a head at the Trident, where Prince Rhaegar and Robert fought fiercely in the riverbanks. With a crushing blow, Robert smashed in Rhaegar's chest with his war hammer, scattering the rubies from his Targaryen armor into the river.

In the books, Daenerys has a series of visions when she visits the House of the Undying. One of these visions showed her brother Rhaegar's death: "Rubies flew like drops of blood from the chest of a dying prince, and he sank to his knees in the water and with his last breath murmured a woman's name."

That woman's name was likely Lyanna Stark.

After the rebellion was won, Ned went looking for his sister and found her in Dorne at a place referred to as the Tower of Joy. In the sixth season of *Game of Thrones*, Bran has a vision of Ned's arrival to the tower. He and Howland Reed kill the Kingsguard stationed there, and Ned goes into the tower only to find Lyanna dying.

In Ned's memories described in the books, she was clutching withering blue rose petals and lying in a bed of blood. She had given birth to a baby boy and begged Ned to take her son and protect him from Robert's wrath. Both Lyanna and Ned knew of Robert's fury. Ned had seen what happened to Elia Martell and her two children, swaddled in bloody fabric and laid at the feet of the new king. He brought Lyanna's baby home and called him his own, naming him Jon, after the man who had a significant hand in raising him.

Catelyn had given birth to Robb by now, so the two newborn babies were raised as half brothers—one a trueborn Stark and the other seen as a bastard of war, begot by Ned on some mystery woman in the South. The secret of this living, legitimate Targaryen prince lay dormant beneath the snows of Winterfell for more than twenty years.

JON SNOW AND THE "PRINCE THAT WAS PROMISED" PROPHECY

Remember how Rhaegar seemed to change after reading a set of scrolls? In the books, Castle Black's Maester Aemon tells Sam Tarly that he and Rhaegar discussed a prophecy known as the Prince That Was Promised, a hero born to fight a great looming darkness. At first, both Aemon and Rhaegar believed the Targaryen prince himself was the prophesied hero. Aemon says Rhaegar later began believing his son would be the one to fulfill that destiny.

The visions experienced by Dany at the House of the Undying include one of Rhaegar and a woman with his newborn son, named Aegon. When the woman asks if Rhaegar will write a song for the baby, the prince says, "He is the prince that was promised, and his is the song of ice and fire." Rhaegar also says, "There must be one more . . . the dragon has three heads."

This is the first time the book series title is found within Martin's text, which gives the scene a lot of added weight when it comes to fans theorizing. Rhaegar had two children with Elia, and it's possible that his "dragon has three heads" line meant he believed he needed three children in order to fulfill the prophecy. Context given by Martin in the books has led some fans to think Elia was experiencing birth complications and was weakened after having two children. If she was unable to carry another child, this might have factored into Rhaeger's decision to leave her. His possible obsession with the Prince That Was Promised prophecy could have consumed him to the point where he was willing to risk civil war and cast aside Elia in order to marry Lyanna and have a third legitimate child.

While all this is easy enough to speculate about for readers, the characters inside A Song of Ice and Fire were never clued in on Rhaegar and Lyanna's true feelings and intentions with each other. This is why the news of their marriage comes as such a shock to Bran and Sam when the pieces of the puzzle come together on the seventh season finale, and Bran is able to see Rhaegar and Lyanna's wedding for the first time.

"Jon wasn't conceived out of some sort of violent encounter between Rhaegar and Lyanna," the finale's director, Jeremy Podeswa, said in an interview with *INSIDER*. "It was actually a romantic relationship, and ... there was a complicitness to their union, and that's [information] that's really new.

"We tried very consciously to create an idyllic atmosphere in that scene, so that the wedding we see is completely antithetical to what their relationship was understood to be," he continued. "That was really the key thing for me—presenting it as a revisionist history."

Up until that big revelatory moment in season seven, Benioff and Weiss were peppering clues for the audiences at home, seeing if fans would be able to piece together the truth just as they had all those years ago before lunch at the Palm with Martin himself.

EVERY R + L = J HINT IN *GAME OF THRONES*

Rhaegar and Lyanna's secret was present from the very first episode, when King Robert arrived at Winterfell and reminisced with Ned Stark in the crypts. This pilot scene established Robert's irrational wrath against the Targaryens while also showing how badly Ned wished to keep the past behind them.

Then in season one, episode two—"The Kingsroad"—after Jon and Ned have said their goodbyes, Robert and Ned reminisce on the good ol' days of their youth and discuss their sexual conquests. "Yours was uh, Meryl? Your bastard's mother?" Robert tries to guess, referring to Jon.

Ned's face looks grim as he simply says the name Wylla. No other details are given, and Robert seems nonplussed by the quick change in Ned's mood.

The context of Ned's honor is key. Throughout the first season we are also shown how Ned's extreme sense of right and wrong can only be compromised when it comes to children. He shows mercy to Cersei when he learns the truth about her children because he knows King Robert will murder Joffrey, Myrcella, and Tommen if he finds out about the incestuous treason.

Even just halfway through the first season, in "The Wolf and the Lion," Robert and Ned have a falling-out over the decision to send cutthroats after the newly pregnant Daenerys. Robert wants to see every last Targaryen dead, but Ned doesn't hold the same hostility for that family. And he cannot abide the harming of children.

Then, as we've already revisited, "Baelor" shows how Ned values the life of his children above his own honor. In the same way he resigns himself to falsely confessing treason in order to save Sansa and Arya, Ned once allowed the realm to believe he was an unfaithful husband for the sake of protecting Jon.

In the second season, Ned's honor comes up again when Jaime taunts Catelyn Stark about Ned's infidelity while being held captive. Benioff and Weiss were repeatedly pointing out how honorable Ned was, and how unusual it had been for him to have a child out of wedlock and then bring him home for the whole realm to see.

By the end of season two, we got another major clue when Benioff and Weiss created their onscreen interpretations of Dany's visions in the House of the Undying. Many of the scenarios they had her walk through were created just for the show because Martin's text had much more surreal imagery.

As she's exploring the magical building and trying to find her dragons, Dany finds herself in the throne room of the Red Keep in King's Landing. The roof has been destroyed, and snow is falling softly onto the Iron Throne itself. When she sees this *snow* (get it?) on the Iron Throne, Dany reaches out to touch it—but she's distracted by the crying of her dragon-children. She turns to walk through a doorway off to the side and goes through a passageway that leads her out beyond the Wall, further connecting her vision to Jon Snow.

In Martin's version of the House of the Undying visions, Dany sees a blue flower growing from "a chink in a wall of ice" that fills "the air with sweetness." Even before the show's version made the snow/Snow connection stronger, book-readers believed that this flower imagery was tying Jon to Rhaegar and Lyanna. The blue flower (from the crown of winter roses Rhaegar gave Lyanna) at the Wall seemed like the clearest symbol of all.

Then there's the way Rhaegar's reputation was handled on *Game of Thrones*. Though King Robert blabbered on and on about what a son of a bitch Rhaegar was, by the third season we started to hear differently. After Barristan Selmy joins Dany's cause, he tells her Rhaegar was the "finest man" he'd ever met.

Aside from Ned Stark, Ser Barristan is probably the last living man in Westeros whose honor is unbesmirched. His praise of Rhaegar should not have landed lightly on the ears of people watching at home. In the same scene, Barristan told Daenerys about the rebellion and the final battle on the Trident. "When your brother Rhaegar led his army into battle at the Trident, men died for him because they believed in him, because they loved him," he says. Ser Jorah Mormont chimes in, saying Rhaegar fought "valiantly" and "nobly."

When we get to the fourth season, Oberyn Martell is introduced with a dramatic scene in a brothel. Tyrion speaks privately with him outside, and the Dornish prince brings up Rhaegar and Elia's marriage. The way Oberyn tells it, Rhaegar "left" Elia for "another woman." This was a far cry from the rape and abduction version of events previously presented, and the first time fans of the show were offered an alternative narrative.

Then the fifth season really ramped things up when it came to hints about Jon's true parentage. Once again Barristan waxes poetic to Dany about how inspiring and kind Rhaegar was—not at all the ruthless killer people sometimes described. Barristan tells Dany how her older brother liked to sing and walk among the people and give money to the lowborn people of King's Landing.

Then, back at the Wall, Jon is elected Lord Commander while Stannis and his wife, Selyse, are staying at Castle Black. At one point in episode four, "Sons of the Harpy," Stannis and Selyse are watching Jon train young recruits and they have a telling conversation. When Selyse refers to Jon as a bastard with a "tavern slut" for a mother, Stannis only says "perhaps" and points out that "wasn't Ned Stark's way."

Similar to the importance of Oberyn giving an alternative narrative, this was the first time someone in the *Game of Thrones* universe cast doubt on the story Ned had told about himself. Then that same episode doubles down on the clues with the memorable scene between Sansa Stark and Littlefinger in the crypts of Winterfell.

While standing in front of Lyanna's tomb, Littlefinger tells Sansa the story of the Tourney at Harrenhal and how Rhaegar had crowned her aunt the Queen of Love and Beauty. When Sansa chimes in for the end of the tale, repeating the oft-told line about how Rhaegar "kidnapped and raped" Lyanna, Littlefinger doesn't reply. He gives Sansa a knowing kind of smirk before changing the subject.

Both this scene and the one before it with Stannis were show-only moments not taken from Martin's texts, which gave them even more weight for the longtime believers in the theory. By this point, Benioff and Weiss had also gone on the record saying they had correctly guessed who Jon Snow's mother was at that 2006 meeting with Martin. More than ever, it was clear that they were adding in hints of their own.

And so we came to the sixth season and the first re-creation of the Tower of Joy scenes. In the books, Ned's chapters include some dreamlike memories of his fight against the Targaryen Kingsguard at the Tower of Joy. *Game of Thrones* brought these to the screen using Bran's greensight visions, and we finally saw Lyanna Stark for the first time.

In the sixth season finale, Bran watches as Lyanna lay dying in her "bed of blood" and whispers something to Ned. In the books, Ned only remembers his sister repeating "promise me," but we never find out what exactly she was asking of him. Now we finally had conclusive proof she had begged him to protect her son.

"If Robert finds out, he'll kill him. You know he will," Lyanna says to Ned. "You have to protect him. Promise me, Ned."

Then, as Ned holds the child for the first time, the camera zooms in carefully to the little boy's face as the emotional music swells, and the shot cuts from the dark-eyed baby's face to Jon Snow, standing in the great hall of Winterfell, about to be crowned King in the North.

In case that wasn't clear enough, HBO confirmed Jon's birth father as Rhaegar with an online chart. Following the sixth season finale in 2016, HBO released a graphic on its "Making *Game of Thrones*" website. The chart showed how various characters were all connected with one another. The bubble for Jon Snow had two black lines leading into it, signaling his parents. Those lines linked to Rhaegar Targaryen and Lyanna Stark. A blue line, marking Jon's guardian, led to the bubble for Ned Stark.

Despite this seemingly overt confirmation, the seventh season proceeded to treat Jon's birth father as a mystery until the finale.

The third episode included a funny little nod to the truth, though. As Jon heads up the pathway to Dragonstone, he and Tyrion discuss how he's not a real Stark by name. A moment later, Jon is startled by Drogon flying overhead. This makes for a pretty great foreshadowing of how freaked out Jon will be when he learns the truth about his own dragon connection.

By the fifth episode of season seven it was time for Jon to properly meet a dragon for the first time. Drogon may have snarled a bit at first, but Jon has the beast practically purring before long. Targaryens have an instinctive connection to dragons, more so than other Westerosi people, so this is yet another sign of the Targaryen blood running through Jon's veins.

Later in the same episode, Gilly uncovers evidence that Rhaegar had his marriage to Elia Martell annulled and wed Lyanna instead. In a comically casual throwaway line, Gilly tells Sam that some dude named "Ragger" had his marriage annulled and was remarried in a secret ceremony. Before she can ask more questions, Sam cuts her off and changes the subject to whine about Oldtown. But those of us sitting at home and watching knew what a huge deal this was, even if Sam didn't.

When Gilly found the record of Rhaegar's annulment, many fans were shocked to realize that meant Jon was a legitimate Targaryen heir, and ahead of Daenerys in the succession line. As much as people had taken R + L = J as gospel, there were always fierce debates in the fandom about what that truth meant for Jon's future. The books provided no evidence that Rhaegar had actually married Lyanna. Was this *Game of Thrones* reveal something that would be unveiled in A Song of Ice and Fire? Fans would have to wait for Martin's next books to know for certain.

But "The Dragon and the Wolf" left everything crystal clear: Jon Snow wasn't simply King in the North. He was King Aegon Targaryen, the White Wolf, King of the Andals and the First Men, Lord of the Seven Kingdoms, and Protector of the Realm.

Of course by the time Jon would learn this, he would be deep in love with his own aunt by blood—the woman who believes herself to be the rightful queen of Westeros. But that complication is for another chapter.

CHAPTER ELEVEN

The UNION of ICE and FIRE

With a simple knock on the door, a montage of a secret wedding, and a camera cut to Kit Harington's perfectly round derrière on a fur-covered bed, the *Game of Thrones* fandom was shaken to the core.

Jon Snow and Daenerys Targaryen—the symbols of ice and fire and of legends reborn—were united in love and lust at the end of season seven. Many fans cheered. Others recoiled at the sight of aunt-on-nephew incest, and others still may not have bought into the sparks between the two young, attractive heroes of our story. Regardless of how you absorbed Jon and Dany's union, the intense and varied reactions were the result of a decades-long campaign to stage this endgame power couple.

Director Alan Taylor was the man behind the camera for one of Jon and Daenerys's most pivotal season-seven scenes: when the King in the North finally bends the knee to the Mother of Dragons after one of her "children" is slain by the Night King. This boat cabin scene was just a tease of what came next, but Taylor knew more than was let on to audiences in that moment. Taylor was one of the directors on hand for the very first season of *Game of Thrones*, which means he was clued into the story of Daenerys and Jon long before most.

"All of the characters have such big arcs, and [George R. R. Martin has] them so mapped out in his head, that the story is functioning moment-to-moment but also in these grand story gestures over several seasons," Taylor said in an interview with *INSIDER*. "That's what makes it so rich."

Taylor directed the ninth episode of the first season, "Baelor," and it was during that 2011 filming that Martin told Taylor how the series was all coming down to Dany and Jon Snow. It's almost unfathomable now for fans to think of the snowy-bearded George R. R. Martin walking around the sunny European set of *Game of Thrones*, just casually mentioning his endgame ideas to the crew of the then unknown hit HBO series.

"He knew from the very beginning where he was driving, and now we're starting to see that come to fruition," Taylor said. "We know that it's circling tighter and tighter on Dany and Jon and their partnership is starting to form—fire and ice."

Clues sprinkled throughout every piece of production lend credence to Taylor's understanding of how Daenerys and Jon are tragically fated—and one of the most subtle hints you would likely never notice comes from Ramin Djawadi's soundtrack.

Both Daenerys and Jon had their own dedicated romantic musical cues in earlier seasons. Dany's love themes of course were played during her scenes with the formidable Khal Drogo, while Jon's underscored the moments shared between him and his wildling first love, Ygritte. As composer and *Game of Thrones* fan Brenna

Noonan pointed out in a tweet sent to *Vanity Fair*'s Joanna Robinson, these early melodies for Jon and Dany's respective love interests were linked to the music Djawadi wrote for season seven.

"Fun fact: Dany/Drogo's theme starts on droning G, Jon/Ygritte's on droning C," Noonan wrote. "First two notes of the opening theme—G perfect 5th down to C."

Following this incredible observation, Robinson spoke with Noonan for a *Vanity Fair* article published just before the seventh season finale. As Robinson broke down all the revelations Djawadi had planted in the score, she cites an email from Noonan that hammered home the importance of those G and C notes.

"Those two notes together, the droning G and C, also kick off the instantly recognizable *Game of Thrones* opening credits song," Robinson wrote. "In other words, together, Jon and Daenerys's love songs form the titular song of ice and fire."

From the literal opening of the series back in 2011, our heroes were embedded in the musical fabric of the core theme.

There were subtle costume clues leading into Jon and Dany's romance, too. Daenerys undergoes several wardrobe evolutions as she progresses from her arranged marriage with Khal Drogo and into Qarth, then Meereen, and more. By the time she kneels down on the sands of Westeros, Daenerys is wearing a costume with the colors of House Targaryen, bloodred and dragonglass black, for the first time in the entire series.

When Dany meets Jon for the first time, she wears a charcoal gown paired with a red sash. During that conversation, the two young leaders clash when it comes to priorities and ideals. But it doesn't take long for Daenerys to soften her resolve against our recently resurrected King in the North.

By the next episode, Dany is clothed in a dark gray dress with a silvery cape—the colors of House Stark's direwolf sigil. Given costume designer Michele Clapton's penchant for embedding a character's inner thoughts in the very fabrics of their costumes, this shift shouldn't be discounted as mere coincidence. This is the first sign of the coming union between the dragon and the wolf.

And Dany isn't the only one signaling a change of heart with her daily outfits. After his resurrection in season six, Jon begins wearing a padded gambeson (a dark-brown jacketlike garment) to symbolize his renewed loyalty to House Stark instead of his Night's Watch blacks. It is the same brown and navy gambeson/tunic combination Ned and Robb Stark had worn in earlier seasons.

But during his scenes with Daenerys and throughout the rest of the seventh season, Jon's gambeson switches to a darker color, almost the same charcoal black as seen on the traditional Targaryen banner. Since many of the characters in season seven wear black, this may have seemed like just another darker palette for another character—but as the Targaryen side of Jon becomes more prevalent, and Dany softens into House Stark, the coloring of their clothing marks them as equals.

Well before all of the season-seven clues, Martin and the *Game of Thrones* showrunners linked Dany and Jon together with their parallel storylines. Both outcasts on opposite edges of the world, the bastard of Winterfell and the last living Targaryen princess have more in common than most of our core characters.

They are each described by their friends and advisers (and even enemies, in the case of Alliser Thorne) as having good hearts. There are even times when Benioff and Weiss used the exact same dialogue for scenes with and about Jon and Dany. In the fifth season, Samwell Tarly tells Maester Aemon he thinks Dany "sounds like quite a woman." Later on the seventh season, Dany returns the compliment when she first hears about Jon Snow, telling Melisandre on Dragonstone that the King in the North "sounds like quite a man."

At the end of the dragonglass cave scene (which in itself was a nod to Jon's first sex scene with Ygritte) Dany presses Jon to bend the knee, and when he refuses she asks if his people's survival was "more important than [his] pride." This was word for word what Jon had asked of Mance Rayder back in the fifth season when King Stannis threatened to burn the King-Beyond-the-Wall alive if the wildling leader didn't bend the knee.

They risk their lives for others and earn the loyalty of those around them by taking up the mantle of leadership for the sake of their people and not for the sake of power alone. They are the king and queen who each rule with a magical living embodiment of their sigil at their side, the dragon and the direwolf.

Each have to contend with their father's legacy—though in Jon's case this burden is doubled. Dany deals with the atrocities committed by the Mad King while Jon is further ostracized when much the realm believes Ned Stark died a traitor.

Even Jon and Dany's differences work in complement to each other. While Jon grew up in the comfort of a castle but without the honor of his family name, Dany struggled in exile with nothing but the Targaryen title to keep her going. Jon's path eventually led him to die and be reborn in the icy shadow of the Wall. Dany walked into fire, twice, and emerged unscathed. People think they are gods. But they are each deeply human.

As Dany and Jon's first meeting neared, the fandom was electric with anticipation. Ahead of the episode in which they'd meet face-to-face (season seven, episode three, "The Queen's Justice") HBO released a small episode promo in which Jon Snow said "Daenerys" for the first time. That little sound clip was enough to start a

#Jonerys Twitter trend. Then Emilia Clarke posted a behind-the-scenes selfie with Kit Harington on Instagram and racked up two million likes in a matter of hours.

At long last, the dragon and the wolf meet in the throne room of Dragonstone. The culmination of all those narrative links in the story, the score, and the costuming came together for the final four episodes of the seventh season. And while the interior storytelling was spot-on, there were meta reasons why this particular *Game of Thrones* union was more fraught than others among the fandom.

First was just the sheer amount of pressure and attention being paid to Jon and Dany's scenes. Because so much of the seventh season storyline had leaked, people knew their shared moments were supposed to be building up to a steamy sex scene. But part of the scrutiny came from the actors' offscreen relationship to each other.

Kit Harington and Emilia Clarke became close friends over the course of *Game of Thrones*. Though they never shared scenes together in the years of filming prior to season seven, they had obviously spent time together doing press and photo shoots. Clarke was also best friends with Rose Leslie (Ygritte), who fell in love with Harington during their time filming seasons two and three together.

Harington and Leslie kept their relationship private as best they could, though photos of the two stars kissing or eating at restaurants were snapped by paparazzi. At the 2016 SAG Awards red carpet, *ET* reporter Nancy O'Dell appeared to get confirmation of the relationship from Clarke.

O'Dell asked Clarke about recent photos showing Harington and Leslie cozied up together. "Oh, were they now? My goodness!" Clarke replied in what we can assume was feigned surprise. "You know, we like to spread the love on our show. It's a beautiful thing. She's one of my best friends, so it's good."

Just a few months later, Harington and Leslie made the relationship public with their debut as a couple on the red carpet of the Olivier Awards. When interviewed by *Vogue Italia* for the May 2016 issue, Harington said his favorite memory of filming *Game of Thrones* was the time spent in Iceland for season three.

"Because the country is beautiful, because the Northern Lights are magical, and because it was there that I fell in love," he said. "If you're already attracted to someone, and then they play your love interest in the show, it becomes very easy to fall in love."

By the summer of 2018, Harington and Leslie tied the knot in a small ceremony in Scotland with most of the *Game of Thrones* cast in attendance.

All this to say, the chemistry between Harington and Leslie was deliciously convincing, and knowing now that the two were actually falling in love with each other makes their scenes even more special. In turn it added a different layer of pressure to the season-seven union of Jon and Dany, because Harington and Clarke were suddenly required to turn their platonic rapport into a convincing romantic chemistry.

On top of that, it wasn't just any romantic relationship they were charged with; they were burdened with bringing together this epic union of the two biggest characters. No pressure at all, right? Both Kit and Emilia spoke about the strangeness of needing to do sex scenes with an actor they were friends with.

"If you've known someone for six years and they're best friends with your girlfriend, and you're best friends with them, there is something unnatural and strange about doing a love scene," Harington told *Vanity Fair*'s Joanna Robinson about filming the famous sex scene on the boat. "We'll end up kissing and then we're just pissing ourselves with laughter because it's so ridiculous."

On top of all this, there was the teensy little added complication of Dany and Jon being related by blood. The aunt/nephew incest wasn't as socially consequential since the two characters hadn't been raised in the same family, but showrunners Benioff and Weiss specifically chose to blend the scenes of Jon's Targaryen parentage reveal with the boat sex for a reason.

"It was about making it clear that this was almost like an information bomb that Jon was heading towards," Weiss said in HBO's post-episode segment. "Just as we're seeing these two people come together, we're hearing the information that will inevitably, if not tear them apart, at least cause real problems in their relationship. And she's his aunt."

"It complicates everything on a political level [and] on a personal level," Benioff said in the same video. "It just takes everything that could have been so neat and perfect for Jon and Dany and it really muddies the waters."

Based on Benioff and Weiss's motivations behind staging the scene the way they did, it doesn't seem as if fans were supposed to be truly comfortable seeing Dany and Jon having sex for the first time. Emilia Clarke echoed similar concerns in the same video segment released after the epic finale episode.

"For us as actors, it's just weird," Clarke said. "The reality of what they are to each other . . . I don't know how that's gonna . . . I mean I think [gagging] might be the reaction."

The weirdness Clarke and Harington felt might have come across on the screen for some fans. But many were moved by the two young rulers finally finding comfort in each other's arms after their tragic first loves had left them more alone and isolated than ever.

THE PRINCE (OR PRINCESS) THAT WAS PROMISED

As many people guessed early on, Jon and Dany's love was destined to be short-lived. The truth about his Targaryen blood causes an irreparable rift in their relationship. When Jon reveals his identity to her in the crypts of Winterfell, Daenerys is so taken aback at first that she doesn't even acknowledge what he told her as the truth. She is skeptical and seething. "*If* it were true," Daenerys says, "it would make you the last male heir of House Targaryen. You'd have a claim to the Iron Throne."

Jon is nonplussed by her reaction; he was unprepared for her first thought to be about the line of succession. "There were so many things we weren't saying whilst saying them," Emilia Clarke said in HBO's behind-the-scenes video for the episode. "And then you've still got the passion that brings them together, and you've still got the need, on both sides, to be loved . . . and to be taken care of. And both characters have that exact thing. And they just can't. It's like the ultimate star-crossed lovers."

Emilia's use of the term "star-crossed lovers," from William Shakespeare's *Romeo and Juliet*, was the clearest hint that the romance between Jon and Daenerys will end in tragedy. Daenerys grows more isolated, and Jon is eventually faced with a distressing choice. As they stand together in the Great Hall of the Red Keep, both within sight of the coveted Iron Throne their shared ancestors had built, Daenerys begs her love to help her create a new world. Jon kisses his queen one last time, then plants his dagger into her heart.

Prophecy played a strong role in *Game of Thrones* from the very beginning, particularly in Jon's and Dany's arcs. In A Song of Ice and Fire, there are multiple accounts told of a legendary hero. Different groups of people have a different moniker for the prophesied person, but the two most common were Azor Ahai and the Prince That Was Promised. The similarities between the tales have led fans to believe that each hero is really the same person.

Melisandre speaks most frequently about Azor Ahai. When we are first introduced to Melisandre and Stannis Baratheon, she proclaims him to be Azor Ahai reborn. The legend of Azor Ahai is found in ancient texts from Asshai, and its believers say that a champion of R'hllor, the Lord of Light, will be reborn to fight a darkness.

The story of Lightbringer is then told to Ser Davos Seaworth in the books by the pirate Salladhor Saan. Azor Ahai forged two swords, both of which shattered when he tried to temper the steel (including the second one, which was stabbed into the heart of a lion). Then came the third blade, which he had to plunge through the heart of the woman he loved, Nissa Nissa, in order to fortify its strength. "Great was his woe and great was his sorrow then, for he knew what he must do," Saan says.

Given the events of the series finale, it now seems clear that Jon Snow was our Azor Ahai all along. But, curiously, the show never mentioned the name Azor Ahai at all. In the sixth season, Melisandre resurrects Jon Snow and tells him he is the Prince That Was Promised, reborn with the power of R'hllor for a reason. Then the High Priestess of R'hllor, Kinvara, is introduced and tells Tyrion and Varys that Daenerys is the chosen hero meant to fight the coming darkness. She doesn't use the name Azor Ahai, either.

This might have been our first warning that *Game of Thrones* would use the Nissa Nissa sacrifice in a surprising way by not having Daenerys's death connected to the fight against the White Walkers. Benioff and Weiss made sure to bring back Melisandre for the seventh season and have her speak with Daenerys about how interpretation of the prophecy is fickle.

"Prophecies are dangerous things," Melisandre tells the Dragon Queen. "I believe you have a role to play, as does another: the King in the North, Jon Snow."

Martin has also spoken about the wavering role of prophecy in his books. "Prophecies are, you know, a double-edge sword," he said in an interview with *Adria's News* in 2012. "You have to handle them very carefully; I mean, they can add depth and interest to a book, but you don't want to be too literal or too easy."

So, as is already clear, Jon and Daenerys aren't a perfect parallel of Azor Ahai and Nissa Nissa. Daenerys was not killed for Jon to forge a new weapon, nor was her death a willing sacrifice in the way Nissa Nissa's was. Jon didn't even stab her with Longclaw, his Valyrian steel sword, which many fans thought could be a stand-in for Lightbringer. Instead, he plunged a dagger into her chest, killing her almost instantly.

But it's interesting how the show wound up fulfilling other parts of Azor Ahai's destiny through Jon Snow. Though fans had long predicted we might see the Azor Ahai/Nissa Nissa legend in the show, and the circumstances of the death (and whether Jon or Daenerys would be the "Nissa Nissa" sacrificed) were always believed to involve the fight against the White Walkers, not the fight for the Iron Throne.

Melisandre's words about Azor Ahai in the books prescribed that "the cold breath of darkness" would fall "heavy on the world" and that this day would happen after "a long summer when the stars bleed." The final seasons of *Game of Thrones* take place during winter, which came after a lengthy summer and a red comet in the sky (a "bleeding star").

Fans believed the "dread hour" and "cold breath of darkness" were unequivocally meant to allude to the White Walkers. And in the books, this might still be the case. But with Daenerys's terrible rise to power and the sack of King's Landing, Benioff and Weiss seem to say her reign as Queen of the Seven Kingdoms was the coming darkness Jon Snow had to prevent.

Martin has yet to finish his book series and lay out all the intricate ways in which these prophecies will (or won't) play out with our main characters. As we saw with Arya Stark and the death of the Night King, Benioff and Weiss had to rework pieces from earlier seasons to fit them into major turning points of the final episode's storylines. So was Jon Snow really Azor Ahai all along, or was Arya Stark also a foretold hero who conquered the darkness when she killed all the White Walkers? Was the Prince That Was Promised prophecy always going to come to a messy realization, or is this convoluted ending just the result of Benioff and Weiss running out of book material?

These questions may go forever unanswered, but we at least feel certain that Daenerys will not survive all of Martin's novels and that Jon Snow will likely play a role in her death. We also know that Benioff and Weiss once again chose to harken back to their own invented scenes as a way of bringing these pivotal finale twists to fruition.

Before her death, Daenerys walks into the throne room of the Red Keep for the first time. The framing and staging of the scene is an almost frame-by-frame callback to the second season finale, when Daenerys visited the House of the Undying. Her trip to the magical building where the Undying of Qarth reside happens in the books, too, but the version we saw in season two was drastically different.

For starters, Benioff and Weiss changed things around so that all three of Dany's dragons were taken from her, instead of just Rhaegal and Viserion. So she walks through a series of rooms, following their cries. The first big room she enters is none other than the Red Keep's Great Hall, where the Iron Throne sits. But it isn't the Red Keep as we'd seen it on the show thus far. The version Daenerys walks into is in ruins, with the ceiling caved in and snow falling to the floor.

Daenerys sees the Iron Throne for the first time. She places her torch on the ground and ascends the steps to the throne she coveted. Daenerys reaches for the seat of power, but then hears the cries of her dragons.

Instead of touching the Iron Throne, she turns and follows the sounds of her dragons, and the vision shifts. She's suddenly beyond the Wall, just past the gate of Castle Black we'd seen the men of the Night's Watch depart from. Daenerys sees a tent amid the snow and enters it. Khal Drogo is inside, holding a small child. It's their son, Rhaego, who would've been born to Daenerys and Drogo if the maegi Mirri Maz Duur hadn't performed her blood-magic curse. Daenerys tells Drogo she's seeing him because of a dark magic. "Maybe I am dead and I just don't know it yet," Daenerys says. "Maybe I am with you in the Night Lands."

Years later, Benioff and Weiss brought Dany's vision to life when she walks into the snowy Red Keep and sees the Iron Throne, only this time she is finally able to place her hand on the seat of power. But just as in the House of the Undying, the dream does not last. She is soon killed, and perhaps goes to the Night Lands where Drogo and her unborn child have been waiting for her ever since their untimely deaths.

Martin's version of the House of the Undying scene contains far, far more prophecies, tableaus, and ominous hints about Dany's future. In the books, Pyat Pree is the person who leads Daenerys to the House of the Undying, but he's not her main adversary once she gets inside. The warlock tells Daenerys she will see "many things that will disturb" her once she ventures into the building.

He gives her Shade of the Evening, a blue wine the warlocks drink that stains their lips, and says it will help her "hear and see the truths that will be laid before" her inside the House of the Undying. Daenerys enters the building and eventually finds herself in a long corridor with doorways and rooms lining the wall.

Inside these rooms Dany sees men and creatures, the staging of which foretell events to come in A Song of Ice and Fire. The most significant of these is the Red Wedding, foreshadowed by Martin when Dany sees "a feast of corpses" and "a dead man with the head of a wolf" sitting on a throne. Dany also sees her father, the Mad King (though she doesn't recognize him, since he died before she was born), sitting on the Iron Throne shortly before his death just before the House of the Undying shows her Rhaegar speaking about his son and calling him "the prince that was promised."

Daenerys eventually makes her way to another chamber, where she finds the Undying themselves. They all speak to her at the same time through a shared whisper and tell her many cryptic warnings. At this point, the Undying say Dany will know three treasons: "once for blood and once for gold and once for love." Most readers believe the blood treason is Mirri Maz Duur's killing of Rhaego and Drogo, while the gold treason is Ser Jorah betraying her trust when he spied on her for King Robert.

And now, thanks to the *Game of Thrones* finale, we know Jon Snow is likely the one who will betray Daenerys "for love." Jon kills Daenerys in part because he came to believe her reign would be one of tyrannical terror, but the more emotional motivation for his choice was the threat she posed to his own beloved Stark family.

Jon is resigned to following his queen's orders, no matter the cost, right up until Tyrion asks about Sansa and Arya. "And your sisters? Do you see them bending the knee?" Tyrion says. Jon says they won't have a choice, but Tyrion persists in making Jon believe Daenerys would kill them. This moment forges a link between Jon's coming choice and the choice Ned Stark made all those years ago when Lord Varys came to visit him in the dungeons of the Red Keep.

After Varys brought up Sansa, Ned made the choice to falsely confess to treason instead of dying with his pride intact. All these years later, Jon Snow wrestles with the same choice: the safety of his family, or a commitment to honor. Just like the man who raised him, Jon chooses to protect the Stark children. Duty became the death of love, and the Mother of Dragons met her fate.

CHAPTER TWELVE

FABRICATING NARRATIVES

With a brilliant style that is both subtle and sensory, Michele Clapton's costume designs in *Game of Thrones* managed to both ground the show in reality and illuminate its fantastical universe. Since she first began working on the series during the failed pilot, Clapton was a key part of the world-building, telling characters' stories through the curve of a neckline or twinkle of embroidery.

"I love the details," Clapton said in an *INSIDER* interview. "Some people say, 'Well, why don't you make it more obvious?' But that's the joy of *Game of Thrones*—you have to search things out."

Her carefully planned designs made it possible to chart the journeys of the characters from season to season, as if following a thread in a bundle of string as it's woven into a brilliant tapestry. To first understand why the *Game of Thrones* costumes look at once familiar and fantastical, it's critical to look at how Clapton was able to pull from and blend different historical aesthetics.

"Our brief was to try and combine interesting visual elements from a lot of different societies and periods," executive producer Frank Doelger said in an HBO behind-the-scenes video posted on YouTube ahead of the first season premiere in 2011.

The Lannister soldiers serve as a key example of this. The Lannister army is made up of mostly Westerosi men descended from the Andals and First Men, which has been interpreted as the equivalent of Anglo-Saxon culture in the real world. But the Lannister *armor* is partly inspired by traditional Japanese style, like the *kusazuri* on samurai armor. Clapton blended this silhouette with medieval elements to create the distinct look of the red, black, and gold Lannister suit of armor.

"We were just trying to create a world that is incredibly gritty and real," Clapton said in HBO's online costume featurette that aired in March 2011. "[Where] you completely believe it but you don't actually know quite where it was . . . we decided to just research across the board. We immersed ourselves in museums and books and paintings. Persian, and Inuit and Mongol, Japanese, everything."

This strategy came with the risk of being disorienting or distracting for audiences at home, but under Clapton's impeccable purview the *Game of Thrones* costumes worked seamlessly with the rest of the world-building.

"I think each [piece] has symbolism, and that's what I find so interesting in designing the costumes," Clapton said in the *INSIDER* interview. "You should be able to look at each character and almost mentally know what they're trying to say."

Certain characters, like Daenerys, Sansa, and Cersei, have clear arcs over each season, and those storylines are reflected in the gowns and coats and jewelry they wear in every scene. By the start of the final season, these three women are among the most powerful people left alive in Westeros. Daenerys, Sansa, and Cersei each have wildly different methods of adapting to their circumstances and status within the *Game of Thrones* universe. With Clapton as our guiding hand, we can trace their characters' journeys and choices along the way through their intricate costumes.

DAENERYS TARGARYEN

Season One

In the pilot episode, Dany is presented to Khal Drogo like a well-dressed piece of horsemeat. She's wearing a sheer lavender gown held up only by two three-headed dragon pins—the sigil of House Targaryen and a physical foreshadowing of her future dragon children. The mechanics of this dress (which we can admit is a generous term for such a thin sheet of fabric) are similar to a dress commonly worn in Ancient Greece called the peplos. Like Dany's dress, a peplos was held together with two pins or brooches at either shoulder. Those dragon pins will become relevant again as we push ahead into later seasons, but first we need to take a closer look at her third outfit of the pilot episode: the wedding dress.

Dany's wedding dress is a similar pale purple, but with a more decorative design and two silver armbands. This early theme of purple and silver is likely linked to the descriptors for Targaryens found in Martin's books, with their silver hair and "lilac" or "indigo" eyes. It would have been too much trouble for the production team to use visual effects and change Emilia Clarke's greenish-blue eyes to purple, so instead we got her amethyst gowns.

As she assimilates to her new predicament, Dany begins dressing in more traditional woven Dothraki clothing, with horsehair and leather in tones of brown and beige. Only once she is pregnant with Drogo's child and more empowered with the khalasar does she show more of her Targaryen side. For the episode in which she orders Mirri Maz Duur to heal Drogo, Dany is wearing a golden-scaled top that is unique from the other Dothraki garb we've seen.

That dragon-inspired outfit is the one she'll remain in throughout the tragic turn of events that leads to Drogo's death. Dany ends up inadvertently sacrificing her unborn son for Drogo's "life." Mourning her husband and child but knowing her path forward, Dany slips back into her lilac wedding dress one final time.

"It was meant to unwrap, as if Drogo is opening a present," Clapton said in HBO's *Inside Game of Thrones* book. "And, of course, she burns in it, which is rather poignant—the end of her story with Drogo."

The delicate gown goes up in flames, reduced to ash in Drogo's funeral pyre—much in the same way the meek, browbeaten Daenerys Targaryen from the pilot episode is no more. The Mother of Dragons emerges, shorn of any need for symbolic fabrics and clutching her new children.

Season Two

Dany's triumph is cut short with the opening of season two. Back in her Dothraki clothing, her victor's braid coming undone, Dany and the small khalasar wander in the Red Waste. It's not until they manage to get inside Qarth that Dany's sense of self, and dress, undergo a new transformation.

She is presented with a thin silk gown from Doreah via Xaro Xhoan Daxos, a gesture mirroring the one Illyrio Mopatis made through Viserys in the first season. She wears the shiny blue-and-gold gown at first, with her hair down in loose waves. Though she's made personal progress, the visual of this costume has much more in common with the bullied Dany we saw in the pilot than the queen we know she'll become.

By the sixth episode of season two, "The Old Gods and the New," Dany has had enough of being patronized by the men of Qarth. She compromises by blending the Qartheen fabrics and gold inlay with the shape and style of her typical Dothraki top and trousers. But when her dragons are stolen, Dany armors herself even more. She ditches the delicate gold metalwork for utilitarian leather—further hiding the lush fabrics of her Qartheen dress and presenting herself as a force to be reckoned with.

But by the next episode, "A Man Without Honor," Daenerys is back in her room speaking with Jorah and the armor has come off. Jorah, perhaps sensing a closer level of intimacy, makes the mistake of speaking with her far too familiarly. He is dismissed, and Dany's leather armor goes back on for the rest of the season. Her guard is up, and now she knows not to balk when faced with men who will underestimate her.

Season Three

The third season is when the pace of Dany's story really starts ramping up. Now with access to new fabrics and resources thanks to her overthrow of Qarth, Dany begins wearing a richer blue gown over pants and boots along with a dragon's-tooth necklace. The color palette of her new costume is reminiscent of Khal Drogo's signature blue-painted shoulders from the first season. Dany still honors her time as a Khaleesi and carries Dothraki elements in her costuming, but Clapton is starting to give Dany more of her own signature style.

In the fourth episode of this season, Dany arrives to the slaver's arena in Astapor wearing the same cape as the slave masters, but with one shoulder purposefully overturned. The destruction she is about to unleash was foreshadowed by her new cloak; their slave-based system of life was about to be overthrown.

Later in the season, once she has fully committed to abolishing slavery in every major city in Essos, Dany starts wearing a pure white dress with a necklace made from a modified version of the slave collars seen in the series. Some have seen this as emblematic of Dany playing into "white savior" tropes. By the season's final scene, when Dany is surrounded by a crowd of former slaves chanting "*Mhysa!*," she is back in her signature blue but with a leather shoulder harness that matches her newly won Unsullied army.

Season Four

Once Dany takes up residency in Meereen, her slave-collar necklace is attached to her draped gown. She declares she will not sail for Westeros but instead stay to rule in Meereen. The costume shift speaks to her choice; she is now tethered to this city and to her mission of establishing an antislavery system of governance.

As Dany and Missandei grow closer over this season and the Mother of Dragons seeks out her advice more and more, Missandei's gowns start matching her queen's. Dany's intimacy with Daario is also reflected in her costumes. Dany's most revealing outfit yet, a sleek X-patterned harness that exposes some serious cleavage and her midriff, is worn after she has sex with Daario, the first time for her since Khal Drogo died.

The color palette and textures of her costumes over the season oscillate between white and blue, with a mix of smooth drapery and pleated skirts and dragon-scale embroidery. The variations and experimental silhouettes mimic Dany's struggles to commit to one method of ruling. By the season finale, the Mother of Dragons makes the choice to lock away her children, and therefore her strongest Targaryen inclinations, and rule on her own.

Season Five

When we catch up with Dany's Meereenese storyline, this time sans dragons, we see she is now fully draped in white. This bright, clean gown could (again) be seen as an on-the-nose reference to the goddesslike "savior" undertone of her story in Meereen. But as Clapton told *Fashionista*, "The idea behind the white and pale gray is the sense of removal, a removal from reality."

There's a secret underneath all those gowns, too. "I still always put trousers underneath because in her psyche anything might go wrong and [she's always thinking], 'I might need to run away,'" Clapton said.

By the season's end, this getaway garb came in handy. Dany flies off on Drogon's back, and her pure white gown is dirtied from the unexpected dragon riding. Her ornate necklace is chipped away, piece by piece, and she drops her precious ring in the grass so Jorah and Daario can find her.

Season Six

Daenerys literally goes back to her roots as she finds herself taken captive by Khal Moro's Dothraki hoard and brought to the city of Vaes Dothrak. Her sullied white gown is stripped from her back and she's dressed in the rough-spun fabric of the tribes. But just as she did in the first season, Dany taps into her inner Targaryen and incinerates her enemies. This invocation of her immunity to fire mirrors the season one finale, where it marks a turning point in her approach to commanding power.

◇◇◇◇◇◇◇◇◇◇◇ **MAESTER'S NOTES** ◇◇◇◇◇◇◇◇◇◇◇

Though Benioff and Weiss chose to use Dany's fireproof powers to get her out of the bind in Vaes Dothrak, this is almost certainly not how Martin's books will play out. In A Song of Ice and Fire, Dany's miracle of emerging unscathed from the pyre was a one-time occurrence. "It was never the case that all Targaryens are immune to all fire at all times," Martin said in 1998, according to a trusty Westeros.org archive called "So Spake Martin."

Another online forum, called Dakka Dakka, published a reference to a Q&A Martin held online in 2000, when a fan asked him if Targaryens became immune to fire once they bonded to their dragons.

"Thanks for asking that," Martin reportedly replied. "It gives me a chance to clear up a common misconception. TARGARYENS ARE NOT IMMUNE TO FIRE! The birth of Dany's dragons was unique, magical, wonderous, a miracle. She is called The Unburnt because she walked into the flames and lived. But her brother sure as hell wasn't immune to that molten gold."

After Dany kills all the khals and takes control of the great khalasar, she spends much of season six back in brown leather and woven tops. But this time the silhouette of her shirt is identical to the blue dresses she wore in the third season—the last time her momentum was this strong. Daenerys earns her bloodriders and heads back to Meereen—this time to rule her way.

The season six finale transitions her gently from a fearsome khaleesi back toward her Targaryen colors. As she prepares to set sail, Dany wears a soft, draped dark gown with a plunging neckline and a wide silver belt. The Grecian influence is there, along with the silver adornments, just as it was in the pilot episode.

This brief stop at season-one Dany is quickly overshadowed by the gown she wears when she finally heads to Westeros. The off-the-shoulder style seen on Dany in the final moments of season six is an exact match for the cut and shape of a white dress she wore in the fifth season—but this time she is adorned in full black fabric with shimmering red-and-black scales on her shoulders. The gown matches the proud Targaryen sails fluttering above her as she stands triumphant on the ship's deck.

Season Seven

The seventh season was an interesting turning point for the costumes in *Game of Thrones*. Nearly everyone's outfits (not just our Targaryen-loyal characters) were switched to a black color palette.

"It's coming to a point [where] everything is almost polarized," Clapton said in an *INSIDER* interview ahead of the seventh season premiere. "So I love the idea that all the women, and actually everything, is almost mono-chromed. It's about winning the throne, all the challenges they have, the threats from over the Wall, everything. Each of the women's costumes have all become quite dark, but there's details within each of them that are incredibly important."

Dany arrives at Dragonstone in a caped gown with dark red thread entwined in little red and black stones. Clapton said she wanted the look to command more "strength" and be "more like a uniform and almost less feminine," to match her Unsullied army.

"With Dany especially, people used to say, 'Well, why doesn't she wear red?'" Clapton said. "Now you do finally start seeing it creeping in through the scaling and embroidery on her dresses. It's just a touch."

Throughout the seventh season, Dany's various outfits have a strong, angular shoulder silhouette often paired with a chain and shoulder sash (held in place by a three-headed dragon brooch that serves as a callback to her sheer purple gown from the pilot).

"With Dany in particular, finally we're getting the [Targaryen] red. She was a confused woman, she was wandering... trying to seek something," Clapton said. "And now she's finally got her armor, she's finally got everything, and she can finally echo the style of her brother with the extended shoulders and the red and the symbolism. He always had the big Targaryen [sigil] on his chest and now she's got the big chain with the dragon's heads on it."

Dany's sash notably changes to a soft bluish-gray color in the third episode of the season, when she and Jon Snow have an intimate conversation in the dragonglass cavern. Just as she's beginning to sense a link to this King in the North, her costume colors switch to become more Stark than Targaryen. An enormous leap in her fashion comes yet again when Dany decides to fly beyond the Wall and wears a lush striped fur coat.

"I felt that there should be a definite shift in her look to reflect her decision to go to the aid of Jon and his team trapped north of the wall," Clapton said in an *INSIDER* interview conducted over email. "I think it's the first time that she has really been to the aid of another individual. And let's face it, she's not going because of the Hound and the other members of the team!

"She is putting herself and her precious dragons at risk and who for? A threat? A King?" Clapton continued. "Dany is elevating her look to that of warrior queen, with the beautiful silver dragon chain completing the look."

Season Eight

The eighth season begins for Daenerys with her wearing an updated version of the indelible white fur coat from season seven, this time even more royally luxurious in its texture and finery. Daenerys is the first Targaryen to come to Winterfell in more than a generation, and her presence in the North is immediately divisive. By the second episode, when Dany's isolation from the rest of the people in Winterfell is more prominent, the pure white of her coat from the premiere gives way to a slightly more gray tone.

Her turn toward a darker path is coming, and her clothing reflects it. While the presence of grays on Dany during the seventh season feels like a signal of her warmth toward Jon Snow and the North (since the colors of House Stark are gray and white), now it signals a warning of her conflicting morals. We first see this in "A Knight of the Seven Kingdoms," when her overcoat is much more gray with prominent red detailing. She wears this darker palette for the trial of Jaime Lannister and her conversation with Sansa, both of which go very poorly for the Mother of Dragons.

Dany wears her white-and-red coat for the Battle of Winterfell, but afterward for the funeral she is back in her greys, leaving behind the acts of altruism she showed during the fight against the Army of the Dead and reembracing her ambition. Later, at the feast, she wears a brand-new Targaryen-red costume, the first time she's worn this much of her house color. This fully red coat has a black panel running down its front, not unlike the white-and-blue gowns she wore in Meereen. Here she is in full Targaryen mode when she manipulates Gendry by legitimizing him and pressures Jon to never speak a word about his claim to the Iron Throne.

Dany returns to her gray-and-red coloring for the entreaty with

Cersei. She's on the cusp, trying to thread the needle between her desire for Cersei's destruction and following her previous moral compass of sparing the innocent. By the time Daenerys has fully succumbed to ruling by fear and attacks King's Landing, she embraces her inner dragon and wears a metallic gown with a scaled pattern. The material is almost iridescent, with blackish-purple hues reflecting in the sunlight as she sits atop Drogon.

Daenerys finally takes Lady Olenna's advice (which we hear in the "previously on" segment before "The Bells") to be a dragon. The episode's director, Miguel Sapochnik, said in HBO's "The Game Revealed" segment that Daenerys pushed forward with the slaughter in part because the surrender felt too easy. She and Grey Worm came for blood, wanting to avenge Missandei and her other fallen followers. "She feels empty," he said. "It wasn't what she thought it was. It's not enough."

Once Daenerys decides to continue punishing the city, she vanishes from the episode's perspective. We only see the dragon and destruction—never our Mother of Dragons herself. And then something interesting happens for Dany's final living moments. She is wearing the same dramatic gown at the start of the finale, "The Iron Throne." But the city sits under a cloud of ash and snow, and in the absence of sunlight and warmth the dress now appears jet-black. The full darkness of Dany's destiny is resting, literally, on her shoulders.

By the time she lies dead in the snow, crimson blood pooling around her, Daenerys is framed just as Jon Snow was in the final moments of season five. In both scenes, the black of their clothing masks the mortal wounds leaving them dead before their time. But Daenerys Stormborn stays lost to oblivion while Jon is gifted back his life. The Mother of Dragons, corrupted in her final hours by the allure of her own power and righteousness, will not rise again.

Sansa Stark

—— ❧ ☙ ——

Season One

One of Sansa's earliest costume metaphors comes by way of her simple Northern-style dress meant to match her sister. Arya and Sansa couldn't be further apart in personality, ambitions, and habits. To that end, on the second episode of the series, both girls wear pale, modest gowns with knotted fabric at the neckline. Sansa's dress is neatly tied with not a stitch out of place, Arya's is more undone as she spars with Prince Joffrey on the banks of the Trident. She's even torn the sleeves off her dress, as Clapton pointed out in a YouTube video feature uploaded by HBO ahead of the first season premiere.

When they get to King's Landing, Sansa's dresses remain modest, but the adornments on them become increasingly intricate to match how she's acclimating to life in the fancy capital. This is noticeable on the fifth episode of season one, when she wears a pale lavender dress with rose embellishments to watch the Hand's tourney.

Sansa continues alternating between her two Northern dresses as Joffrey and Cersei Lannister masterfully manipulate her. After Ned is arrested and Sansa is pressured by the small council to appear before King Joffrey and beg for mercy on her father's behalf, Cersei has dressed Sansa in a new blue gown, much like the ones the Queen Regent herself wears. Sansa is now visibly a pawn in Cersei's game at court.

Season Two

Sansa continues to wear the fanciful dresses of a southern lady as the Lannisters hold her prisoner in King's Landing. She alternates between pale blue and pink gowns, mirroring the colors Cersei tends to wear when she's presenting her softer side as a façade.

On the seventh episode, when Sansa wakes up to the horrifying realization that she's started her period, she wears a simple sky-blue embroidered dress. The color palette for both Sansa and Cersei in this scene matches the dresses they wore to Ned Stark's sentencing in the first season. New pain, blood, and terror are present in the season two scene as Sansa's loss of innocence is made more literal. From this point on, the blue of Sansa's early costumes gives way to a deep purple as her sense of identity is further muddled between Stark (and the bluish gray of the North) and Lannister (red and gold) during her captivity.

During the Battle of Blackwater, this aesthetic of a purple and gold brocade stands out as she steps into a position of slight confidence. She messes with Joffrey before he goes out to the ramparts, trying to goad him into fighting on the frontlines. And inside Maegor's Holdfast, Sansa holds her own against Cersei and steps into a leading role when the Queen Regent loses hope.

Season Three

Throughout the first several episodes of season three, Sansa wears new variations of purple gowns with gold detailing. The Lannisters' grip on her is tightening, but it's happening gradually without Sansa (or the audience) realizing what's to come. The rug is ripped from beneath Sansa's feet when she's forced to marry Tyrion. On that day, Sansa wears an ornate gown covered so thoroughly in gold patterning that the underlying purple is almost imperceptible.

Though her relationship with Tyrion was starting to look amicable, by the season's conclusion Sansa is retraumatized by the murder of her mother and brother at the hands of the Lannisters and Freys. Her purple-and-gold gowns become the only markers of mourning she is allowed to wear in the capital.

Season Four

In the opening episode, "Two Swords," Sansa is back to the very first iteration of her purple gown we saw in the second season. The progress in confidence she'd made over the last two seasons was cut from underneath her. But all is not lost for Sansa. The dark amethyst color of her dress is linked to the purple crystal necklace that poisons Joffrey in the next episode. Though Sansa did not have a hand in the Purple Wedding, it's no coincidence her unique dress palette (by King's Landing standards) is the color sign of King Joffrey's death.

Sansa stays in this purple gown once Littlefinger whisks her away to the Vale. Thanks to Littlefinger's manipulations and mentorship in all things deceptive, Sansa begins to regain her confidence. She lies to the lords and ladies of the Vale in a cunning move that surprises even the slippery Littlefinger. When he goes to her room to talk about her achievement in trickery, Littlefinger finds Sansa sewing. For the first time since she was a girl in Winterfell, Sansa is shown making her own clothes, threading her needle into the dark fabric just as she starts to pierce the steely exterior of Littlefinger.

"Dark Sansa," as her new look is called, is fittingly black—the mourning color she was unable to wear in King's Landing because her dead family members were considered traitors. Here the black becomes Sansa's display of strength and resilience instead of grief.

Season Five

Dark Sansa is out in full force for the opening episodes of the fifth season. A new element to the design is a black caped overcoat that matches Littlefinger, her mentor in manipulation. Once he brings her back to Winterfell and idiotically delivers her into the hands of the Boltons, we see Sansa is wearing the same hand-sewn black gown and striking necklace she wore on the fourth season finale.

As Clapton revealed in an interview with *The Cut*, this necklace—the chain of which ends in a long spike—is meant to be Sansa's version of Arya's Needle. Interestingly, the circular brooch design with a chain running through it looks very similar to a necklace Clapton herself wore in behind-the-scenes videos from 2011, when *Game of Thrones* was first being filmed.

Clapton shared a photo of herself wearing both Sansa's needle necklace and another circular iteration on Instagram in December 2016. When a fan asked Clapton if she could explain the meaning behind Sansa's necklace in the comments, the costume designer obliged.

"The chain is 'stitched' through a dark stone circle with a large metal 'needle,'" Clapton wrote, noting how this "needle" weighs down the necklace and holds it in place. "The process of stitching reflects Sansa's youth; she has always created her own looks, but the needle is now a weapon, a miniature of her sister's sword; Sansa now understands her sister's desire to fight. The dark circle represents the seemingly never-ending darkness in Sansa's life..."

Season Six

For the start of the sixth season, Sansa stays in her slate-gray and light-stone-colored dress and brocade-patterned cloak. Only once she is safely in Castle Black with Jon does Sansa find the time—and presumably finds resources, though gods know why the Night's Watch has fancy fabrics lying around—to make a new dress. For the first time since the second season, Sansa steps back into the color blue.

This time her dress is a deep, rich blue with a direwolf sigil embroidered along the front. Sansa pairs it with a thick fur cape (she makes Jon a new cape, too). Together they are ready to show the North that the Starks are far from gone. Sansa wants to reclaim her home, and has the aesthetic to prove it. She and Jon scrape together a victory with a major boost from Littlefinger and the knights of the Vale.

The finale gives us Sansa standing on the ramparts of the Starks' castle once more and later sitting in the godswood. Littlefinger approaches Sansa in that sacred Northern place, and finally reveals for the first time his creeptastic dream of sitting on the Iron Throne with her at his side. But he's overestimated the esteem Sansa holds for him. Sansa is visually separated from his machinations in this moment, standing gloriously in her velvet dress and lush fur cape. Dark Sansa is laid to rest. Sansa Stark, Lady of Winterfell, has joined the game.

Season Seven

In the seventh season, Sansa wears a darker palette of colors, just like the rest of our characters. But she's not in full black the way Dark Sansa always had been. Her needle necklace remains, but now Sansa has added a brown leather belt that crosses around her back and wraps her torso.

"This is her taking back control of her body," Clapton said in an HBO interview for the *Making Game of Thrones* website. "I designed it to wrap around over her side-laced dress to represent the absolute removal of any possible physical touch. Her dresses are also tightly laced on, incredibly difficult to remove; it's a message to Littlefinger."

Sansa was physically abused for much of the series, but the seventh season is when she finally finds herself in a place of safety.

"[Sansa] has the chain, she has the circle, she's bringing all that she's been through to her costume," Clapton said in an *INSIDER* interview. "You need to look at the story. Her strength and the way that she's clothed to protect herself from the things that have happened. At the same time, she's beginning to assert herself as an independent woman and not actually being manipulated by anyone anymore."

By this seventh season, Clapton was hyperaware of the meaning she was imbuing in the smallest of details for the characters' costumes.

"At this stage, everything has reached such a zenith in their character development that everything they do and say symbolically means something," Clapton said. "Every single bit says something about the character."

In that spirit, the detailing on Sansa's dress pattern is worth noting. At a glance you could mistake it for light lines making up triangles on the dark fabric. But really it appears to be made up of a bunch of X-figures—just like the House Bolton sigil of a flayed man. When Sansa had Ramsay killed, he told her he would always be a part of her now. As we watch Sansa's resolve harden, eventually leading her to sentence Littlefinger to death as well, the pattern on her dress becomes representative of this newer capacity Sansa has for violence. Of course, Sansa exacts that vengeance on wholly deserving parties, which separates her from the cruelty of Ramsay.

Season Eight

Sansa is first seen in the eighth season in a distinctive silhouetted top, the squared shoulders of which match the tunic stylings of both King Joffrey, Ned Stark, and other men who influenced Sansa's life. That same shoulder design was seen on Margaery Tyrell's gowns when she started exerting more influence on King Joffrey. Though this garment is hidden beneath her fur cape when she greets Jon and Daenerys in the Winterfell courtyard, it is seen more clearly when she's speaking privately with Jon and first reveals just how little trust she has in Daenerys. The Bolton patterning is still visible, along with her trusty needle necklace.

Then, aware of the threat Daenerys poses to the independence of the North, Sansa gets into full battle gear for the first time on the show in episode two, when Daenerys comes to her to discuss their alliance. In an interview with *Vox*, Clapton said this new leather look was sending a different message compared to the protective subtext of Sansa's leather belt from the seventh season. "It's not about protection, it's a statement!" Clapton said. "Sansa's armor is a direct reaction to Dany's assertion of power."

It's also interesting that Sansa flips to the fully black-and-silver color scheme as Winterfell prepares for war. We hear Sansa tell Yohn Royce to keep the castle gates open for as long as possible because people from the countryside are still coming to find shelter. This action is in direct opposition to the order we see Cersei give later, telling Qyburn to keep the gates of King's Landing open so that more innocent people can flood into the city. Cersei's creation of a human shield is done for purely selfish reasons and leads to the massacre of thousands, while Sansa is genuinely trying to help the people of the North.

Then comes the true pièce de résistance in the series finale, when Sansa Stark is crowned Queen in the North. This poignant end to her journey in Westeros is enhanced by a stunning coronation gown and the reveal of a new Stark crown. Sansa's new look has—literally—layers of meaning, from the fabric used on her gown to a cameo by Clapton.

As Clapton revealed in an Instagram post, Sansa's coronation dress was made from the same fabric we had seen twice before. First it was used to create Margaery's wedding gown when she married Joffrey. "Sansa had a bond with her," Clapton wrote in her caption.

Margaery and her grandmother Olenna Tyrell were protective of Sansa and wanted to help get her out from under the Lannisters' control. So Sansa's dark look, which we saw throughout season five as well, was the same fabric as Margaery's lush, light blue wedding dress—just dyed black. Her coronation dress was also crafted from the same material, but its light hues were able to shine.

The intricate bodice of Sansa's finale dress looks almost like a delicate armor. "The metal bodice features the growing branches of the weirwood tree," Clapton said on Instagram. In that finale montage, we see a pair of hands tying Sansa's dress to the weirwood bodice. According to her Instagram, those were Clapton's own hands making a small cameo.

The dress also has red-beaded weirwood leaves on one of its draping sleeves. Weirwoods are ancient trees associated with the old gods of the North. They have white bark and deep-red leaves, and each weirwood has a face carved into its trunk.

Weirwoods once grew all throughout Westeros, but centuries before the events of *Game of Thrones*, men who followed the new gods had them cut down. But the great weirwood of Winterfell still stands at the center of House Stark's godswood. When she was held captive in King's Landing, Sansa used to go to the godswood, where there was only a stump of a once mighty weirwood. Now her coronation gown is imbued with the symbols of the weirwood, displaying the power of the North and its ancient traditions.

"The sleeves are textured like the fur on the first sigil," Clapton said on Instagram. The direwolf sigil of House Stark is drawn with a pointed pattern that appears almost scalelike, though the design is meant to represent the fur of a wolf.

Sansa still has part of her needle necklace for the ceremony. Its chain is still connected to the bottom of the bodice, just barely visible as we see her walking down the aisle toward her direwolf throne.

The direwolf of House Stark is also represented in Sansa's gown on the cape draped over her shoulders. The wolf's head has little feathers coming out of it, matching the feathers on the sleeves of Sansa's gown. In a second Instagram post, Clapton implied that the "asymmetry of the cut" was a reference to Arya Stark's one-shouldered cape she wore for the final two seasons of *Game of Thrones*.

Sansa's Queen in the North crown also appears designed to blend the Stark direwolves with Sansa's underlying connection to Cersei. We first see Sansa's crown from behind, and the delicate weaving pattern looks very similar to Cersei Lannister's crown for the last couple of seasons. Cersei was a ruthless, evil ruler who tormented Sansa for years. But Sansa eventually realized she had learned a lot from Cersei, and she adapts the Lannister queen's traits into her own methods of more compassionate but firm leadership.

Clapton made no mention of Cersei in her Instagram post, but the link is there visually.

Once we see the front of Sansa's crown, it becomes clear that the new Queen in the North is celebrating House Stark through and through. Clapton said Sansa's crown is two howling direwolves, and once again you can see the abstract fur pattern from the House Stark sigil. The smaller direwolf head is propping the other up—a gesture we'd like to believe signals how the last of the Stark children all supported one another and helped keep their great house alive through the turmoil of the final wars on *Game of Thrones*.

"The lone wolf dies, but the pack survives," Ned Stark used to tell his children. Sansa Stark, the Queen in the North, honors her late father's words with the two direwolves on her crown. Long may she reign.

CERSEI LANNISTER

Season One

Clapton was very cognizant of the in-universe resources available to Cersei Lannister, the first queen we meet in the series. As a member of royalty living in a port city, Cersei is able to wear a larger variety of fabrics than many other women we see in *Game of Thrones*. She's introduced in the pilot wearing soft pinks and rich, deep reds adorned with golden finery. Lannister soldiers wear armor inspired by samurai, and many of Cersei's gowns (particularly in the early seasons) have Japanese origins.

"[Cersei] tends to wear very soft, wrapped silks which are embroidered," Clapton said in a video shared by HBO ahead of the first season premiere. "It's like a kimono-style but with a slightly medieval cut. And she has a lot of metal belts because I quite like the idea that she's armored in a sense."

Cersei's softer side is made visible when she is with those she truly loves. She wears a light blue gown embroidered with birds for her scenes with Joffrey and Jaime in the third episode. The birds are given added meaning when we consider how Cersei has spent her whole life feeling slighted and caged by her gender, cursed at birth for being born a girl. She also frequently calls Sansa a "little dove," which is again reflected on her gowns.

When Cersei and Joffrey take the Iron Throne in the wake of King Robert's death, the newly widowed queen wears a deep-green caped gown for the first time on the series. Her delicate gold crown, which she wore at the feast in Winterfell in the pilot episode, is set with an emerald.

Once she takes control of King's Landing by crowning Joffrey and beheading poor Ned, Cersei is all Lannister all the time in vibrant reds and shimmering golds.

Season Two

Cersei starts the second season back in her embroidered blue gown, squaring off against Tyrion as he tells her that her love for her children is her one redeeming quality ("That, and your cheekbones," he says).

The Queen Regent spends much of the season in pink, gold, and red gowns, with increasingly elaborate stitched lions on her sleeves and bodices. Freed of King Robert, she drops the half-Baratheon front. Cersei only returns to her ornate light blue coloring for her wrenching goodbye to Myrcella in the sixth episode, the final time she'll see her only daughter alive.

Then we come to "Blackwater," and the moment when Clapton

was able to give Cersei her most literal armored gown. There are still birds embroidered on this dress, framing her shoulders and connecting her mini-arc in this episode to Sansa's, her little dove. But the intricate golden corset dominates the aesthetic of this outfit. Cersei is making her stand as a fighter, even if only the men are allowed to bloody the shores of King's Landing.

Season Three

The third season of *Game of Thrones* begins with Cersei Lannister backed against a wall as Tywin plants himself in King's Landing and Margaery begins sinking her claws into Joffrey. Margaery's battle tactics are all about her power as a lady of court and future wife. Her gowns are more modern, sleek, and revealing, with softer toned fabrics that evoke gardens and greenery and the rose of House Tyrell.

Cersei is on defense, and she knows it. In the very first episode of the season, when the Queen Regent hosts the young Tyrells for dinner, she wears a bloodred gown with new, armored gold plating. The young queen-to-be has never encountered an embittered and ambitious woman like Cersei, one who is so desperate to have been born with the advantages of a man that she'll stop at nothing to impress her cold father and turn to violence in situations when diplomacy would do.

Cersei will continue losing to Margaery throughout this season. You can see the way Margaery's manipulations are working on Joffrey in each of their shared scenes, and their clothing even begins to match. On the fourth episode, which follows the one where Margaery seductively visits Joffrey's room and has him show her how his crossbow works, the sleeves of the blue-and-gold gown she wears in the Sept of Baelor are the same squared shoulder silhouette as Joffrey's for the first time.

During this season, the necklines and structure of Cersei's dresses start to mimic the modernity of Margaery's season-two gowns, with high backs and stiff, rounded shoulders. The Lannisters are reaching the height of their power, and Cersei's ornamental costumes reflect her new status even as she claws for full control.

Season Four

The fourth season opens with Cersei still peacocking around Margaery and the rest of the King's Landing court in her Lannister reds and golds, insistent on retaining her power even though a new queen has come along. But the floor falls out from under her when Joffrey is murdered at the Purple Wedding.

Cersei immediately begins wearing black mourning gowns, a sign of respect and grief she never gave to her husband. The cut and gold embroidery are the same as the pink and red gowns we've seen on her, but with an inky black fabric that seems to swallow her aura of power. Cersei still tries to exude control, but a bitter rage now dominates any softness she used to have.

Though Cersei refuses to wear any color but black for the remainder of the season, her clothing influence is seen in other characters. At Tyrion's trial, Shae trades in her handmaiden uniform for a lady's dress when she testifies against Tyrion. This indicates she was dressed (and likely bribed or coerced) by either Cersei or Tywin. A similar subplot appears to play out in the following episode when Bronn visits Tyrion in his cell. "You have new clothes," Tyrion tells his sellsword. Bronn reveals he's betrothed to Lollys Stokeworth thanks to another successful Cersei bribe that came with fancy new clothes.

Season Five

The fifth season begins with a flashback of young Cersei, reminding us of the reddish-mauve gowns she used to wear. But in the present day, Cersei remains in mourning blacks. She is adorned with more gold finery and bolder jewelry to go along with her dour gowns. Her necklines continue to be structured like Margaery's earlier dresses. Cersei would of course see this as a power move, but in fact it betrays her insecurity and paranoia regarding Margaery (worsened when the younger and more beautiful queen—in Cersei's mind the very one she was forewarned of by the woods witch—marries Tommen).

Cersei's braids and hairstyles in this season could rival Daenerys's at her most Dothraki-victorious. As she flounces about King's Landing, certain she is in command of everything from King Tommen to the High Sparrow, Cersei's outward appearance shows her hubris.

Of course, she is stripped of all pride and dignity, right down to those beautifully coiled locks of golden hair, by the season finale. Her walk of atonement lays Cersei's worst nightmare of humiliation and disrespect at her bloodied feet. She is served a valuable lesson about underestimating her enemies and overestimating her own cunning—but will she take it to heart?

Season Six

Now is a good time to note that Michele Clapton didn't actually craft most of the sixth season's costumes. After completing the costume designs for season five, Clapton left the *Game of Thrones* production team for a spell.

"I feel like we've covered all bases now," she told *Fashionista*. "It was really important to me, knowing that I was going to leave, to actually design the costumes for each [geographic] area so it's complete. In my head anyway, it's a complete look that I left."

The opening episode of season six has Cersei back in her pale-red wrap dress for the first time since season two. She wears it to the bay, where she thinks she will welcome back Myrcella. But to her dismay, it's time to wear mourning colors once again. For the rest of the season, Cersei's costume is just her simpler black wrap dress, in the same kimono style first introduced in season one, with gold thread detailing. She wears her staple oval Lannister necklace, and quietly plots her way back to power.

Everything changes for the sixth season finale, "The Winds of Winter," when Clapton returned triumphantly for the finale episode to craft Cersei's two gowns. The episode opens with Cersei in a new black dress with ostentatious jeweled silver lions on either shoulder. The tight, textured black leather and high collar look just like the tunics her father, Tywin, wore in earlier seasons.

"When they sent me the script, I just read it and said, 'I know what she's going to wear.' I knew instantly the moment I saw it," Clapton said in an interview with *Tech Insider*'s Melia Robinson. She never explained exactly why she opted to return, but clearly inspiration struck.

With her enemies smote by wildfire and her last child dead, Cersei ascends to the Iron Throne. Her coronation gown is similar to the one she wears in the opening scenes, but with more armored shoulders and a new crown. The intertwining silver barbs are an abstract representation of the Lannister lion and the Iron Throne itself. With her children stripped from her, there are no more redeeming qualities left for her to lean into. Cersei is ready to rule with fear, and the severity of this gown proves it.

Season Seven

For the seventh season, Clapton returned in full force. She designed Cersei's new series of black gowns to be even more gaudy and lavish, while keeping with the general theme of black and silver.

"With Cersei, at this point, she's attained the throne, and there's a strength in her embroidery," Clapton said in an *INSIDER* interview. "It's actually quite ornate and over the top and that's a precursor in a funny way—it's the last gasp before something else, in my sense. It's a weird flamboyance, but it's quite hard as well."

In scenes where Cersei walks across a room, you can see that her dresses are now a bit shorter than in previous seasons.

"[We] shortened her dress so it makes her less vulnerable," Clapton said. "She can move and she can be a little bit like Dany in a way, because it's not quite as restrictive. [Cersei] always had strong collars and strong shoulders, so I thought this [dress] should take it the furthest I can take it before it's not there."

In an Instagram post from December 7, 2016, Clapton shared a painting from a nineteenth-century French artist with the vague caption "Gustave Moreau inspiration." The piece was *Les Lincornes* (The Unicorns), a lavish depiction of women and the titular mythical creatures, which Clapton had cropped down to focus on the most ornately dressed lady in the foreground. "In [Moreau's] paintings, often of mythological or biblical subjects, a powerful, seductive, evil woman often appears," the J. Paul Getty Museum writes of Moreau on its website.

In December 2016, production was well under way for *Game of Thrones* season seven, the season in which Cersei Lannister is no longer burdened with her love for her children and at her most ruthless. Cersei spent the first six seasons building up her literal armor against the world. Clapton's Instagram post about Moreau came sandwiched between photos of the sketches for Cersei's black coronation gown and other pieces. It's not hard to understand why Moreau's "powerful" and "evil" painting subjects served as inspiration for Clapton's Cersei designs.

On the finale, Clapton used a new dark fabric for Cersei's dragon pit scene. The matte black overcoat swallows all light and aptly conveys the queen's cold indifference toward the great war heading her way. But the real kicker was the detail in the back; a twisted silver texture runs down the spine of her gown, barely visible when she turns to walk away from Jon and Dany.

"I knew she was lying," Clapton said in an interview with HBO for its *Making Game of Thrones.* "Something about the slashing and the twisting told you a lot about her character, a contradiction of the costume from the front. It's almost like a sting in the tail, something on edge as you see her walk away: there's something really disturbing about this woman."

Cersei's lie was of course that she would join the fight. As her final scene of the season with Jaime shows, she had no intention of helping despite the agreement she made with Tyrion. We'd have to wait until the eighth season to see how this cowardice and selfish instinct served Queen Cersei.

Season Eight

Cersei begins the eighth season in a new take on her flamboyant black gown styling. Now the metal shoulder adornments are a burnished gold and connected to her golden Lannister lion pendant. The twisted detailing from her season-seven-finale dress goes all the way down the front of her dress now instead of the back. The deception is no longer a subtlety—Cersei is overt in her cruelty and lack of honor.

She's self-assured and powerful as she lords over Captain Harry Strickland of the Golden Company and Euron Greyjoy in the throne room. But then Euron effectively blackmails her into sleeping with him, and we cut to her back in the soft blue dressing gowns we previously only saw her wear around Jaime in the seventh season.

By the time we see her next, on the fourth episode of season eight, she's wearing a velvety red gown. No longer the pure-dark queen, Cersei is embracing the colors of House Lannister for the first time since Joffrey died. The golden hue of her armorlike accessories now fits with her "hear me roar" stance. As she raises a hand, threatening to kill Tyrion, we can see a bulging crystal ring on one finger. The hulking silhouette of this jewelry conjures up imagery of Casterly Rock—House Lannister's ancestral castle that looms over a coastal bluff. But despite all her gaudy Lannister pride, Cersei is also unknowingly wearing her own funeral garb.

Cersei will die (somewhat ironically) when she's crushed by a pile of brick and stone, the literal weight of the Red Keep falling on top of her. But she's given an unexpected peace in her final moments as she folds into the full embrace of her twin, the man whom she most desperately desired to be born as. Wrapped in the metaphorical fabric of House Lannister, Cersei meets her doom.

CHAPTER THIRTEEN

HIDDEN DETAILS

One of the most rewarding things about being a fan of a meticulously crafted series like *Game of Thrones* is how themes and details reveal themselves to you with each viewing of the show. Much in the same way Martin laid down breadcrumbs of plot twists in his novels, Benioff and Weiss found ways to foreshadow future revelations or give meaningful winks to the audience. You might have spotted some of these yourself right away the first time around, while others become crystal clear only upon a rewatch. From clever prop placements to loaded dialogue and links to Martin's books, these are some of the best hidden details you might have missed along the way.

SEASON ONE

Episode One: "Winter Is Coming"

The inner workings of the pilot episode of *Game of Thrones* are already covered in our third chapter, but here is one final Easter egg highlighted in the script for "Winter Is Coming." Remember the gratuitous shot of Jon Snow, Robb Stark, and Theon Greyjoy all standing around shirtless (and clearly flexing their abs as hard as possible) while they get haircuts? The man with the shears wasn't played by your average extra. That was Tommy Dunne, the weapons master who designed all the badass swords you see on the show.

Episode Two: "The Kingsroad"

Jon and Ned's final goodbyes don't appear anywhere in Martin's books. So when Jon asks Ned about his mother, the scene immediately grabbed the attention of any book-readers watching. Ned replies carefully: "You are a Stark. You might not have my name, but you have my blood."

The Stark family blood does indeed run through Jon. It just happens to be Lyanna's blood, not Ned's. This tiptoeing around the truth immediately stood out to those who believed fervently in R + L = J.

Episode Three: "Lord Snow"

In the opening scene of this episode, we see Ned enter the throne room of the Red Keep for the first time. A curiously designed set of stained-glass windows adorn the walls of this room. They each show a round circle enclosing a seven-pointed star, the sign of the Faith of the Seven, with a blue flower in its center.

It's easy to dismiss this blue shape as an indistinct blob of color, but as *Watchers on the Wall* contributing writer and artist Vanessa Cole once pointed out on Twitter, the windows are often framed just behind Ned whenever he's in this particular room, and this is likely a nod to the iconic blue roses associated with Lyanna Stark.

At this point Benioff and Weiss nixed the idea of flashbacks, which meant they couldn't use Ned's memories in the books to explain the connection between Lyanna Stark and blue winter roses—the flower that made up the crown Rhaegar had bestowed upon her at the Tourney of Harrenhal. In the books, Ned has dreams of his confrontation at the Tower of Joy and of Lyanna's death in the tower, and of rose petals.

"As they came together in a rush of steel and shadow, he could hear Lyanna screaming," Martin writes in *A Game of Thrones.* "'Eddard!' she called. A storm of rose petals blew across a blood-streaked sky, as blue as the eyes of death."

These potent symbols of Jon's secret parentage and Lyanna's love for Rhaegar are relegated to the far background of the throne room. But if you watch closely for frames of Ned in "Lord Snow" and "You Win or You Die," the blue rose motif is ever-present.

Episode Four: "Cripples, Bastards, and Broken Things"

In yet another show-invented scene, Ned Stark's trusted man Jory Cassel has a conversation with Jaime Lannister outside King Robert's chambers. The two men reminisce over the Siege of Pyke, and Jory laments about how a Greyjoy almost "took his eye." This is rather bleak foreshadowing of how Jaime will kill Jory by the end of the next episode. How does he do it? By plunging a dagger through his eye.

Episode Five: "The Lion and the Wolf"

Littlefinger is in the small council meeting where Robert Baratheon and Ned Stark square off over how the newly pregnant Daenerys Targaryen should be dealt with. A Faceless Man is put forth as an option; in the previous episode, "Cripples, Bastards, and Broken Things," Daenerys's handmaid Doreah first mentions the people who can change faces the way one changes clothes. Both of these references to Faceless Men are made long before we meet Jaqen H'ghar in the second season.

But most important, Littlefinger's brutal approach to Daenerys's assassination foreshadows his own demise. "Cut her throat and be done with it," he callously says to King Robert Baratheon. Little (ha) does he know, Arya Stark will do the same to him many years later.

In this same scene, the rose mosaic glass is once again centered behind Ned Stark as he faces a blustering King Robert, who is intent on killing every last person in the world with Targaryen blood, even a baby. This was yet another message to the audience that Ned Stark would have needed to keep Jon Snow safe and away from any Targaryen association—otherwise Robert surely would have had the baby boy killed.

Episode Six: "A Golden Crown"

When Ser Jorah Mormont stops Viserys from leaving Vaes Dothrak with Dany's precious dragon eggs, the young Targaryen is incredulous that the knight who swore his service to both him and Daenerys would behave like this. Viserys reminds Jorah of the promise he made, and Jorah responds with an invocation of the House Mormont words.

Though Jorah says "Here I stand" and not "Here We Stand"

(the formal phrase), it was a slick way for Benioff and Weiss to give a nod to book-readers. The House Mormont words are never directly referenced within the show's universe in this season, but anyone who had read A Song of Ice and Fire likely smiled at the inclusion of Jorah's line.

Episode Seven: "You Win or You Die"

One of the series' most memorable and downright badass character introductions came when Jaime enters his lord father's tent to find him skinning a stag (a metaphor you hopefully don't need explained). This scene was another one that didn't appear directly in the books, and only made it into the show thanks to a series of mishaps.

"A strange thing happened midway through shooting the first season," Benioff said in HBO's Inside Game of Thrones. "We realized several of the episodes were coming in with short running times, which meant we had to come up with a slew of new scenes. Unfortunately, our budget was also coming up short, which meant these new scenes generally had to be two-handers, shot interior, without action or VFX or horses or anything, really, but two actors and some dialogue."

Benioff and Weiss eagerly accepted this challenge because it meant they could really focus in on character development without stressing over plot or epic scale. Which brings us back to Tywin skinning a stag as he lectures Jaime on the importance of their family legacy. Charles Dance, the dynamite actor who played Tywin, told the Daily Beast's Marlow Stern about how Benioff and Weiss made sure he wasn't a vegetarian before having a butcher come in to show the actor how to properly gut and skin an animal.

"The next day, they gave me another dead animal, and we shot it," Dance said. "It was a bloody good time, but it took me two days to get the smell off my hands."

"That scene was one of the last we wrote for the show and one of our favorites," Benioff said. "Watching Charles in that scene, you'd think he skinned three stags a day. He managed to deliver a riveting, note-perfect performance while gutting a dead beast. After watching that, Dan and I looked at each other. We were both thinking the same thing: 'We need more Tywin scenes.'"

Episode Eight: "The Pointy End"

For the first four seasons of *Game of Thrones*, George R. R. Martin put his scriptwriting talents to work for one episode per season. This is the episode he wrote for the first season, in which Sansa appears before the newly crowned King Joffrey to plead for mercy on her father's behalf. Martin found a clever way to reference his own writing with this line from Varys on the show: "And yet they say wisdom oft comes from the mouths of babes."

In the book, Ned first realizes the truth about Cersei and Jaime's incestuous relationship in a chapter told from Sansa's point of view. When Sansa points out how different King Robert and Prince Joffrey are, Ned Stark goes quiet.

"Father looked at her strangely. 'Gods,' he swore softly, 'out of the mouth of babes . . .'"

The show opted for a more visual showing of Ned's realization. After speaking with Sansa and Arya, he dismisses the girls and immediately goes through the lineage book, talking to himself out loud about the Baratheon and Lannister hair color. Since this scene (which takes place in episode seven) omitted Martin's words, he added them back in with Varys telling the gathered court that wisdom can indeed come from the mouths of babes.

Episode Nine: "Baelor"

Book-readers noticed a significant change when the time came for Tyrion's first big battle. After he spends a night with Shae and Bronn, getting properly drunk ahead of what he thinks could be his last day on Planetos (the nickname fans have given to the world of *Game of Thrones*), Tyrion wakes up to the news that Stark forces are on the horizon.

He gives a rousing speech to the mountain clans but is swiftly knocked out with a battle axe as the troops make their way to the field. Martin's novel shows the entire brutal battle from Tyrion's point of view, but Benioff and Weiss were completely hamstrung when it came time to film this episode.

"Frankly we just ran out of money and we couldn't do it," they revealed on the *UFC Unfiltered* podcast. "So that was one of the big battles from the book that we hoped we could get onscreen, and we never managed to do it."

The showrunnners lucked out with the second Lannister fight of the episode, when Robb Stark surprises Jaime's camp in the Whispering Wood. That battle is told from Catelyn's perspective in the books, where she waits in the forest nearby and only hears snippets of the fight.

Episode Ten: "Fire and Blood"

When Joffrey brings Sansa out to the walls of the Red Keep so he can torment her by showing off the heads of her father and Septa Mordane, there are several other rotting heads on spikes. As one fan on Reddit shared, the first season DVD commentary from Benioff and Weiss revealed that a prosthetic head of George W. Bush had been used for one of these faces.

"The last head on the left is George Bush," they said. "George Bush's head appears in a couple of beheading scenes. It's not a choice, it's not a political statement. We just had to use whatever head we had around."

Once this little fact was spread online, both Benioff and Weiss and HBO issued statements clarifying the use of the prosthetic and apologized.

"We use a lot of prosthetic body parts on the show: heads, arms, etc. We can't afford to have these all made from scratch, especially in scenes where we need a lot of them, so we rent them in bulk," Benioff and Weiss said in a joint statement published by *The Hollywood Reporter*. "After the scene was already shot, someone pointed out that one of the heads looked like George W. Bush. In the DVD commentary, we mentioned this, though we should not have. We meant no disrespect to the former president and apologize if anything we said or did suggested otherwise."

"We were deeply dismayed to see this and find it unacceptable, disrespectful and in very bad taste," HBO added in its own statement. "We made this clear to the executive producers of the series, who apologized immediately for this inadvertent, careless mistake. We are sorry this happened and will have it removed from any future DVD production."

If you watch the scene now on HBO's streaming services, that shot has been digitally altered. Now the head to the left of Septa Mordane's appears turned away, so the Bush-identifying features are indiscernible.

SEASON TWO

Episode One: "The North Remembers"

One of the best subtleties found in the second season of *Game of Thrones* comes by way of song. When Tyrion first arrives at King's Landing in the season two premiere, he enters the small council chambers while whistling "The Rains of Castamere"—a song that became very significant by the third season's Red Wedding episode. This little whistle, so casually performed by Peter Dinklage, was the very first time fans heard the ominous tune.

Episode Two: "The Night Lands"

When Jon follows Craster into the forest and hears the White Walkers for the first time, the subtitles on the episode note that there's a "guttural clicking" noise along with a "creature chittering." This indicates that Benioff and Weiss were still planning on having the White Walkers use a language in the series at this point.

David J. Peterson, the linguist who created Dothraki and the other fictional languages spoken on the show, wrote a White Walker language called Skroth. This plan of a clear ice language was later ditched, as Peterson eventually revealed at a San Diego Comic-Con event. By the time the sixth season rolled around, Benioff and Weiss decided against giving the Night King a speaking line.

"We don't think of The Night King as a villain as much as Death," Benioff and Weiss said in a 2016 interview with *Deadline*. "In some ways, it's appropriate he doesn't speak. What's Death going to say? Anything would diminish him. He's just a force of destruction. I don't think we've ever been tempted to write dialogue for The Night King. Anything he said would be anticlimactic."

Episode Three: "What Is Dead May Never Die"

Benioff and Weiss made another book reference when Varys tells Tyrion "a very small man can cast a very large shadow." In Martin's *A Game of Thrones*, after Jon meets Tyrion for the first time, the chapter ends with Tyrion walking away. "When he opened the door, the light from within threw his shadow clear across the yard, and for just a moment Tyrion Lannister stood as tall as a king," Martin writes.

Tyrion is one of the most powerful players in the game of thrones, of course, but it's noteworthy that Varys is one of the first people to acknowledge it within the series.

Episode Four: "Garden of Bones"

Several times throughout the show, Benioff and Weiss used small throwaway lines to acknowledge longstanding debates or points of contention within the ASOIAF fandom. One of these comes in "Garden of Bones," when the Spice King greets Dany and her Dothraki followers at the gates of Qarth.

"Oh, my name is quite long and quite impossible for foreigners to pronounce," he tells her. "I am simply a trader of spices."

Many believe this was a reference to how many names of minor characters in Martin's novels are phonetically tricky to readers, like Ynys Yronwood or Hizdahr zo Loraq or all of the "Ae-" name variations found in the Targaryen dynasty.

Episode Five: "The Ghost of Harrenhal"

In this episode we are introduced to the makers of wildfire for the first time. The pyromancer Hallyne tells Tyrion and Bronn they "have been working tirelessly, day and night," but he fails to account for why their production of wildfire has been so much more successful as of late. In the show, the warlocks in the House of the Undying will later tell Daenerys that her dragons make their magic stronger. This comes up in the books, as well.

"His powers grow, Khaleesi, and you are the cause of it," the mysterious character called Quaithe tells Dany in the books when they see a man performing magic in the streets.

Just as with the street performer's magic, it is implied in Martin's books that the birth of Dany's children has made the creation of wildfire easier.

Episode Six: "The Old Gods and the New"

When Jon and Qhorin Halfhand encounter a band of wildlings and capture Ygritte, the Halfhand interrogates her with several questions to prove to Jon that she won't spill any wildling beans. One of the things he wants to know is why the wildlings have come to the Frostfangs. She doesn't answer, and the subject isn't really explored again in the show. But from the books, we know that Mance Rayder, the King Beyond the Wall, had the wildlings gather in the Frostfangs area because he was trying to find the Horn of Joramun, also called the Horn of Winter.

In Martin's third book, *A Storm of Swords*, Ygritte eventually tells Jon Snow that the wildlings were searching for the legendary horn, the one that was said to have the power to bring down the Wall once blown. Martin mentioned this object again in his fictional encyclopedic text, *The World of Ice and Fire*.

Though the horn was never referenced directly on the show, Benioff and Weiss made the curious choice of placing a horn with the cache of dragonglass found by Sam Tarly and Pyp and Grenn at the Fist of the First Men. In the books, Jon is the one who finds this stash of dragonglass (thanks to Ghost sniffing it out). Among the obsidian arrowheads and daggers he finds a broken horn and gives it to Sam. Many people have long theorized that this is the real Horn of Joramun, and the one Mance claims to have in the books was a fake.

Sam, Eddison Tollett, and Grenn find the horn and dragonglass stash in the eighth episode of season two, "The Prince of Winterfell." They discuss the obsidian, but not the horn, and we've no indication of where it is now. Book-readers will have to wait for Martin's next installments to see if that horn holds any importance, since the Wall came down in the show's seventh season thanks to the Night King's resurrected wight-dragon, Viserion.

Episode Seven: "A Man Without Honor"

Here Quaithe comes into play once again. This time the show-version of her character is used to foreshadow Jorah's eventual travels to Valyria. He finds her painting a man's back with a series of patterns, and Quaithe tells him that "all who travel too close to the Doom must have protection."

When Jorah takes Tyrion through the Smoking Sea in the fifth season, neither of them have protection of any kind and they are attacked by the Stone Men. Jorah contracts greyscale there, which threatens his life for the next two seasons until he's cured by Sam Tarly in the seventh season.

Episode Eight: "The Prince of Winterfell"

Proving yet again how much Ned Stark influences the characters of *Game of Thrones*, the eighth episode of season two includes an important line taken from the books. As Robb and Talisa take a walk together, their conversation turns to Ned. When Talisa says all the northmen she speaks to say they loved Robb's father, he tells a story about how Ned tried to prepare Robb for lordship by explaining how the people he ruled were like children to him, and that fear ruled him from dawn to dusk.

Robb remembering his father saying "a man can only be brave when he is afraid" comes straight from the first book, *A Game of Thrones*. In the book's version of events, Ned says the line to Bran instead. Bringing that conversation back into the plot for season two was not only a poignant way of reminding viewers how special Ned was but also was a good use of the book material being reconfigured into a show-invented scene with Talisa.

Though Robb indeed marries a non-Frey girl and breaks his oath in the books, that courtship happens outside the perspective of any point-of-view characters. Robb is one of the rare book characters who contributes greatly to the core storyline but doesn't have his own point-of-view chapters (Stannis is another important one).

In the books, Robb marries a highborn girl named Jeyne Westerling, who takes care of him when he's wounded after a battle. Robb gets word of Bran's and Rickon's alleged deaths, and winds up in Jeyne's bed as he's grieving and in desperate need of comfort. Ever the son of Ned Stark, Robb marries Jeyne partly out of affection but also out of duty—now that they've had sex, it would be greatly dishonorable to her and her family for him to simply leave.

Benioff and Weiss changed the character of Robb's wife significantly, so the audience got to know her along with Robb. By making her a foreigner with no particular allegiance to the war, it's more understandable that Robb's men are distrustful of her. With his choice to marry her purely out of love (and well before he knows what Theon has presumably done to Bran and Rickon), the showrunners made the *Game of Thrones* version of Robb much more foolish. But it also added an element of romance and optimism we might not have otherwise seen in the Young Wolf.

Episode Nine: "Blackwater"

The gloriously constructed battle episode of "Blackwater" comes to an end when Tywin Lannister's army arrives in King's Landing to crush Stannis's forces. Loras Tyrell leads the Highgarden troops and is at Tywin's side when they enter the throne room. The young knight is wearing Renly Baratheon's armor, which we saw on the would-be king throughout the earlier episodes of the second season.

Nobody within the show's universe points this out, but in the books this becomes part of the lore of battle. News of Renly's murder had reached King's Landing by then, so when people saw Loras riding into battle with Renly's armor, many of them thought he was Renly Baratheon's ghost coming to kill them all. This small costume detail is also an added note on the tragedy of Loras's love for Renly and the way he wanted to honor him and avenge his death.

Episode Ten: "Valar Morghulis"

Remember the blue roses in the windows of the throne room in King's Landing? Even after Joffrey has the throne room redecorated at the start of season two, the blue rose window makes another appearance during Dany's visit to the House of the Undying. While she's inside she walks through a destroyed version of the throne room. Snowflakes drift through the air and cover the Iron Throne as Dany, for the first time in her life, sees this royal seat of power she so dearly covets.

But as she reaches for the throne, with the blue flower visible in the windows behind her, Dany hears her dragons screech and she withdraws her hand, never quite getting to her goal. Dany then turns and walks through a gate, finding herself at the Wall, once again linking Jon Snow to the vision of ice, the Iron Throne, and that blue rose.

SEASON THREE

Episode One: "Valar Dohaeris"

At the start of the third season, Tyrion is still recovering from the wounds given to him by a member of the Kingsguard during the Battle of Blackwater. When Cersei comes to visit him for the first time, she looks at the gash across his cheek, brow, and nose.

"They said you'd lost your nose, but it's not as gruesome as all that," Cersei tells him.

This is yet another time Benioff and Weiss had fun with book-readers in a way that wouldn't appear obvious to show-only fans. In the book's version of events, Tyrion's nose is almost completely cut off when he's attacked, leaving him much more disfigured than the show's version of his wound. But it would have been tough for HBO to pull off the CGI or prosthetics needed for that, and there was no point in ruining Peter Dinklage's good looks. Besides, Dinklage's Tyrion already differed from the books, where he's described as having one green and one black eye, as well as white-blond hair.

Episode Two: "Dark Wings, Dark Words"

The early episodes of season three included the mysterious buildup around who had captured Theon and why. Book-readers watching knew it was Ramsay Snow, the bastard son of Roose Bolton, but the showrunners left a lot of hints for show-only fans as well. In the books, much of Theon's transformation into Reek was left to the imagination, so Benioff and Weiss had a lot to play with when it came to the show-invented scenes.

The biggest of these happens when Ramsay comes to Theon and pretends he was sent by Yara. At the end of that scene, as Ramsay walks away, we see a wide shot of the crossed beams Theon is tied to for the first time.

Later in the episode, Jaime and Brienne are found by a group of soldiers. "The flayed man of House Bolton," Jaime says, drawing attention to the men's banners. If you had paid close enough attention to connect these two dots, you would have realized Theon was being held by the Boltons long before Theon himself knew it. This was also a good foreshadowing of Roose Bolton's betrayal of Robb—if he were truly loyal, surely Roose would have told his king that his son had captured Theon Greyjoy.

Episode Three: "Walk of Punishment"

The third season might have been a record-setter when it came to ASOIAF fandom references. This episode's example comes when Tyrion takes Podrick to a brothel and introduces him to the sex workers he's hired.

"Kayla is famous from here to Volantis in certain circles," Tyrion says. "One of four women in the world who can perform a proper Meereenese Knot."

The "Meereenese Knot" is the term used by Martin and his fans to explain part of why it took so long for *A Dance with Dragons*, the fifth ASOIAF book, to get published. The years-long delay in publishing was partly due to his struggle to sort out the intertwining stories all crossing paths in Slaver's Bay. The major characters either in or headed to Meereen included Tyrion, Jorah, Victarion Greyjoy (one of Theon's uncles who was cut from the show), and Quentyn Martell (a Dornish character also cut from the show). Then Martin had to contend with the different armies attacking Daenerys, and Drogon's reappearance, and a nasty plague that spreads in the city (another cut storyline). And that's all just the tip of the iceberg.

Martin dubbed this particularly nasty iceberg "the Meereenese Knot" before *A Dance with Dragons* came out in 2011. Years later, Benioff and Weiss took it upon themselves to repurpose the phrase so it alluded to the flexibility and talents of a sex worker, which is really the best possible summation of *Game of Thrones* you can find.

Episode Four: "And Now His Watch Is Ended"

Knowing the Red Wedding is coming while rewatching the third season of *Game of Thrones* is an intense lesson in noticing subtext. In this episode, Tywin sits writing letters in front of Cersei while she waits to talk with him. He does the same thing to Tyrion earlier in the season. These moments are meant to show readers that Tywin was plotting the Red Wedding long before it actually happened.

"The contents of a man's letters are more important than his purse," Varys helpfully says in this same episode.

Tywin is forming an alliance with Walder Frey and Roose Bolton, and since he remains in King's Landing the entire time, he has to conduct all of this business via raven. In the books, this subtext is made clear when Tyrion thinks back to his father's actions after news of the Red Wedding reaches him. Tyrion remembers Tywin telling him once that some battles are won with "quills and ravens" instead of weapons. The Lord of Casterly Rock may have won this battle, but he'd wind up losing the war.

Episode Five: "Kissed by Fire"

Benioff and Weiss had to cut many smaller book characters for the show, and one of these was Patchface, a court fool who serves as a companion to Shireen Baratheon. Patchface was supposedly in a shipwreck where he was the only survivor—only he didn't wash ashore until several days after the boat sank. He talks only in eerie sing-song rhymes, some of which seem oddly prophetic.

As a way of referencing Patchface, the *Game of Thrones* writing team instead had Kerry Ingram (Shireen) sing one of Patchface's songs in her introductory scene. "Under the sea, I know I know, oh oh oh," she sings. "The birds have scales and the fish take wing."

In the books, one of Patchface's songs seems to foreshadow the Red Wedding ("Fool's blood, king's blood, blood on the maiden's thigh, but chains for the guests and chains for the bridegroom, aye aye aye.") We can be grateful the show chose a slightly less creepy song for Shireen to sing.

Episode Six: "The Climb"

Ramsay torments Theon in this episode by blowing a loud horn and keeping his prisoner from sleeping. This is a callback to the second season finale, in which Theon is under siege by the Bolton forces at Winterfell. Someone outside the walls of the castle is blowing a horn, day and night, driving Theon absolutely up the wall. At the time, the horn-blower's identity goes undiscovered. But with this little torture technique seen in season three, we can safely assume Ramsay was getting the best of Theon from the very beginning.

Episode Seven: "The Bear and the Maiden Fair"

This episode's title is derived from a popular tavern song in Westeros. We'd heard it already on the show, when rock band The Hold Steady recorded a cover version that was used over the dramatic cut-to-credits after Jaime's hand was chopped off in the third episode of the season. A soldier (played by Gary Lightbody of Snow Patrol) sings the song in an earlier episode, too.

"The Bear and the Maiden Fair" takes on a new meaning in this episode when "Brienne the Beauty" is forced to fight a literal bear with nothing but a wooden sword. Thankfully Jaime finds it in himself to rescue her. Just as the song played earlier in the season after Jaime had prevented her from being sexually assaulted, here the tune is once again made synonymous with their growing affection for each other.

Episode Eight: "Second Sons"

On the day of her wedding to Tyrion Lannister, Sansa sits at her dresser and looks in a mirror. The camera briefly focuses on a doll—the very same doll Ned gave her on season one's "Lord Snow." We saw it a second time on season two's "Blackwater" episode as Sansa fled to her room when it seemed like the city was lost.

Ned had given Sansa that doll when he was trying to make peace between Sansa and Arya, and cheer the former up after her direwolf, Lady, was sentenced to death by King Robert at the behest of Cersei. Sansa sneered at the gift, still furious at her family.

We can't blame Sansa then for being angry with her father. Of course a silly doll cannot replace her beloved, innocent wolf. But knowing Sansa has kept the doll this entire time as a reminder of her now dead father is heartbreaking. Particularly cruel is the reminder of it on the day she is being forced to marry a grown man when she is only fourteen years old.

Episode Nine: "The Rains of Castamere"

In Martin's *A Storm of Swords*, during the buildup to the Red Wedding, Catelyn makes a very big point to tell Robb he needs to get salt and bread from Walder Frey as soon as they cross the castle threshold. She does not trust Walder Frey, and places all of her faith in what is known in Westerosi culture as "guest right."

"Robb, *listen to me*," Catelyn tells her eldest son. "Once you have eaten of his bread and salt, you have the guest right, and the laws of hospitality protect you beneath his roof."

The show passed over this bit of foreshadowing, and also opted to not include the moment when Robb and Catelyn wind up having to ask Walder Frey specifically for some food and salt because the Lord of the Twins fails to offer it.

Instead, without explaining it at the time, the camera focuses in on a plate of salt and bread being passed from Robb to Catelyn and to the rest of the guests when they stand before Walder. Which brings us to an important story Bran tells in the following episode.

Episode Ten: "Mhysa"

When sitting with Meera and Jojen in the dark, Bran tells them the legend of the Rat Cook. Long ago there was a man who worked as a cook in the Nightfort kitchens, and when a king came to the Wall the cook killed his guest's son and baked him into a pie. The cook served this pie to the king, who ate a second helping of his own son. As punishment, the gods turned the murdering cook into a giant rat.

"It wasn't for murder the gods cursed the Rat Cook, or for

serving the king's son in a pie," Bran says. "He killed a guest beneath his roof. That's something the gods can't forgive."

This was Benioff and Weiss's way of contextualizing the crime committed by Walder Frey at the Red Wedding. The Rat Cook story also wound up foreshadowing the way Arya killed Walder Frey's two sons and fed them to him in a pie on the sixth season finale.

SEASON FOUR

Episode One: "Two Swords"

The opening of the fourth season brings us yet another reference to Jon Snow, Lyanna Stark, and those icy blue roses. Daario cheekily comes up with an excuse to give Daenerys three flowers—a Dusk Rose, Lady's Lace, and a Harpy's Gold. Though this could seem like innocent flirtation, there's no way Benioff and Weiss put a blue rose in Dany's hands by coincidence. This was yet another fore-shadowing of Jon and Dany's romantic union of ice and fire.

Episode Two: "The Lion and the Rose"

Though much of the conversation around this episode is right-fully centered on King Joffrey's death (and all the clues pointing to Olenna Tyrell being the mind behind the murder), it's worth taking the time to closely examine the visions Bran has when he touches a weirwood tree in this episode.

He gets flashes of many important things: the tree where Bloodraven is, the crypts of Winterfell, Varys visiting Ned in the dungeon, the Night King turning a baby into a White Walker. There is also a brief shot of Ned pouring water on Ice, his ancestral sword, in this sequence—a shot we never saw in the pilot but that was filmed back in 2011 with Sean Bean.

In the behind-the-scenes segment following this episode, Weiss says that "every image in [Bran's vision] is there for a reason, and it does have some bearing on his story specifically and the story in general going forward."

Part of the importance of the shots like Ned in the dungeons is that these are things Bran most certainly couldn't have known about. Which means there is a power of sight coursing through him like he's never known before.

"Maybe the most crucial shot to us was the shadow of a dragon flying over King's Landing. And we don't know yet ... is that from the past? Is it from the future? We'll find out," Benioff also said while grinning. "But it's not clear yet. Nor should it be clear to Bran. But the one thing that does make sense is that someone is trying to guide him."

Benioff and Weiss wouldn't make this flash of the future clear to fans until the second-to-last episode of the series, when we see Drogon's shadow passing over the rooftops of King's Landing.

In addition to that dragon shot, Bran also sees snow falling in the throne room, just as Dany did back in the second season. This shared vision between them seems extra-prophetic, and likely linked to Jon Snow.

Episode Three: "Breaker of Chains"

When Meereen sends a champion to challenge the Mother of Dragons and her army, their chosen man yells at Dany in Low Valyrian. The show's language inventor, David J. Peterson, revealed in an HBO interview that the man is actually quoting a scene from *Monty Python and the Holy Grail*.

"He's shouting and Nathalie Emmanuel [Missandei] is translating—but she's not translating what he's saying," Peterson said. "He's actually saying a Low Valyrian translation of the French guy's insults in *Monty Python and the Holy Grail*. That was Dan Weiss's idea, and it was so hilarious that I had to do it."

Some very smart fans knew enough Valyrian by then to realize something was up.

"Right after that episode aired, I was getting tweets like, 'Is he saying a "your momma" joke?'" Peterson said. "Close . . . But no, he's actually starting out with, 'Your mother is a hamster.'" The full line from the movie is of course: "Your mother was a hamster and your father smelt of elderberries."

Episode Four: "Oathkeeper"

One of the many disturbing parts of the Night's Watch mutiny at Craster's Keep comes with the revelation that Karl Tanner (the "fookin' legend") is literally drinking out of Lord Commander Mormont's skull. This is a callback to the scene from the ninth episode of the previous season, when Rickon recounts a story he heard about wildlings.

"Old Nan said they turn your skull into a cup and drink your blood from it," Rickon says in front of Osha.

But as "Oathkeeper" makes clear, there are evildoers in every walk of life; wildlings, the Night's Watch, lords and ladies and low-born alike are all capable of human horrors. Karl and Craster are two sides of the same coin, but at least all men must die, in the end.

Episode Five: "First of His Name"

When Karl is finally killed thanks to one of Craster's daughter-wives stabbing him and giving Jon enough time to recover, the staging of that scene is pulled straight from a part of *A Feast for Crows* that never made it to the show.

Jon stabs Karl through the back of the head, making the point of Longclaw come out of his mouth in grotesque fashion. This echoes a scene from the fourth book when Brienne of Tarth is fighting a band of brigands and Gendry (whom she's run into in the River-lands) saves her by stabbing the attacker, a man named Biter, through the skull.

Brienne is underneath Biter when this happens, and from her dazed perspective she thinks to herself that his sharp, pointed, bleeding "tongue" looks "almost like a sword." Since Brienne's big season-four showdown happens with the Hound instead of Biter, Benioff and Weiss repurposed this visual for Karl and Jon instead.

Episode Six: "The Laws of Gods and Men"

During Tyrion's trial, Grand Maester Pycelle ticks off a list of poisons found in his stores, including basilisk venom, widow's blood, wolfsbane, sweetsleep, and demon's dance. During this recitation, he offhandedly mentions the poison that killed Jon Arryn: the tears of Lys.

In the episode prior, Lysa reminds Littlefinger of the way he instructed her to pour the drops he gave her "into Jon's wine." The death of Jon Arryn, Lysa's first husband, is the inciting incident of the current war between House Stark and House Lannister. Though neither Littlefinger nor Lysa says the name of the deadly liquid during this game-changing revelation, the audience knows what it's called. And thanks to Pycelle, we also know where Littlefinger procured it.

Episode Seven: "Mockingbird"

When Bronn is explaining to Tyrion why he doesn't want to risk his life fighting Gregor Clegane in trial by combat, the sellsword describes almost the exact way Oberyn will soon fight and die at the Mountain's hands. Bronn guesses that the only way to beat him would be to "dance around" until the much larger man wears out, but the sellsword also tells Tyrion that if he makes even the slightest mistake, he'll be toast.

Oberyn winds up doing precisely that. His superior spear and acrobatic talents give him the advantage over Ser Gregor Clegane, but as we see in the next episode the Dornish prince will make a huge, prideful, fatal mistake.

Episode Eight: "The Mountain and the Viper"

Littlefinger has a mini monologue in this episode that can be interpreted as a meta commentary of how characters die in *Game of Thrones*.

"People die at their dinner tables, they die in their beds, they die squatting over their chamber pots," he says to the young Lord Arryn. "Everybody dies, sooner or later."

Dying at "dinner tables" is of course a reference to the Red Wedding, but Littlefinger's note about chamber pots foreshadows Tywin Lannister's coming death inside his privy.

Episode Nine: "The Watchers on the Wall"

Karl Tanner is basically the worst, but he does seem to prove useful when it comes to Benioff and Weiss giving little nods and details to viewers. Remember when Jon was fighting Karl at Craster's Keep and the mutineering scumbag taunts Jon about his proper fight-training in a castle? Karl spat in Jon's face, dishonorably getting the upper hand in their fight and very nearly killing Jon as a result.

By the time Jon is fighting the wildlings at Castle Black, he has taken this lesson to heart. While battling one-on-one with Styr, the Magnar of Thenn, Jon is close to dying when he spits his own blood in the Thenn's face, instantly gaining the upper hand. This is a great small moment where we can see how Jon's abilities and leadership have grown throughout the seasons.

Episode Ten: "The Children"

The Hound's return was heavily winked at when, after being beaten bloody in a ruthless fight against Brienne, he is left for dead by Arya. A similar scene plays out in the books (sans Brienne), and fans of A Song of Ice and Fire had long debated whether Sandor Clegane had survived. After all, no body, no death, right?

Well, the Hound himself tells Arya that "unless there's a maester hiding behind that rock" then he's toast. By the sixth season, we'll know that there actually was a healer nearby, and whoever it was got that gnarly femur break mostly healed up.

Season Five

Episode One: "The Wars to Come"

The fifth season of Game of Thrones begins with a very unusual cold open. For the first time, Benioff and Weiss decided to film a flashback. This one shows Cersei and her friend visiting a woods witch called Maggy the Frog. When Cersei says "I've been promised to the prince," she is referring to Rhaegar Targaryen—Dany's brother and Jon Snow's father.

When she was a young girl, Cersei was told by Tywin that she'd marry Prince Rhaegar and become queen. But the Mad King Aerys grew distrustful of Tywin and refused the proposed betrothal. Instead, just as Maggy predicts, Cersei winds up marrying the new king, Robert Baratheon, after the Targaryens are overthrown.

Episode Two: "The House of Black and White"

By the fifth season, Arya Stark's kill list had grown shorter. She repeats her mantra while waiting outside the House of Black and White in Braavos: "Cersei, Walder Frey, The Mountain, Meryn Trant." You might have realized Ser Ilyn Payne was suddenly gone from the list, and from the series. This character cut happened because of unfortunate real-world circumstances.

Wilko Johnson, the actor who played Ilyn Payne, was diagnosed with pancreatic cancer in late 2012. Johnson initially issued a statement saying that he would not be seeking chemotherapy treatment, and the showrunners were left to decide how best to respect Johnson in light of the tragic news. In the books, Ser Ilyn is the one who helps train Jaime to fight with his left hand. Benioff and Weiss decided to write Bronn into that role instead.

In 2014, Johnson announced that he had undergone surgery and doctors successfully removed a tumor. As of 2018, he is cancer free after initially being given just ten months to live. He never did return to *Game of Thrones*, though, and so Arya's list remained just a bit shorter.

Episode Three: "High Sparrow"

There is a coincidental link between the scene where Jon Snow executes Janos Slynt and an early book chapter told from Sansa

Stark's point of view. Slynt was the leader of the City Watch in King's Landing before Tyrion sent him to the Wall. Back when Joffrey ordered Ned Stark beheaded, Janos was one of the men who grabbed him and held him at the execution block.

In the chapter of *A Game of Thrones* immediately following Ned's beheading, Sansa is forced by Joffrey to attend court, and she sees Janos there. The book text reads: "Sansa stared hard at his ugly face, remembering how he had thrown down her father for Ser Ilyn to behead, wishing she could hurt him, wishing that some hero would throw him down and cut off his head."

Jon, without knowing it, becomes Sansa's hero all those years later. Martin has later explained that this wasn't a planned moment of foreshadowing in his books, because he originally wrote that Jon hanged Slynt. When Martin read a preview of this chapter at a convention, a fan pointed out that Jon would likely follow Ned's ethos of "the man who passes the sentence should swing the sword." Martin changed the scene in time for *A Dance with Dragons*'s publication, leaving us with a lovely full-circle moment.

Episode Four: "Sons of the Harpy"

When Jaime and Bronn mull over the ways they'd prefer to die, Jaime touchingly says he wants to go "in the arms of the woman I love." Interestingly, he does *not* specifically say Cersei's name in this scene, which left fans with the hope he might be referencing the one and only Brienne of Tarth. But by the end of the series, Jaime would get his wish. He died embracing Cersei, the hateful woman he loves.

Episode Five: "Kill the Boy"

Sam Tarly and Maester Aemon receive a raven at Castle Black with news of Dany's struggling conquest of Slaver's Bay. Maester Aemon is one of Dany's last living relatives, and he expresses regret about not being by her side during her time of need.

"A Targaryen alone in the world," Aemon says. "It's a terrible thing."

As soon as Aemon finishes his line, Jon Snow conveniently walks through the door and into the camera's focus. This is probably one of the most amusing nods to R + L = J we get in the entire series.

Episode Six: "Unbowed, Unbent, Unbroken"

Tyrion and Jorah talk about cynicism and Daenerys and the power of witnessing magic while on their way to Meereen. "Have you ever heard baby dragons singing?" Jorah asks Tyrion.

This is yet another way Benioff and Weiss found to reference Martin's books. Back in the very first novel of A Song of Ice and Fire, the book's final paragraph references how the "music of dragons" was heard in the air after Dany hatched her dragon eggs. The dragons on the show may sound more screechy than musical, but Jorah referencing this memorable Martin passage is a lovely (if small) homage to *A Game of Thrones*.

Episode Seven: "The Gift"

Back in the third season's sixth episode, "The Climb," Cersei called Margaery a "little doe-eyed whore" while she was talking to Tyrion. Now, a couple of seasons later, Cersei believes she's beaten Margaery once and for all by having her imprisoned by the Faith of the Seven. As her way of gloating, Cersei brings the younger queen a piece of deer meat on a silver platter.

"Venison. It's quite good," she says with a smirk. "I had it myself for supper only last night."

Unfortunately, Cersei is unable to relish the metaphor of devouring Margaery for long. The High Sparrow arrests the Queen Regent just minutes later.

Episode Eight: "Hardhome"

Arya's time in Braavos comes toward the end of her arc in Martin's fourth and fifth published books. As she begins her Faceless Man training, the chapter titles stop reading "Arya" at their beginning and instead lead with the name of whatever persona she has adopted.

In the show, Arya plays the game of faces with Jaqen, and tells him about being a girl named Lana. Right as her voiceover mentions heading down to the canals, a cat runs by in the alleyway.

This is a nod to her *A Feast for Crows* chapters titled "Cat of the Canals," in which she sells her "oysters, clams, and cockles!" at the harbor. Perhaps Benioff and Weiss thought Arya calling herself "Cat" would be too confusing for the show since that was her mother's nickname, but it was nice of them to include a cat by the canals anyways.

The canal scene isn't the only reference to Martin's fourth book in the ASOIAF series. This is the episode where Ramsay Bolton, now legitimized by his father, says his army should leave a "feast for the crows" by attacking Stannis's forces in the field.

Episode Nine: "The Dance of Dragons"

The burning of Shireen Baratheon was the first *Game of Thrones* plot point that actually spoiled something major for book-readers. When this episode aired in the summer of 2015, Martin's sixth novel, *The Winds of Winter*, had not yet been published (and in fact would not be published before the series ended in May 2019). But in HBO's post-episode segment, Benioff revealed that Martin was the one who came up with Shireen's mode of death.

"When George first told us about this, it was one of those moments where I remember looking at Dan and it was just like 'Ugh that's so horrible and so good in a story sense,'" Benioff said. "Because it all comes together from the beginning—from the very first time we saw Stannis and Melisandre, they were burning people alive on the beaches of Dragonstone, and it's really all come to this."

Stannis and Melisandre were actually only burning effigies of the Seven when we first saw them (in the second season premiere, "The North Remembers"). It's not until the fourth season that Stannis gets burn-happy in the show, starting with his brother-in-law Ser Axell Florent.

Episode Ten: "Mother's Mercy"

Jon Snow's assassination is one of the biggest cliffhangers in both the books and the TV adaptation. Thankfully, book-readers had much more time (about five years) to mull over what the Night's Watch mutiny meant and how Jon would be brought back to life.

But Benioff and Weiss and pretty much everyone at HBO seem to have wanted the show audience to really, truly believe Jon was dead and that was that. Benioff and Weiss even spent extra money on the CGI budget to make Kit Harington's eyes dilate as the camera pushes in on Jon's bleeding, stab-wound-covered body.

"Your pupillary muscles relax when your body gives up," Weiss told *Variety* ahead of the sixth season premiere, when the talking points among the cast and crew were still focused on Jon's death.

"Like your sphincter," Benioff added.

"It's called a 'pupillary sphincter,' as a matter of fact, we looked this up on the Internets," Weiss continued. "And it said that your pupillary sphincter relaxes [when you die] and that your eyes dilate, and if you look carefully, Jon's pupil dilates."

Now let's stick a pin in the recap of the show's details you might have missed and take a break to explore *why* book-readers were so convinced Jon Snow wouldn't stay dead for long.

HOW (AND WHY)
HIS WATCH WAS ENDED

Jon's death scene comes toward the end of *A Dance with Dragons*. This was the last book Martin was able to get published before all of *Game of Thrones* aired on HBO. For readers of Martin's series, Jon's fate had been one of the biggest burning mysteries since *A Dance with Dragons* was first published in the summer of 2011.

Forums like Westeros.org and *Watchers on the Wall* and the A Song of Ice and Fire subreddit were chock-full of debates and clue-gathering sessions built around optimistically cataloging the available evidence that Jon would live on as one of the story's heroes.

We should begin with Jon's untapped ability to warg. In the books, Martin makes it clear that all the Stark children are wargs, meaning they can take over the minds of their direwolves. In the books, there's a delineation between wargs, people with connections to wolves or dogs, and skinchangers, people who can inhabit the mind of any animal or even another human.

The show includes Bran's skinchanging as a core part of his character, but only gives implicit clues about Robb (like when men tell stories of Robb Stark "turning into a wolf" on the battlefield). Benioff and Weiss scrapped all hints about Jon or Arya or Rickon also being wargs. Sansa of course lost her direwolf early, and this lost connection is a wrenching metaphor for her isolation from her family.

Both the show and the books have a wildling character with exceptional skinchanging abilities. His name was Orell in the show, but in the book he's named Varamyr Sixskins. In *A Dance with Dragons*, Varamyr is the point-of-view character for the prologue. In all five of Martin's novels, the prologue and epilogue introduce a point-of-view character who is always killed by the end of that chapter. More significantly, these chapters almost always include a piece of vital information that links thematically to the book's events.

Varamyr's chapter is an in-depth look at how his skinchanging powers have enabled him to survive thus far. He spends much of the time pondering his "second life"—the life he will live through either an animal or another person after his human body is dead. Varamyr also thinks about Jon Snow and directly references his direwolf, saying to himself that he knew Jon was a warg as soon as he'd seen him with Ghost. Varamyr believes Jon has skinchanging abilities, but simply hasn't been shown how to use them yet.

Martin's likely narrative intention for including Varamyr's prologue was to establish a precedent for characters "living" after death via skinchanging. It is also worth noting that, in the books, the last word Jon says before falling unconscious is "Ghost." Some fans take this as a sign that Jon's energy in his final moments is directed at his direwolf, and he will subconsciously manage to skinchange into Ghost out of sheer survival instinct.

But the show changed his final line to "Olly," much to the frustration of many book-readers. A similar change was made for Robb Stark's final words at the Red Wedding. In *A Storm of Swords*, Robb says, "Grey Wind," the name of his direwolf, just before his death. This has led many to the gutting conclusion that Robb might have warged into Grey Wind before he died, and was thus murdered a second time when the Freys killed the direwolf, too. (But the show's version of the Red Wedding has the Freys kill Grey Wind before Robb, and then Robb's final word is simply, "Mother.")

Hand in hand with this warg theory was the guess that Melisandre would have something to do with Jon's potential resurrection. By the time Jon Snow was assassinated, Martin had laid down a lot of groundwork with Melisandre and her Lord of Light's abilities. The show proved this too, with Melisandre's shadow-baby and blood-leeches and so forth.

Melisandre makes many claims about the power of blood magic and her ability to "see" the future through fire. She believes Stannis Baratheon is the prophesied hero Azor Ahai, a legendary figure who is the Lord of Light's champion and will be reborn in order to fight a coming darkness. She wrongfully puts her faith in Stannis, but the books make it clear that several others fit the possible description of this prophecy, which is also interchangeable with the lore of The Prince That Was Promised—the very same prophecy Prince Rhaegar Targaryen likely subscribed to.

Leading up to his assassination in the books, several of the key markers for Azor Ahai were made present in Jon's chapters. Melisandre says in her point-of-view chapter that the Lord of Light showed her "Snow" when she prayed for a "glimpse of Azor Ahai," and then Jon's stab wounds were described as smoking, while the man attacking him was crying salty, remorseful tears.

And then there is Thoros. In both the books and the show, Beric Dondarrion is introduced alongside a man known as Thoros of Myr, a red priest. Thoros uses the Lord of Light's prayer to resurrect Beric after he is killed in combat a total of six times. But the real thumb-on-the-scale moment for book-readers came when Benioff and Weiss manipulated the storyline in season three so Melisandre actually meets Thoros and learns of this power. Nothing of the sort takes place in the books, so this

was a loaded clue about Melisandre's importance in Jon's coming death and rebirth.

And then of course there was the fifth season finale itself. Again, Benioff and Weiss changed the book events and made it so Melisandre rides to Castle Black just before Jon's death (in the books, she's still at a different castle).

So many people grew confident, ahead of the show's portrayal of Jon's return, that he would warg into Ghost just before dying, and maybe hang out in the direwolf's body until Melisandre was able to work the Lord of Light's magic on his body. Once Jon's regular body was brought back to life, he would reenter it and be almost good as new.

This theory worked neatly, since a big concern among fans stemmed from the way Beric Dondarrion admits he is not the same man when he returns, as if the rebirth causes his spirit to fade. This is where the warging theory becomes important again, because if Jon can move his spirit into Ghost temporarily, then when Melisandre revives him there should be no loss of Jon's essence.

Another book quote that supports the theory of Jon warging into Ghost and then returning to his body comes from a Melisandre chapter in *A Dance with Dragons*. She is looking into the flames and sees a vision of Jon Snow. Melisandre watches and notes that his figure changes: "Now he was a man, now a wolf, now a man again."

In case all of this wasn't enough, there were the cryptic words from Martin himself. In 2011, just after *A Dance with Dragons* was released in the summer following the first season's finale, Martin was interviewed by *Entertainment Weekly*.

"So why did you kill Jon Snow?" reporter James Hibberd asked the author.

"Oh, you think he's dead, do you?" Martin replied.

"Well, I guess," Hibberd said. "Yes. That's how I took it. The way it was written, it sounded like he was mortally wounded—and, you know, it's you!"

"Well. I'm not going to address whether he's dead or not," Martin said.

This coy answer seemed to be a pretty clear way of dodging any definitive confirmation. If Jon were truly dead and never coming back, why would it matter what the reader thought happened?

By then Martin was known to leave characters in cliffhanger situations, intentionally leading readers to think the worst had happened. Amid the chaos of the Red Wedding, Arya's point-of-view chapter concludes with her getting smashed in the back of the head with an axe. The chapter left readers in a momentary lurch, thinking Robb wasn't the only Stark child killed in the massacre. Arya's chapters pick up again several pages later, revealing she had simply been knocked unconscious. Fool us once, George.

Another shock came when, through a different character's perspective, readers were led to believe Ser Davos Seaworth was dead. A character off-handedly mentions Davos has been caught and executed for his allegiance to Stannis. Lo and behold, Davos's point-of-view chapter appears later in the book, assuring readers that his head was fully intact, and the rumor of his death was an intentional misdirection tactic. Fool us twice, George.

Lastly, Tyrion fans had quite the scare in one of his chapters as well, when he fell overboard from a ship and into the watery realm of the Stone Men. His chapter ended with the cryptic line "black water filled his lungs, and the dark closed in around him." The show actually mimicked this scene in season five when Jorah and Tyrion are attacked by Stone Men and the scene fades to black as Tyrion is dragged deep into the water. But the show revealed, similar to the book, that Tyrion was rescued and spared from any lasting damage.

By the time we get to the coup against Jon, book-readers refused to be tricked, once again, into thinking that a key character has died when their chapter ending is left unfinished. The last line in the chapter where Jon is stabbed says, "He never felt the fourth knife. Only the cold . . ."

The trailing off implies Jon falls unconscious. None of the following chapters are from the perspective of characters located at the Wall. This means we have no evidence of what happens beyond the attack in Martin's books, but his history of writing white-knuckle chapter endings gave fans strong optimism this was another false alarm.

Despite these many, many, many hints pointing at Jon Snow's return, Benioff and Weiss and HBO executives and all the cast and crew spent the better part of a year breathlessly telling anybody who asked that Jon was definitely, tragically, super-duper dead.

We know what happens next, even if it wound up being a simplified version of all the many fan theories. Ghost and warging never came into play for the show's version of Jon's resurrection. Not to say it won't in the books, but Benioff and Weiss went the simpler route. Melisandre said a humble prayer to the Lord of Light, snipped Jon's hair and tossed the locks into the flames, and that was pretty much that.

The only consolation for fans of the Ghost-warging theory was that Jon's direwolf seemed to sense his beloved owner's return to life a few seconds before Jon opened his eyes and took those shocked, gasping breaths. With this revelation, *Game of Thrones* once again surpassed Martin's story and (at least partially) confirmed a long-debated fan theory.

Season Six

❦ ❧

Episode One: *"The Red Woman"*

In yet another moment that Benioff and Weiss say was laid out by Martin himself, the sixth season premiere ends with the disturbing revelation that Melisandre is a very old woman. Her necklace seems to give her the appearance of youth (though there was a bathtub scene back in the fourth season that showed her not wearing it and still looking young, but no matter).

As HBO's post-episode segment revealed, Melisandre isn't just a secretly old lady—she's hundreds of years old. "There have been a few hints before that Melisandre is much older than she appears," Benioff said. "[This is] going back to a very early conversation with George R. R. Martin about her: She's supposed to be several centuries old."

Episode Two: *"Home"*

When Bran's greensight takes him back to the court of Winterfell, he watches as young Ned Stark spars with his brother Benjen. Encouraging his little brother to fix his form, Ned says, "Get your shield up, or I'll ring your head like a bell."

Back in the fifth season, Jon Snow says the exact same words to Olly when helping him train. Jon even musses up his hair in the same way. That line is too specific for Jon to randomly say it—he likely heard it from Ned as a young boy and was passing on the Stark lesson to Olly. It's a moment that shows just how much protective affection Jon had for Olly, in turn making it all the worse that Olly literally stabbed him in the heart.

Episode Three: "Oathbreaker"

In this episode, we finally got our first Tower of Joy flashback, courtesy of another Bran vision. As young Ned Stark and Howland Reed engage in a gruesome battle against Ser Arthur Dayne and Gerold Hightower, we see the latter brutally stab one of Ned's men. The scene holds ever so slightly on the frame as Hightower stabs a man through his torso, the blade of his sword red and bloody and visible behind him.

This fight choreography is a callback to season one, episode three, "Lord Snow," when Ned watches as Syrio Forel trains Arya. In that scene, Syrio and Arya strike the same pose as Hightower and the man he kills. As Ned looks on, the sound of Syrio's and Arya's wooden swords turns into clashing metal and his face falls, as if Ned is experiencing PTSD.

Rewatching that first scene, knowing what Ned experienced at the Tower of Joy, it's not hard to connect the concern he has for his youngest daughter with his little sister's untimely death.

Episode Four: "Book of the Stranger"

Theon's return to the Iron Islands is shot in a way that directly matches the camera angles of his season-two journey home. While here the day is bleak and foggy, and Theon is clearly a broken man with little hope left, back in season two he was a swaggering young prince. That day was bright and sunny and Theon hadn't a care in the world. Unfortunately winter came for our princeling, and he made many regretful choices between that fateful day and this one. Theon is a changed man, and at least he learned his lesson a thousand times over.

Episode Five: "The Door"

The title of George R. R. Martin's planned sixth book in the series, *The Winds of Winter,* is mentioned during the Braavosi play about King's Landing. Arya Stark watches a play about Robert Baratheon's death and Ned Stark's execution. Aside from being a wonderful look at how the Lannisters are regarded outside of Westeros (Who knew Cersei's PR team had turned her into a sympathetic victim in Braavos?), there was a little Easter egg for book-readers. "I feel the winds of winter as they lick across the land," Lady Crane says.

Episode Six: "Blood of My Blood"

Just as Bran's flashing weirwood visions on the fourth season contained important revelations, the series of greensight visions he has in the opening scene of this episode are worth a closer look. In them we see a glimpse of the Mad King Aerys Targaryen—Daenerys's father and ruler of the Seven Kingdoms before Robert Baratheon. Not only was this the first time we saw the Mad King, but Bran's vision includes a shot of Jaime Lannister stabbing his king in the back.

We know Jaime killed the Mad King before he could carry out a plan to burn King's Landing to the ground with wildfire. And up to this point, the only other time we'd seen wildfire in the show was during the attack on Blackwater Bay—when Tyrion blew up Stannis Baratheon's fleet with it.

But Bran's vision included a shot of wildfire exploding in an underground passageway, which is a piece of footage straight from the explosion at the Sept of Baelor that hasn't happened yet at this point in season six. Careful observers would have noticed this scene, and put two and two together with Cersei's frequent mentioning of how she would "burn cities to the ground" for her children.

Episode Seven: "The Broken Man"

This episode featured the brief role of Ian McShane's Brother Ray and the return of Sandor Clegane. Benioff and Weiss changed up several roles to create the amalgamated storyline, since Sandor Clegane is not confirmed as alive in the books yet.

"The Broken Man" is a reference to a beloved monologue delivered by a godly man in Martin's books named Septon Meribald, who links up with Brienne and Podrick while they're traveling in *A Feast for Crows*. The subject of "broken men" (soldiers who have defected or deserted their armies) and what follows is one of the best commentaries on war given in all of A Song of Ice and Fire. It's worth reading in its entirety, and there are even people online who have recorded themselves reading it in character because it is considered such a seminal part of Martin's novels.

In the monologue, Septon Meribald describes the fathers and sons and brothers who were sent away from their homes to fight brutal battles on behalf of their lords. He describes the ways glorification of war through song and speeches leaves new soldiers unprepared for the reality of death and starvation and having to steal shoes from a corpse just to march another day. People like Brienne should be wary of broken men, he explains, but she should also pity them. They are not criminals for the hell of it, but traumatized souls reduced to their most base instincts of survival.

"The Broken Man" speech is Martin at his most melancholic and empathetic. The series spends much time revolving around the highborn lords and ladies, giving very few smallfolk or lowborn characters any meaningful time onscreen. When we did see them, they were often under attack from either cutthroat soldiers or the Free Folk or, in the end, during the sack of King's Landing. It is in the speech about broken men that we are reminded of what the War of the Five Kings has cost the realm, and how, at this moment, it no longer matters who wins the Iron Throne. The suffering and pain and damage inflicted on a war-torn country cannot be undone.

Many of his avid readers believe this chapter was inspired by Martin's own views on war, particularly the Vietnam War. In his twenties at the time, Martin applied for the status of "conscientious objector." His request was granted, and he was able to stay out of the draft.

"I don't think America has ever quite recovered from Vietnam," Martin said in a *Rolling Stone* interview. "The divisions in our society still linger to this day. For my generation it was a deeply disillusioning experience, and it had a definite effect on me."

McShane's Brother Ray gives an adaptation of the speech in this episode, though the message winds up being much more cynical thanks to Ray's death by the episode's end and Sandor Clegane's return to killing. The show's context makes violence seem as if it's the only viable solution, whereas Martin's words included much more nuance about the choices we can make in times of conflict.

Episode Eight: "No One"

In this episode Tyrion, attempting to bond with Missandei and Grey Worm, tries to tell a joke. He starts by saying, "I once walked into a brothel with a honeycomb and a jackass. The madame says—"

But then Tyrion is cut off by the arrival of the Sons of the Harpy. This isn't the first time Tyrion has been interrupted while telling that story. Back in season one, Tyrion was captured by Catelyn Tully for the attempted murder of Bran and was taken to the Eyrie. There he was forced to confess to his crimes.

But instead of talking about Bran, Tyrion chooses to admit to silly instances of pranks he pulled as a child. The last thing he says, before getting cut off by Lysa Arryn, is: "I once brought a jackass and a honeycomb into a brothel." Unfortunately the punch line is lost to the wind both times. The joke will resurface (and remain unfinished) for the third and final time on the series finale as we see Tyrion leading one last meeting on the show.

Episode Nine: "Battle of the Bastards"

Roose Bolton foreshadowed the way Ramsay would ultimately meet his death at the end of the Battle of the Bastards. At the start of the season, Roose tried to put Ramsay in his place and guide him down a path lined with less torture and more leadership. Even though Ramsay's, uh, "talents" for manipulating people were effective, Roose was able to see the potential backlash that came with flaying and torturing your subjects without mercy.

Just minutes before Ramsay shoves a dagger into his abdomen, Roose tells his son: "If you acquire a reputation as a mad dog, you'll be treated as a mad dog—taken out back and slaughtered for pig feed."

Ramsay is indeed taken to the kennels and slaughtered by his own hounds, thanks to Sansa Stark. Though we never saw him fed to the pigs, it's best to leave that one to the imagination.

Episode Ten: "The Winds of Winter"

Speaking of the great Bolton-ousting of season six, the sigil sitting atop Winterfell in the opening credits was finally changed for this episode. Ever since the fourth season, the flayed man of House Bolton had sat atop Winterfell during the animated title sequence while the broken Stark sigil lay on the ground next to the tower.

But all that changed with the Battle of the Bastards. Jon and

Sansa finally defeated the Boltons, and fans were thrilled to see the Starks officially returned to power in the North.

Speaking of sigils, a bonus detail comes with Jon Snow's new nickname bestowed upon him by Lord Wyman Manderly: the White Wolf. When Robb Stark was crowned King in the North, his men called him the Young Wolf. Jon's new pseudo-title is more than just an allusion to his albino direwolf, Ghost—it has ties to his supposed bastard status.

In Westeros, bastards who take up their house banners typically reverse the colors of the sigil. House Stark's sigil is a gray direwolf on a white background, which means Jon Snow's banners would be a white wolf on a gray background.

Season Seven

Episode One: "Dragonstone"

Sandor Clegane's grave-digging scene in the seventh season premiere was yet another nod to book-readers, and it has to do with one of the most hyped theories of all time. The Hound was left for dead by Arya in both the books and on the show. Many people began theorizing about ways in which the Hound might return, and one such theory was referred to as "Gravedigger."

In the books, Brienne of Tarth visits a monastery and speaks to the Elder Brother, who claims to have found the Hound and laid him to rest. But Brienne spots a huge man (around the Hound's height) digging graves, and notices that the Hound's horse is being kept in the stables nearby. Many believe Sandor Clegane is alive in the books but disguising himself as a gravedigger in this monastery.

The gravedigger theory then spawned a second, more extreme theory called Cleganebowl.

The Cleganebowl theory posited that Sandor and Gregor Clegane (the Hound and the Mountain) would fight to the death in an epic one-on-one combat. Benioff and Weiss seem to be aware of this theory, because having the Hound literally dig a grave in the opening episode of season seven felt like a not-so-sly reference to the fight for the ages fans were dying to see. The showrunners finally delivered on the hype during season eight's "The Bells," when the two brothers meet a fiery end.

Episode Two: "Stormborn"

Arya's reunion with her direwolf, Nymeria, ends with a bittersweet goodbye. After trying to get Nymeria to come with her to Winterfell, Arya realizes the wolf has no intention of following her ever again. She smiles sadly and says, "That's not you." Arya doesn't mean that literally—she is referring to the fact that Nymeria isn't a pet who will trot behind Arya, in the same way Arya isn't following the rules a highborn girl should.

"Arya's not domesticated and it makes total sense that her wolf wouldn't be, either," Weiss said in HBO's post-episode segment.

The line was also a direct reference to a season-one scene where Ned and Arya have a heart-to-heart about her future as a lady and she rejects the idea outright. Ned tells Arya that Bran will grow up to be the lord of a castle, and Arya asks if she could be a lord, too. "You will marry a high lord and rule his castle," Ned says. "And your sons shall be knights and princes and lords."

"No," Arya replies. "That's not me."

Episode Three: "The Queen's Justice"

As the R + L = J hints piled up in the seventh season, Jon made an accidental connection between himself and Rhaegar. When Daenerys and Jon are talking about Tyrion and his love for conversation, Daenerys says, "We all enjoy what we're good at."

"I don't," Jon replied.

This was likely a reference to his skills with a sword. We've watched as Jon has cut down many foes, and even some friends. But Jon has never appeared to take pleasure in killing, even when it's clearly the right thing to do. Without realizing it, Jon drew a parallel between himself and his birth father, Rhaegar.

Back in the fifth season, Ser Barristan told Daenerys about her brother Rhaegar's love of singing, and Dany was surprised to hear about this side of her late brother. "[Viserys] told me Rhaegar was good at killing people," she says.

Barristan assures her Rhaegar never liked killing, but he loved to sing. Though Ned will always be Jon's true father in spirit, the blood he shares with Rhaegar also holds a significant narrative meaning. With this small line of dialogue, Benioff and Weiss were bringing Jon closer to his Targaryen identity.

Episode Four: "The Spoils of War"

When Jon takes Daenerys into the dragonglass caves to show her ancient drawings on the wall made by the Children of the Forest, there are two familiar patterns carved into the rock.

The first is a circle with a line through it—the same pattern the White Walkers used to arrange the wildling bodies in the cold open of the pilot episode. The second important shape is a sunburst-style swirl, which was first shown on season three. Mance Rayder called the White Walkers "artists" because they left the carcasses of horses and men in a spiral shape after the massacre of the Night's Watch at the Fist of the First Men.

The pattern appeared again in the fifth season, when we watched the Children of the Forest create the very first White Walker (who is also the Night King) by plunging a dragonglass dagger into his heart. He is tied to a tree that stands at the center of a rock formation in the same spiral shape.

Episode Five: "Eastwatch"

Gendry's triumphant return was a pretty meta form of fan service. Davos even has a line of dialogue directly referencing the many memes that had cropped up in the three seasons since Gendry, played by Joe Dempsie, departed from Dragonstone.

"I remember, about six or eight months after I'd said goodbye to Joe Dempsie, that a tweet came through from his Twitter account," actor Liam Cunningham, who plays Ser Davos, said in an *INSIDER* interview. "It was just two words: 'Still rowing.' I laughed my head off."

Cunningham was as thrilled as anyone for Gendry's return.

"So when they wrote the scene and Davos said 'I thought you might still be rowing,' there was a tongue-in-cheek aspect to it," he said. "It was just great. Joe is a fantastic actor and Gendry is a wonderful, wonderful character. And he's very similar to Jon Snow. I just love these beautiful touches of humanity and these wonderfully written characterizations—they're just undeniable and fun to play. It was really lovely."

Gendry's newly forged weapon was another nod to fans. The warhammer was King Robert's weapon of choice, and now his bastard son would wield one. Gendry even crafted a Baratheon stag sigil to wrap around the center of the warhammer.

Episode Six: "Beyond the Wall"

The seventh season was full of weighty retcons when it came to Dany's ability (or lack thereof) to have children. In this episode, Dany tells Jon her dragons will always be her only children.

"The dragons are my children," Daenerys told Jon. "They're the only children I'll ever have—do you understand?"

Dany believes she's infertile after Mirri Maz Duur "saved" Khal Drogo in the first season. At the time, Mirri Maz Duur told Daenerys she'd save Khal Drogo's life—but there was a terrible price. The blood magic she conjured killed Dany's unborn child, Rhaego, and when Daenerys awoke she asked to see Drogo. The great Khal was effectively in a vegetative state—alive but without life. Daenerys asks Duur when he would return to her.

Here's where the weird retcon comes in. Back in the first season, Benioff and Weiss omitted a significant portion of Duur's reply. In the books, the witch says, "When the sun rises in the west and sets in the east. When the seas go dry and mountains blow in the wind like leaves. *When your womb quickens again and you bear a living child.* Then he will return, and not before."

The show's version of Duur's pseudo-prophecy ends before she says anything about Dany's womb. So why did the seventh-season scripts work so hard to claim that Duur had told Dany this? It seemed as if Benioff and Weiss wanted to replant the seeds for Dany to get pregnant with Jon's child, even though she believed herself to be infertile. This became a very common prediction among fans in the year leading up to the final season of *Game of Thrones*.

Strangely, Dany's alleged infertility never came up in the final season at all, nor did she become pregnant. The mystery of this retcon is still an open case.

Episode Seven: "The Dragon and the Wolf"

Game of Thrones often thrived when the script slowed down the action and pushed character arcs forward with weighty conversations. Just as the introduction of Tywin Lannister in season one was a fantastic move by Benioff and Weiss, the conversation between Jon and Theon in "The Dragon and the Wolf" is an incredibly well-done character study.

When speaking with Jon, Theon laments about his identity struggles, born from spending half his life as Ned Stark's ward. "It always seemed like there was an impossible choice I had to make: Stark or Greyjoy," Theon says.

In a beautifully magnanimous gesture, Jon assures Theon that the nurture he received from Ned Stark was just as important to his character as the blood that runs in his veins. He tells Theon that he doesn't have to choose—he can be both Greyjoy and Stark.

Jon himself will be confronted with these identity struggles in the eighth season once he finally learns that he's the son of Rhaegar Targaryen and Lyanna Stark.

During a post-season interview, *INSIDER* asked the episode's director, Jeremy Podeswa, whether this touching scene was supposed to foreshadow Jon's future identity crisis.

"I think it is very much a possibility that [the scene] was a foreshadowing of that," Podeswa said. "The show has so much to do with questions of 'What is family? Who is family? How do you identify yourself?' It's something that runs through [season seven] with the Stark children and figuring out what their relationship is to each other after all the things they've been through.

"For Theon, his identity has been a major quest for the entire series," Podeswa continued. "So certainly now that we know everything there is to know about Jon, I think that's going to raise all kinds of questions in terms of how he deals with this knowledge and where that takes him going forward."

Ideally Jon won't have to choose between Stark and Targaryen. Ned will always be his father, even as he contends with the truth about his birth parents and how he is the heir to the Iron Throne.

Season Eight

Episode One: "Winterfell"

Even if you were aware of the reasons behind each name Daenerys gave to her dragons before, those monikers are made more meaningful when Jon Snow hops on the back of Rhaegal. Drogon was named for Khal Drogo, Daenerys's first great love. Viserion was named for Viserys, the cruel brother who was the only family Daenerys ever had. And Rhaegal was named for Rhaegar, the older brother she never knew. Without knowing it, Jon has connected with the mystical creature who is most linked to his birth father.

Episode Two: "A Knight of the Seven Kingdoms"

Both Davos and Gilly are visibly moved by the sight of a young girl who reminds them of Princess Shireen Baratheon. The young girl has burn marks on her face, in the same place where Shireen's greyscale covered her cheek. Davos thought of Shireen as a daughter and was devastated not only to learn of her death but to hear she was executed by Stannis and Melisandre. Shireen helped both Davos and Gilly learn how to read. We saw the young princess bond with Gilly in season five, when they were both at Castle Black.

Though this link may be clear, what you might have missed was the meaning of the quiet music playing in the background. Composer Ramin Djawadi wrote an instrumental version of Shireen's haunting song, the same one from her season-three introductory song, called "It's Always Summer Under the Sea" (which was introduced in "Kissed by Fire," a Bryan Cogman–penned episodes).

Episode Three: "The Long Night"

Theon's final moments in the godswood have a poignant connection to a key chapter Martin's fifth ASOIAF book, *A Dance with Dragons*. In the last published chapters told from Theon's perspective, he's only just barely breaking out of his tormented "Reek" persona. Theon ponders death as "the sweetest deliverance he could hope for" and also thinks about Winterfell as his home. "Not a true home, but the best I ever knew," he says to himself. Theon wanders around Winterfell and finds himself in the godswood, where he speaks with the weirwood tree there. "Please. A sword, that's all I ask," he says. "Let me die as Theon, not as Reek."

In the books at this same time, Bran is still beyond the Wall and learning to use his powers. Theon in the books thinks he sees Bran's face in the weirwood tree and hears whispers on the wind. This was most likely Bran using his greensight powers through the weirwood tree. Though the events that lead Theon to the godswood in "The Long Night" are very different from his arc in Martin's book, the moment when Bran tells Theon that Winterfell is his "home" had extra meaning for people familiar with the book series.

Theon's manner of death is also a callback to the rousing speech he once gave at Winterfell in the second season finale. After Theon takes Winterfell from Bran, the Boltons come to reclaim the castle in the name of Robb Stark. Seeing he is surrounded, Theon thinks they'll make a stand against the army outside Winterfell's walls and tries to rally the Ironborn.

"We die today brothers," Theon says to his men. "We die bleeding from a hundred wounds, with arrows in our necks and spears in our guts. But our war cries will echo through eternity. They will sing about the Battle of Winterfell until the Iron Islands have slipped beneath the waves. Every man, woman, and child will know who we were and how long we stood."

Theon is promptly knocked out and betrayed by those men, and receives no glory on that day. But in the *real* Battle of Winterfell, Theon dies after charging at the Night King, who grabs Theon's spear and plunges it into his gut. People will know his name for centuries to come as the man who helped save Bran the Broken.

Episode Four: "The Last of the Starks"

While talking to Tyrion about his wheelchair, Bran brings up Daeron Targaryen, one of Jon's ancestors who was crowned king as a young teen. In George R. R. Martin's books, Jon Snow mentions Daeron in one of his very first chapters. While talking to his Uncle Benjen about joining the Night's Watch, Jon insists he's not too young because "Daeron Targaryen was only fourteen when he conquered Dorne." Benjen points out that Daeron was also assassinated when he was eighteen. This was the earliest possible foreshadowing of Jon's own coming death at the hands of the Night's Watch when he is little more than a teenager (in the books).

Given how the finale plays out, we can also see this as a clear hint of how Bran will be crowned king in short order. This is the same conversation in which Bran tells Tyrion he doesn't "want" for much of anything anymore, and by the next episode Varys is pondering if the best possible ruler would be a person who "doesn't want" the crown.

Episode Five: "The Bells"

Throughout the entire series, various directors would frame important trios of characters in the same "angel and devil" motif, with one central character in the center of the frame and two people shown out of focus over each of their shoulders. This happens in the pilot, "Winter is Coming," when Ned Stark is being counseled by both Catelyn and Maester Luwin about the cryptic letter sent by Lysa Arryn. We see it again in season two's "What Is Dead May Never Die," when Theon supplicates to his cruel and indifferent father. Balon Greyjoy's back is turned to both Yara and Theon, who frame him as he chooses to ignore his last living son. The tableau is there again in the third season finale, "Mhysa," when Melisandre and Davos each make their case to King Stannis about the value of Gendry's life against the possibility of winning the kingdom.

It surfaced once more on the season eight premiere, "Winterfell." As Tyrion stands before the Northern lords and defends Jon Snow, both Sansa and Daenerys are positioned behind his shoulders, a shot that precludes the way Tyrion's allegiance will become divided between the two power players.

But here, in "The Bells," we get a twisted variation of this framing when Daenerys and Tyrion are broken from each other's trust at last. "No, it doesn't matter now," Daenerys tells Tyrion after he admits to making mistakes but insists he and Varys only wanted to do what was right.

Daenerys turns to face the window overlooking Dragonstone's bay, the same window Stannis stood in front of in that fourth season finale. Instead of being centered in the shot, Daenerys is much closer and all the way to the right. Tyrion, her last living adviser who hasn't actively committed treason against her, fades into the unfocused background. We watch as he turns and walks away, visible over Dany's shoulder, a final sign that Daenerys is truly isolated now, and will stop at nothing to reach her goal.

Episode Six: "The Iron Throne"

The series finale reveals Ser Brienne of Tarth as the new Lord Commander of Bran's Kingsguard, and her armor bears his new raven sigil. It is seen for the first time as Brienne fills out the remainder of Jaime Lannister's pages in the White Book. In the fourth season, Brienne and Jaime stand in this very room and talk about how he still has room left in the book for great deeds. "It's the duty of the Lord Commander to fill those pages," Jaime tells Brienne when he gifts her armor and a sword and tasks her with finding the Stark girls. "There's still room left on mine."

The sword Jaime gives her in that scene, Oathkeeper, is sitting next to the White Book as she writes. Unfortunately, the show never reveals what happened to Widow's Wail. How about we collectively agree it was recovered, renamed Knightmaker, and gifted to the newly knighted Ser Podrick?

EVERY CHANGE MADE TO THE SEASON EIGHT OPENING CREDITS

Fans may have been expecting surprising turns in the story, but Benioff and Weiss managed to shock everyone even before the actual premiere episode began. After seven steady seasons of opening credits showing a rotating set of castle locations, the animated sequence got a complete overhaul for the final six episodes. In addition to this one massive change at the season's start, the credits were given tiny updates based on the events of every episode.

Episode One: "Winterfell"

Previously the astrolabe (that spinning, da Vinci–looking device rotating around a sun) had bands of artwork showing historic Westerosi events, such as Robert's Rebellion, that all occurred before *Game of Thrones*. But now it highlights three major events from the first seven seasons of the show.

The first band shows the most recent cataclysmic event on the continent: the Night King bringing down the Wall at Eastwatch by the Sea. You can see a row of the Army of the Dead in the lower right corner and birds flying off from the top left side, which symbolize both the Night's Watch "crows" and Bran Stark's ravens fleeing.

The second band depicts the Red Wedding. A dead wolf (Catelyn Stark) hangs from the towers of the Twins (House Frey's castle) while a Flayed Man (House Bolton) holds up another wolf's head (Robb Stark). To the left, a lion (Tywin Lannister) holds a fish in its jaws (House Tully).

The last band shows the birth of Daenerys Targaryen's

dragons, with Dany herself represented as a large dragon and three small babies flying around her. The band even has a little comet visible, representing the actual comet that was in the sky when Dany built Khal Drogo's funeral pyre.

When it comes to the actual map and castles, the first episode of season eight shows the Army of the Dead creeping toward Last Hearth, the castle of House Umber. The Night King's army is symbolized with blue tiles.

Episode Two: "A Knight of the Seven Kingdoms"

After we learn in the season premiere that the Army of the Dead had already overtaken House Umber's castle, the opening credits for episode two show the blue tiles surrounding Last Hearth. New defenses are also shown around Winterfell, with trenches built around the border of the castle.

Episode Three: "The Long Night"

At the start of episode three, the blue tiles have crept all the way up to the grounds of House Stark's beloved castle to show the Army of the Dead about to attack. The Winterfell crypts are also changed slightly for episode three's opening. For the first two episodes, the sweeping shot of the crypts showed flickering torches lining the hallway. But for episode three, the torches start going out at the end of the hallway. This is an early signal that the Army of the Dead would inflict its horror on the people inside the crypts, too.

Episode Four: "The Last of the Starks"

The fourth episode shows Winterfell's post-battle destruction. Near where the Army of the Dead was marked before, little burning funeral pyres dot the landscape. The main tower of Winterfell is also visibly damaged in this version of the credits. The interior of Winterfell shows piles of rubble, too. The main hall of Winterfell is left in shambles for episode four's opening credits, even though once the episode begins all seems well inside for the celebratory feast.

Episode Five: "The Bells"

The fifth episode brought a change to King's Landing for the first time in the season. At the start of "The Bells," Cersei's scorpion crossbows pop up on the ramparts. The dragon-slaying devices are all destroyed by Daenerys in short order, though.

Episode Six: "The Iron Throne"

For the final episode of the series, we see the devastation of King's Landing. As anticipated, the gates of King's Landing are in ruins for the opening credits. The entryway to the Red Keep is also shown in disarray before the camera sweeps to the interior shots of the castle.

The little map of Westeros inside the Red Keep has a big crack across it. This is the most important detail in the new opening credits for "The Iron Throne." We later see Tyrion walking in that very room, and the broken map splits almost precisely where the North is marked. This is in-episode foreshadowing of Sansa Stark's coronation as Queen in the North and the future of that kingdom being independent once more.

When the animated sequence zooms into Cersei's spiral staircase, you can see how chunks of the architecture are missing, including pieces of the stairs where Sandor and Gregor Clegane's had fought to the death. As the credits move into the secret passageway where Jaime and Cersei meet their doom, we see that one of the previously intact dragon skulls has crumbled.

And last but not least, the episode's title object itself: the Iron Throne. The lion sigil of House Lannister has broken away from the window above the Iron Throne at the start of the episode.

CHAPTER FOURTEEN

CAMEOS, PRANKS, *and* LIFELONG FRIENDSHIPS

Game *of Thrones* was a life-defining series for many of its fans, but within the production family it was also a breeding ground for incredible bonds and friendships between the cast and crew.

After both Sophie Turner and Maisie Williams had nailed their individual auditions, the two preteens were brought in for a chemistry read together. The Stark sisters have important roles very early on in the series, so Benioff and Weiss had to be sure they would play well off each other onscreen. Williams recalls meeting other young girls in the running for Sansa, but Sophie Turner stood out.

"I just remember her being, like, super tall and then after everything we'd do she'd be like, 'Aw you're really cute,'" Williams said at the 2013 Emmys panel while sitting next to Turner and grinning. "And I was a bit like, 'Yeah, I'm only one year younger than you.'"

Williams, who made a stern little side-eye face at this comment, went on to reveal that she was Team Sophie right away. "But yeah, we got on really, really well," she continued. "I came out of the audition and said to my mum, 'Even if I don't get the part, I really want that girl to because she's really cool.'"

The two became fast friends, and soon were inseparable offscreen in all the ways their characters failed to develop closeness onscreen. By 2013, when both young women had Instagram accounts and were just starting to test out their social media prowess, they often shared photos of each other at dinners and sleepovers and nights out.

By 2016, Turner arrived to the Emmys red carpet and revealed to *E! News* she and Williams had their best friendship sealed with ink. They were now sporting matching tattoos that read "07.08.09," or August 7, 2009—the date they were both cast in *Game of Thrones*, written out in British date format.

That same year, the young women celebrated Halloween together. They dressed as "Hash Brownies," wearing Girl Scout uniforms decorated with weed leaves. They partied and rocked red-carpet events together, helping each other adjust their dress trains for photos and always sharing supportive words about the other in on-camera interviews. Sophie and Maisie even coined their own celebrity portmanteau hashtag, #Mophie, which accompanied most of the tweets and Instagrams of their many hangouts.

"We have sleepovers whenever we're in Belfast at the same time, which is nice," Turner told *INSIDER* on the red carpet ahead of the seventh season premiere. "She's my best friend, she's my soul mate. I love that girl to pieces."

Two years later, Williams announced in a *Radio Times* interview she would be a bridesmaid in Turner's wedding to pop singer

Joe Jonas. What began as a fluke audition for an unknown show turned into one of the purest public displays of friendship to ever grace the red carpets of Hollywood.

Williams's behind-the-scenes relationship with the *Game of Thrones* crew also led to one of the most standout cameos in the series: Ed Sheeran. At a SXSW event in 2016, Benioff and Weiss said Sheeran had agreed to a small role in the coming season as a gift to Maisie Williams.

"For years, we tried to get Ed Sheeran on the show to surprise Maisie [Williams], and this year we finally did it," Benioff said.

Williams was a longtime superfan of Sheeran's. Nearly three years earlier, she had met him for the first time and posted a photo on Instagram with the caption: "Lovely to finally meet you. Playin it cool."

But Sheeran's appearance as "Ed" the Lannister soldier was a far more involved visit that left Williams grinning from ear to ear. Sheeran's character was introduced while he was singing a song to a group of fellow Lannister soldiers. And not just any song, but a ballad straight from Martin's A Song of Ice and Fire known colloquially as "Hands of Gold."

In the books, a singer named Symon Silver Tongue tries to blackmail Tyrion Lannister by writing a ballad about his secret affair with Shae. The song is meant to be a direct threat to Tyrion and Shae. In the books, Shae isn't given to Sansa as a handmaid as a cover for her presence. Instead she's kept hidden in a house in King's Landing, and Tyrion must secretly travel outside the Red Keep's walls each time he wants to see her.

One of the times Tyrion goes to visit, he finds Symon Silver Tongue inside the house with Shae. Symon recognizes him right away, which throws Tyrion off. If this singer knows about Tyrion and Shae, who else does? And what if he says something? Both Tyrion and Shae would be in grave danger if the secret of their relationship made its way to Tywin Lannister.

And so Symon makes the grave mistake of blackmailing Tyrion. He wants to be able to sing at an upcoming royal wedding, and demands that Tyrion make it happen or else he'll spill the beans. Symon sings the "Hands of Gold" song for Tyrion, which tells the story of a man who rides into a city for a woman he calls "his secret treasure" and "his shame and bliss." The song's title refers to the chorus about the "hands of gold."

In the books, the Hand of the King doesn't just wear a pin, but also an ornate necklace made of golden hands linking together to form a chain. We saw a variation of this golden chain on Tyrion's armor in the season two "Blackwater" episode.

But most important, the "hands of gold" are what Tyrion uses to kill Shae in the books when he finds her in Tywin's bed in *A Storm of Swords*. She's wearing the golden necklace, and Tyrion grabs the chain and twists. As he kills her, Symon Silver Tongue's lyrics come into his head: "For hands of gold are always cold but a woman's hands are warm."

On the show, Shae is wearing a plain gold chain when Tyrion strangles her—not one made of hands. Benioff and Weiss also changed the staging of the scene so that Shae grabs a knife when she sees Tyrion, effectively making her murder an act of self-defense (which it very much is not in the books).

When Arya hears Ed Sheeran's character singing "Hands of Gold" on the season seven premiere, she remarks that she's never heard it before. Ed's soldier says, "It's new," implying that it might still be meant to reference Tyrion and Shae within the show. But it's long past the time in the series where anyone would be trying to blackmail Tyrion about Shae. Instead it was likely just a fun way to give book-readers a nod at a point when the series had gone far beyond Martin's published books.

Of all the musician cameos in *Game of Thrones*, Ed Sheeran's definitely had the best hidden meaning. Most of the seasons prior had musical cameos of their own. Perhaps most memorable was when a member of Coldplay was present for the Red Wedding in season three.

Drummer Will Champion played, well, a drummer in "The Rains of Castamere." His role was that of a musician-turned-traitor—the band at the Red Wedding swaps their instruments for crossbows and helps murder the Starks.

Earlier in that same season, Gary Lightbody of Snow Patrol led a group of Bolton men in a sing-along on the "Walk of Punishment" episode. While Brienne and Jaime are being transported by an unfriendly group of Bolton men, the scene opens with Lightbody leading his fellow soldiers in the tune "The Bear and the Maiden Fair."

Then in the fourth season, Icelandic band Sigur Rós performed a somber version of the Lannister tune "The Rains of Castamere" for King Joffrey at his wedding shortly before his death. The full song plays over the credits of the episode as well. One regular member of the *Game of Thrones* cast was starstruck to have Sigur Rós on set.

"I met them on the red carpet a few years ago," Kristian Nairn (Hodor) told *Spin*. "I had so much to say . . . and it translated into nothing. You know how that happens sometimes? I made a fool out of myself. I just basically turned into Hodor—I couldn't say a word." (Kristian Nairn is a musician himself. He tours the world performing DJ sets at events now dubbed "Rave of Thrones.")

On season six's fifth episode, "The Door," another Icelandic group had a cameo. The pop-folk band Of Monsters and Men can be spotted playing music during the Braavosi play Arya attends. Band member Ragnar "Raggi" Þórhallsson spoke with the *Wall Street Journal* about the experience of being on set for a full day.

"I didn't realize how much work being an actor is," he said. "They're at it all day, repeating the same line for different camera angles over and over again, and they have to keep up the same high energy the whole day."

Then there's American metal band Mastodon. Bandmates Brann Dailor, Bill Kelliher, and Brent Hinds suited up for the epic massacre on season five's "Hardhome." Each man played a wildling who is slaughtered and then reanimated into a wight. The Mastodon band members reprised their roles as wights for the season seven finale. As reported by *Pitchfork*, this time they got to be a part of the army of the dead. You can catch a glimpse of them when the flashing blue flames from Viserion light up the gathered army waiting to march south into Westeros.

The last of the show's musical-based cameos came when country singer Chris Stapleton got dressed up as a soldier for the massive Battle of Winterfell in season eight's third episode, "The Long Night." Unfortunately, the chaos of the fight between the living and the dead made it just about impossible to spot Stapleton on your screen. You'll have to take his Instagram photo from the costume fitting and HBO's word for it.

The most overt cameo of the final season came from Benioff and Weiss themselves. They're both standing just next to Tormund Giantsbane while he drunkenly brags about Jon Snow during Winterfell's celebration feast in the episode "The Last of the Starks."

THE GREAT *GAME OF THRONES* PRANK WARS

Benioff and Weiss did more than just enlist the occasional cool musician for appearances on the show. As the cast tells it, the two showrunners got a kick out of pranking their stars.

"David and Dan are the pranksters, like completely," Hannah Murray, who plays Gilly, told *INSIDER* at the second annual Con of Thrones. "They're really, *really* bad, and they've done a whole bunch of different things to people. The one really fun one that I was involved in was on season six. So at the season-five premiere, Dan Weiss came up to me and was like, 'I have two words for you: New costume.' Because I had had the same costume the whole show, and I was really excited."

Who can forget the literal rags Gilly wore for four seasons until Sam (played by John Bradley West) traveled south with her in the sixth season? Of course Murray was thrilled to finally have a proper costume after all those years! But Murray decided to take advantage of this news and pull the wool over her costar's eyes.

"I went up to Kit and I told him [about the new costume] and he was like 'This means John [Sam] gets a new costume too. We can have so much fun with this,'" Murray recalled. "And so we emailed David and Dan and were like, 'We think John should get long robes, maybe pink,' and they wrote back to us and were like, 'We're into it.'

"We did this whole elaborate thing where they got wardrobe to design this absurd costume for John and told him it was his," Murray said, holding back laughter. "They sent pictures from his fitting and he looked like a crazy clown version of Henry the VIII—that's the best way I can describe it. It was like a multicolored patchwork thing with a codpiece, like really, really absurd, and a hat."

The word "codpiece" derives from the Middle English "cod" (scrotum) and refers to basically jockstraps worn primarily around the 1500s by fancy men who felt like accentuating their man-parts while also keeping them from being accidentally exposed.

You can imagine why John Bradley West would be less than thrilled about this costume.

"He kept trying to talk to me about it and was like, 'What's your costume like?' and I was like, 'It's fine! It's fine,'" Murray said. "And he said, 'Mine's really weird, I think my hat has been made comically small.' And I just had to go, 'Oh, hmm, I don't know, that's strange.'"

Murray and Kit Harington kept the bit up for more than a month, and even got other cast members in on the joke.

"David and Dan are the worst for this sort of thing," Joe Dempsie (Gendry) told *INSIDER* during the same Con of Thrones weekend. He laughed when recalling the picture of Bradley West at the costume fitting. That photo was eventually shared exclusively with James Hibberd at *Entertainment Weekly*, so anyone can also share in Bradley West's poor costume humiliation.

"He looked like a really sad jester," Dempsie said, laughing. "And I know John, and you can see in his eyes that he's fuming, but he can't say anything because he just thinks this is going to be his outfit."

Dempsie empathized with his costar, though. "I mean if it happened to me, I would fall for it hook, line, and sinker," he said. "Everyone's fair game."

Murray eventually took mercy on her friend and costar. "I went to David and said, 'We need to tell him at some point,'" Murray said. "So we went up to him and told him that it was a joke, and he was very upset but then saw the funny side pretty quickly as well."

The tradition of pranking began all the way back on the first season when Benioff and Weiss decided to have a go at resident pretty-boy Kit Harington.

"We assumed that, like most good-looking guys, he likes being a good-looking guy," Benioff revealed in the *Inside Game of Thrones* book. "So while we were shooting the first season, when we distributed new drafts of Episode 108, we gave Kit a copy with these Jon Snow scenes in place of the actual scenes."

Episode 108 (season one, episode eight) is the one where Jon Snow fights off a wight and saves Lord Commander Mormont. He only manages to kill the undead man when he grabs a lit lantern with his bare hand and throws it on the creature. As a result, his hand is horribly burned. But the prank script had Jon completely engulfed in flames instead of just his hand, resulting in his hair being burned away and the skin of his upper lip completely sloughed off, "exposing the top row of his teeth."

According to Weiss's telling of the tale, Kit took the horrible turn of events for Jon in stride. This adds up, given that the first season of *Game of Thrones* was Kit's first major acting gig, and he likely had no cause for diva-ish behavior.

"He was a remarkably good sport about the whole thing," Weiss said in *Inside Game of Thrones*. "I think he had actually resigned himself to possibly spending years and years on the show with no hair and no upper lip."

Another great prank comes from the second season, when Benioff and Weiss turned their sights on Alfie Allen (Theon Greyjoy). Allen was one of the cast members who had read all the books, so he knew Theon is taken out of sight for all of books three and four, and only resurfaces for the fifth book when he is then "Reek." Weiss and Benioff planned on showing the TV audiences

Theon's full transformation at the hands of Ramsay Bolton, but Allen didn't know that yet.

Instead, he received a fake script from Benioff and Weiss that had Theon dying at the hands of Bran after he took over Winterfell. If the showrunners expected a drastic reaction out of Allen, they must have been let down.

"We didn't hear from Alfie for two weeks," Benioff said in *Inside Game of Thrones*. "Finally we called him. He was on holiday in Ibiza, on a sailboat. He said he was fine with it. He thought it was a good way to go."

Alfie Allen literally just went on vacation after hearing he was killed off the show. Not a care in the world. What an icon. But Benioff and Weiss weren't giving up that easily. They tried to pivot with another prank, asking him if he'd be okay with coming back onto the show as a wight version of Theon.

"After a long silence on the line, he said he'd consider it," Benioff added. "'It would mean having no dialogue and being naked most of the time,' we said, 'but it would still be acting.' He drew the line at naked zombie. So we told him there was no way we were killing him off."

Only once (in the public record) did anyone manage to flip the script on Benioff and Weiss and their dastardly pranks. Nikolaj Coster-Waldau (Jaime Lannister) pulled a joke so serious that lawyers almost got involved. Between the third and fourth seasons, Benioff and Weiss gave Nikolaj a heads-up that Jaime would be getting a haircut.

His longer blond locks had become filthy thanks to long-term imprisonment, and so the styling department wanted to give him a shorter, more modern look. As Weiss revealed in a 2016 interview with *Entertainment Weekly*, Nikolaj appeared *very* disgruntled with this decision.

"Nikolaj wrote this Angry Actor Email about how he was very upset that we were changing his hairstyle," Weiss told *EW*. "He said he felt the need to own his hair because his hair was part of his character, and he was going to take it upon himself to get his own haircut that he felt best reflected Jaime Lannister as he saw him. He said he hoped we'd understand and he'd send us a picture shortly."

Almost three days later, he emailed them a picture that showed him with a military-level shaved head. Benioff and Weiss became "alarmed," according to *EW*, because Nikolaj was still scheduled to film some reshoots and this would throw a major wrench into the look of his character.

"We thought we'll have to get a Jaime Lannister wig at last-minute at tremendous expense," Weiss said. "HBO's lawyers were calling his lawyers . . ."

But before everything went totally to shit, a second email came through. The photo he had sent was from several years earlier—long before *Game of Thrones*. How the tables had turned.

CHAPTER FIFTEEN

✧✧✧✧✧✧✧✧✧✧✧✧✧✧✧

VALAR MORGHULIS

Prank scripts aside, every actor on *Game of Thrones* knew Benioff and Weiss didn't call you unless they had bad news. The worst news. The "yeah, this is finally it" news. But unlike with a wholly original TV series, the *Game of Thrones* cast went through a unique evolution of how they found out their characters were going to kick the bucket. For the first batches of doomed protagonists, all they had to do was walk into a bookstore and pick up one of the ASOIAF books to discover their fate.

That's precisely what Jason Momoa did when he was cast for the first season as the terrifyingly hunky Khal Drogo. As he later told *Access Hollywood*, the script description of Khal Drogo was so impressive that he decided to go buy the first book.

"It took me four days [to read]," Momoa said. "When Drogo died, I literally freaked out, set down the book, went to Barnes & Noble, bought the second book."

According to *Access Hollywood*, Momoa then flipped through the second book to see if Drogo somehow came back, but there was no happy news to be found. "I was super bummed," he said. Momoa did get to come back on the season two finale for a brief appearance during one of Dany's mystical visions in the House of the Undying, but Drogo remained firmly dead.

Sean Bean (Ned Stark) of course knew his death was coming, even if many people tuning into the show weren't expecting it. But the shock was there in the script nonetheless. During his Reddit AMA (Ask Me Anything) in 2014, a fan asked Bean if he was shocked about Ned Stark's beheading.

"Yes," Bean replied. "Yeah. I mean, I knew it was coming, you know? But when I read it, you know, it just comes out of the blue and was a nasty shock. Especially after Ned Stark thought he'd got some agreement between Joffrey and the various factions, and for them to renege on that deal was pretty shocking.

"Because they made a cast of my head with hair on it, I've got some pictures of me holding my head. And it was fun. I don't know, you kind of just have to imagine what it's like to have your head chopped off, [Anne] Boleyn and how she must have felt. But it was the manner in which it was done, it was all the more tragic for that."

But not all of the show's actors had read Martin's book series. For many, staying wholly within the TV script was more useful for their process. That way they weren't playing a scene in season two in a way that might inform what happens to their character in season seven. But this left those actors vulnerable to fans who took it upon themselves to tell the stars their roles on the show had a set expiration date.

Richard Madden, who played Robb, actually had his death spoiled by fans of the series, since the published books already

included the dreaded Red Wedding. "A thousand people spoiled it for me before I had a chance to pick up the third book," he told *Entertainment Weekly*.

Madden had been reading each book as the seasons went, but apparently book-readers hadn't been able to help themselves when it came to telling Madden that something bad was coming for Robb.

"I also made the fatal flaw of Googling," Madden continued in his *Entertainment Weekly* interview. "So that kind of reinforced what people were hinting—saying that something terrible was going to happen and giggling."

Michelle Fairley's character, Catelyn Stark, is also murdered at the Red Wedding. Fairley and Madden worked together often as Robb and Catelyn grew closer following Ned Stark's death on the series. But unlike Madden, Fairley had decided to read ahead.

"I read the series so I knew what was coming and I also knew how many years I signed for," Fairley told *EW*. "And [the Red Wedding is] something that anyone who's read the books will talk about."

Partial vengeance for Robb and Catelyn comes just three episodes later when King Joffrey is killed at the christened "Purple Wedding" (so named for the poisoned wine Joffrey drinks, the color of the deadly crystal placed in his glass, and his purpled, strangled face). Jack Gleeson had played the sadistic teen with impressive bravado for four years, but his time on the show was coming to an end. Like his predecessors, Gleeson knew Joffrey's fate because of the books (and the internet).

"That was one of the first things I did when I heard I got the part: I looked at the Wikipedia summary of the books and my character," Gleeson said during a New York Comic Con panel in 2016. "If you get a new job and you know that at some point you're definitely going to be fired from it, you're going to check online when you're going to be fired. I think that's a pretty reasonable thing to do. So the whole thing wasn't a surprise."

After Joffrey's death, the next major character to go was Lysa Arryn. Littlefinger shoves his wife unceremoniously through the Eyrie's moon door, then claims her death was a suicide.

"Lysa's [death] was challenging for me as I'm scared of heights and I had to be hanging from a harness very high up while I was filmed from below," actress Kate Dickie said in an interview with *Watchers on the Wall*. "But it's good to be out of your comfort zone and do things that scare you."

Before fans could catch their breath from Lysa's surprising murder, "The Mountain and the Viper" aired, bringing to life one of the most devastating turns of any *Game of Thrones* fight. Oberyn having his head squeezed into a pulp left audiences shocked and disgusted. The memorably dashing man who played Oberyn, Pedro Pascal, says he knew from the very first audition his character was doomed.

"I didn't know *how* he died, until I met David Benioff and Dan Weiss in Belfast," Pascal said in an interview posted on HBO's *Making Game of Thrones* site. "They mentioned the crushing of my head in three steps: First the teeth, then the eyes, and finally the entire melon head. My first thought was, 'Hopefully I'll be able to compete for a top spot for the most gruesome death on *Game of Thrones*,' which is saying a lot."

Next on the chopping block was Rose Leslie, who starred as Ygritte—Jon Snow's first love. Leslie revealed in an interview with *Entertainment Weekly* that she knew coming in to *Game of Thrones* that Ygritte was toast. Her death happens in the third novel of the series, *A Storm of Swords*. Though the death of Ygritte itself is tragic, Leslie has fond memories of that day on set.

"It was really lovely. I know that everybody mentions this but we are very much a close-knit unit on set," Leslie told *Entertainment Weekly*. "After my final take I was given [Ygritte's] bow and arrow ... on one side of the handle is an emblem of a red rose, on the other was a silver placard that read, 'Kissed by Fire.' Everybody huddled around. I felt very privileged. It was absolutely beautiful."

"Kissed by Fire" is of course the nickname given to redheads by wildling tribes. The phrase was also used as the title of the episode in which Ygritte and Jon Snow have sex for the first time.

The fourth season was the last major installment in the series when the actors were able to easily discern their fates. Charles Dance, who played Tywin Lannister, had a similar experience to Richard Madden in that a fan ruined the surprise of his death for him.

"Someone in the street came up and said, 'You got this great death scene,'" Dance told *Entertainment Weekly*. "So then I went into a bookshop ... grabbed a book and I said, 'Oh, I see.' It's quite spectacular."

The sight of Tyrion aiming a crossbow at his father sitting on the chamber pot is one we won't soon forget. Not many *Game of Thrones* actors can claim such an unusual (and frankly gross) setting for their deaths.

By the fifth season, you'd expect fans to be used to the brute ways *Game of Thrones* axed characters. But the limit was tested with the burning of Shireen Baratheon. At a Con of Thrones panel moderated by *A Cast of Kings* podcast hosts Joanna Robinson and David Chen, several of the killed-off cast members dished on their final moments in the series. Among the actors on the panel was Kerry Ingram, who played the young Shireen.

"I found out about halfway through season five," Ingram said. "I was really, really excited. I knew exactly what the reaction was going to be and I was so excited for it."

Shireen, as you'll remember well, was burned alive at the stake on her father's orders by Melisandre in one of the bleakest points in the whole series. Ingram and her costars managed to inject some lightness into the whole affair by posting a few choice photos on Instagram.

First Ingram posted a picture on her social media accounts taken at a backyard barbeque. The photo was staged so it looked like the grill's flames were surrounding Ingram, who has her hands up in mock anguish.

"Oh ffs [for fuck's sake] not again . . ." Ingram wrote in the caption.

Then, almost a year after Shireen's untimely demise, actress Carice van Houten (Melisandre) tweeted a darkly hilarious throwback picture. The photo was clearly taken on set the day Ingram was filming her death scene. In it we see the two stars huddled close in a tent, and van Houten is holding a box of Duraflame Quick Start firestarters. Her choice caption simply read: "Awkward farewell presents."

Perhaps the only *Game of Thrones* death scene that can top Shireen's in terms of tragedy is the fate that befalls Hodor. On the sixth season, Benioff and Weiss shocked the fandom once again when they revealed the meaning behind Hodor's name ("Hold the door!") at the same moment he was killed.

Actor Kristian Nairn accidentally ruined the reveal for himself before Benioff and Weiss could give him the dreaded call. As reported by *INSIDER*, the *Game of Thrones* scripts that season were passed out to the actors in order of episode appearance. Nairn was good friends with Finn Jones (Loras Tyrell), so he gave him a call because he knew Jones would get the scripts first.

"I said, 'So, do I make it through the end?' not expecting that his answer would be silence," Nairn said in an *INSIDER* interview. "Yeah . . . it was an awkward silence for a few seconds. I said, 'Are you serious?' And his response was just, 'You're going to absolutely love it. You're going to be so pleased when you read this.'"

Jones wouldn't give up any more details. A few days later, the script was sent to Nairn. "That same day the showrunners called me, and that's the sign of impending doom," he said.

Hodor's death will remain one of the more heartbreaking losses of innocent life on *Game of Thrones*, memorable in part because of how meme-able it was. Within days, online stores were selling Hodor doorstops. Nairn played along too, appearing in one viral video from UNILAD where a man ran to a closing elevator, yelling "Hold the door!" only to find Nairn standing there looking properly peeved.

Next on the season-six chopping block was poor Rickon Stark, played by Art Parkinson. He hadn't been seen on the series since Bran and Rickon parted ways at the end of season three. Rickon is still very much alive in Martin's published books (as are Hodor and most of the characters left on our list here), so Parkinson had to wait for the dreaded call.

"When I was originally told I was coming back to the show, I didn't actually know [Rickon] died," Parkinson said in an interview with *The Hollywood Reporter*. "But before they sent me the script [for "Battle of the Bastards"], they filled me in. They said, 'Listen, just so you know and don't get too shocked, you do die this season.' It was sad to finally let the character go."

Though Parkinson was given precisely zero speaking lines for his sixth-season appearances, he went down in history for not zig-zagging as Rickon fled from Ramsay's arrows at the Battle of the Bastards. Following the episode's debut and the clamor from fans online about Rickon running in a straight line, Parkinson simply tweeted "had a good run" with #shouldazigzagged.

We didn't have to wait long for Jon and Sansa to exact revenge on Ramsay. By the end of "The Battle of the Bastards," Sansa has Ramsay's own hounds rip his face apart and presumably eat him alive. Filming that scene was tricky, as actor Iwan Rheon revealed at the Con of Thrones panel with *A Cast of Kings*.

"They had to protect my face, even though it was my last scene and I thought they might just be like, 'Eh,'" Rheon said. "The dogs we used were *not* pet dogs. They aren't the kind of dogs you want near your face. The first time I saw them I was like 'Ohhh, hello!' [mimes waving] and they were like 'God no! Don't touch the dogs!'"

Mat Krentz, the visual effects supervisor who oversaw Ramsay's death scene, told *Variety* the scene was originally supposed to be more gory. "Artists also created a CG jaw for Bolton, and animated it to reveal the flesh ripping between Ramsay's skin and gums," *Variety*'s Lawrence Yee reported. The final version was more toned down, and no dogs or Iwan Rheon were harmed in the making.

Next came one of the biggest slew of named characters to die at the same time in the show's history. The sixth season finale opens with Cersei's twisted massacre of Margaery, Loras, and Mace Tyrell, the High Sparrow, Kevan Lannister, and dozens of other King's Landing characters. Natalie Dormer (Margaery) told

Entertainment Weekly she accidentally preempted the call from Benioff and Weiss when she asked them about possibly leaving the show earlier so she could take on another acting project.

"They ended up phoning me—and that was The Call," Dormer said. "But I got it six months ahead of normal."

Dormer wound up having a good news/bad news version of the call, because Benioff and Weiss had to tell her she was locked in for the sixth season (and therefore couldn't do the mystery project she was trying to schedule), but then afterward would be freed up for any other TV or movie roles she'd want.

Dormer's onscreen brother was played by Finn Jones. Though he wound up accidentally spoiling Hodor's death for Kristian Nairn, Jones was in the dark about his own fate for a bit longer. Benioff and Weiss gave him the first nine scripts for season six, but held the tenth one back for a suspiciously long amount of time.

"I was like, 'Why didn't I get episode 10 yet? That's really weird. It's 5 p.m. and we're doing it tomorrow. Why haven't I received it?'" Jones recounted in an *Entertainment Weekly* interview. "And just as I was saying that I get a call from [Benioff and Weiss]. And as I'm picking up, I'm staying positive, thinking, 'Maybe they're checking in to say "Hi."' And they were just like [a long pause of dead silence]. And I was like 'Ahhhh, God no! I was so close to season 7!'"

Shortly after watching his wife get blown up by his mother, young King Tommen dies from self-defenestration. As he drops from the tower in the Red Keep, *Game of Thrones* loses yet another innocent character. Dean-Charles Chapman, the actor who played Tommen, was grateful for his time on the show (especially, as noted in our casting chapter, given that he had two roles).

"I first found out when we got flown out to Belfast for a table read with the cast," Chapman recalled during an interview with

Vulture. "The night before, I got a call from [Benioff and Weiss]. As soon as I saw it was them, I knew it was over. I answered the phone, 'Hey, how are you doing? You're going to kill me, aren't you?'"

Chapman said he was grateful Tommen at least had a "peaceful" death. The same cannot be said for one of the biggest character departures on the seventh season—Petyr "Littlefinger" Baelish. After a buildup of tension between Sansa and Arya Stark, the sisters team up with Bran Stark (who by then was really the three-eyed raven) and take down the man responsible for much of the realm's chaos.

"The infamous call. It's so obvious what it is," actor Aidan Gillen said in an *Entertainment Weekly* interview. "[Benioff and Weiss] never ring you up—maybe once in six years. I learned about that call from [Roose Bolton actor Michael McElhatton] when he told me about his call."

Gillen's call came, and it left him feeling a bit "bereft" but also validated. He told *Entertainment Weekly* he had been saying he'd like for Arya to be the one to kill him since 2015, two years before the script was sent to him. Littlefinger would wind up being the last major character death before the final six episodes, when the game started *really* whittling down to a few key players.

For the eighth and final season, the phone-call method went completely out the window. The stars wouldn't be coddled through the last pages of *Game of Thrones* scripts. Everyone was tossed into the deep end at the same time, when encrypted files of all six episode scripts were emailed out to the cast just a few days before they were scheduled to come to Belfast.

In a set of days both celebratory and melancholy, the *Game of Thrones* cast sat down in a room with the show's executives and writers, and read through the final season together. Bryan Cogman read the scene descriptions and actions written out between the actors' dialogue. Many of the people in the room already knew what would happen, since it would have taken a special level of self-control to not read those final scripts the moment you received them. But a few key actors arrived in Belfast with no idea of what would happen. Most notable of these rogues was Kit Harington himself.

"I walked in saying, 'Don't tell me, I don't want to know,'" Harington told *Entertainment Weekly*. "What's the point of reading it to myself in my own head when I can listen to people do it and find out with my friends?"

This meant the gut-wrenching moment when Jon kills Daenerys was revealed to Harington as the whole room watched. HBO's documentary about the final season's production, *Game of Thrones: The Last Watch*, includes footage of the Jon Snow actor realizing in real time what his character did. As Bryan Cogman reads, "We see Jon with his hand still on the hilt of the dagger he just lodged in Dany's heart." Harington pushes away from the table with his hand on his mouth and tears welling in his eyes.

He is sitting across the table from Emilia Clarke (Daenerys), who had already read the heartbreaking scene. She sinks in her chair and makes horrified faces at Harington, while others around them looked both surprised or gleeful to see Harington's real-time response. Clarke looks at Harington and gives him a little nod as if to say, "Yeah, that really happens."

Her cherished costar is sitting in a state of shock, but Clarke had been processing the shock and trauma of Daenerys Targaryen's final scenes for days at that point. She had read all of the scripts the moment they were sent, and was completely blindsided by Dany's downfall and death.

"I took a very long walk around London in a daze, not quite knowing how to digest the news," Clarke told the *New Yorker* in an interview that ran right after the series finale. "Now, finally, people are going, 'Oh, now we understand why this season hit you hard.' I had no idea what to expect for this last season. I hoped for some juicy things to get into, as I always do for each season, but I didn't see this coming."

MAESTER'S NOTES

One *Game of Thrones* actor took a rather unique and rebellious approach to handling his character's death. Pilou Asbæk, the Danish actor who brought the bombastic pirate Euron Greyjoy to life, just straight-up refused to actually die on camera during his last scene.

"I had a long conversation with [director] Miguel Sapochnik about it," Asbæk told HBO for its *Making Game of Thrones* blog. "Dan and David were like, 'and then Euron dies' and I was like, 'No he doesn't.' And they said, 'What do you mean?' I said, 'I'm not going to close my eyes. I want to smile up at the sky like life is beautiful, and then you guys have to cut away.' Miguel kept saying, 'Close your eyes!' but I was like, 'No.'"

Euron Greyjoy's final moments show his eyes open and gazing toward the sky as he smiles through bloody teeth, mischievous until the very end.

Clarke knew Dany's fate in 2017, and had to try her best not to drop hints about the oncoming tragedy. But the mask slipped several times in now-viral video and print interviews. The first big hint for fans came in a cover story by *Vanity Fair*'s Joanna Robinson published in the spring of 2018. While promoting *Solo: A Star Wars Story*, Clarke said she had already filmed the last onscreen moments for Daenerys Targaryen. "It f—ed me up," Clarke said. "Knowing that is going to be a lasting flavor in someone's mouth of what Daenerys is . . ."

Clarke trailed off and didn't get into more specifics, but that was the first major warning sign that people were likely to be upset with Daenerys's turn on the season. The next big clue came from the night of the Emmy Awards. On September 17, 2018, Clarke attended HBO's Emmys after-party with costars Jacob Anderson (Grey Worm) and Nathalie Emmanuel (Missandei). *Entertainment Tonight* spoke with them on the party's red carpet, and asked all three actors what they could say about the final season.

Clarke started out the interview by saying it was "the best season ever." But a couple questions later, Clarke was asked if she had shot her final scenes yet and if so, was she happy with how things had ended? Emmanuel says "Yes" almost immediately, but Clarke instead raised her eyebrows and made a small noise of laughter.

When pressed, Clarke repeated the phrase "Best season ever" loudly into the microphone, but this time it sounded a bit sarcastic. Anderson, who was standing next to her, started laughing. Knowing now that Missandei and Daenerys would die rather horrible deaths, and Grey Worm would take a concerning turn into vengeance, it's clear the three actors were trying to refrain from revealing too much while also letting fans know things were going to be rough for their characters.

Missandei meets her death after she is captured by Cersei's armies, which means Emmanuel was one of the last actors whose characters met an untimely end on *Game of Thrones*. "To be honest with you, when I read the script for it, I was like, not surprised that she died because I had been expecting it for a really long time," Emmanuel told *Entertainment Weekly's* Piya Sinha-Roy. "So many people die in that show, and I guess I didn't think I was any safer than anybody else in that respect. But I am fully aware and engaged in the conversation of representation because I am the only woman of color in this show that has been on there regularly for many seasons."

Missandei's death was part of the narrative impetus for Dany's descent into morally problematic territory. She had been Dany's sole female friend for years and her loyal adviser. Missandei was also the only woman of color with a recurring role on *Game of Thrones*, and was a former slave. Seeing her beheaded with her hands bound in chains made this scene even more difficult to watch.

"It's a really complex conversation and it always astounds me how much it meant to people and how much my being in that show has meant to people in terms of representation," Emmanuel said. "The fact that I've been able to do that for people literally makes me want to up and cry every time someone says it to me."

To borrow a phrase from another fantasy tale, at least death (in this case) is but the next great adventure. The brutal ending of *Game of Thrones* for these actors did not mean fading into TV history, but launching forward into bright new spotlights and projects. Fans had to reckon with saying goodbye to the beloved characters as the curtain fell on the epic series. Was it bittersweet, as promised? Well, that depends on who you ask . . .

CHAPTER SIXTEEN

◇◇◇◇◇◇◇◇◇◇◇◇◇◇◇

A BITTERSWEET ENDING

The day before HBO aired its eighth season finale of *Game of Thrones*, CBS debuted a *60 Minutes* special featuring the cast of the series and George R. R. Martin himself. This was a very different setting and tone from Martin's appearance on *Conan* six years earlier. Back then, Martin was giddy and grinning as he sat in the spotlight and soaked in the fervor created by the Red Wedding. He didn't know then he would fail to meet deadline after deadline, missing his opportunities to publish the final two ASOIAF books before Benioff and Weiss would cross the finish line with *Game of Thrones*.

But here he was in 2019, sitting in front of Anderson Cooper and talking about how the world was about to tune into a version of his planned ending. "It was a blow when the series caught up," Martin told Cooper after letting out a hollow laugh. "I didn't think it would happen."

Martin had long touted the word "bittersweet" as the best way to describe his planned ending for the books. He had no way of knowing the term would apply so well to the extra-textual events of his series, too. To understand how Martin, the *Game of Thrones* showrunners, and fans all found themselves in this murky circumstance, we first have to revisit how Martin's writing styles and issues with deadlines plagued the progress of A Song of Ice and Fire.

As explored in the second chapter of this book, the genesis of A Song of Ice and Fire is dotted with changes in the plan for the number of books and the years in which they'd be published. This stems from Martin's "gardening" approach to writing.

"I think there are two types of writers, the architects and the gardeners," Martin said in a 2011 interview with the *Guardian*. "The architects plan everything ahead of time, like an architect building a house. They know how many rooms are going to be in the house, what kind of roof they're going to have, where the wires are going to run, what kind of plumbing there's going to be. They have the whole thing designed and blueprinted out before they even nail the first board up."

J. K. Rowling is one of the most famous examples of an "architect" writer. She spent at least three years outlining the main plot trajectory for all seven Harry Potter books before she began writing 1997's *Harry Potter and the Sorcerer's Stone*. Martin, on the other hand, is a gardener.

"The gardeners dig a hole, drop in a seed and water it," he told the *Guardian*. "They kind of know what seed it is, they know if [they] planted a fantasy seed or mystery seed or whatever. But as the plant comes up and they water it, they don't know how many branches it's going to have; they find out as it grows."

This creative process means it can take longer to flesh out Martin's novels, some of which reach almost 1,500 pages in length. This style of avoiding outlines isn't just a preference for Martin—it's at the heart of how his characters come to life. If he does outline a story, then he can sometimes lose all motivation for fleshing it out into a full novel. When he submitted the original proposal for the ASOIAF books, Martin made his process clear.

"As you know, I don't outline my novels," Martin wrote to his publisher in 1993. "I find that if I know exactly where a book is going, I lose all interest in writing it. I do, however, have some strong notions as to the overall structure of the story I'm telling, and the eventual fate of many of the principal characters in the drama."

In an interview with *INSIDER*, one of Martin's friends and the coauthor of *The World of Ice and Fire*, Linda Antonsson, expanded on this particular writing habit of Martin's.

"He feels that once he has outlined it, once he has explored all the details of the story, all the beats of the story, he can't go back and revisit it," Antonsson said. "He can do general notes about characters . . . But once he goes and puts it all into a cohesive story, then he says 'I've done it, I can't revisit it because I'm going to be bored.' He experiences the story as he writes it, and he wants to be able to surprise himself to some extent or get new ideas along the way."

Some people have worried about the effect Martin's meeting with Benioff and Weiss about his plan for the ending might have had on his motivation to actually write thousands of pages about it. But there can be no doubt that the mere existence and popularity of *Game of Thrones* impacted Martin's progress with the final two books.

As the HBO show took off, Martin became a celebrity in ways he never expected or dreamed of. *Game of Thrones* brought an unprecedented level of attention and success to his writing, and he became far busier than he was when previously trying to write installments for A Song of Ice and Fire. "As the books have become increasingly complicated, there have [also] been increasing demands on his time," Antonsson said in an *INSIDER* interview. "With the attention from *Game of Thrones* publicity [and] all these other things, it's certainly true that he has a lot of irons in the fire."

Suddenly Martin couldn't walk the floor of a convention hall without being mobbed by fans. He was invited onto shows like *Conan* and parodied in *South Park*. No one can blame him for soaking in the love and adoration of millions of new fans who came to *A Song of Ice and Fire* because of *Game of Thrones*. But as the years went by, it suddenly became clear that his lack of progress with *The Winds of Winter* was going to overshadow everything.

"I'm hopeful that I can not let them catch up with me," Martin said in a 2014 interview with *Vanity Fair* ahead of the fourth season. "The season that's about to debut covers the second half of the third book." The fourth season would be the final time Martin helped write a script for *Game of Thrones*. In the intervening year, it became clear that he needed to cut down on extraneous commitments and try to crank out *The Winds of Winter*.

"Writing a script takes me three weeks, minimum, and longer when it is not a straight adaptation from the novels," Martin wrote in a March 2015 blog post announcing his plan to cancel some convention appearances. "Writing a season six script would cost me a month's work on WINDS, and maybe as much as six weeks, and I cannot afford that. With David Benioff, D. B. Weiss, and Bryan Cogman on board, the script writing chores for season six should be well covered. My energies are best devoted to WINDS."

But the rest of 2015 would come and go with no *Winds of Winter*. On January 2, 2016, Martin published a new blog post at 12:24 a.m. It read: "You wanted an update. Here's the update. You won't like it. THE WINDS OF WINTER is not finished." The nearly two-thousand-word post went on to explain how he had missed two deadlines from his publishers that would have made it possible to release the sixth book in his ASOIAF series before the sixth season of *Game of Thrones* aired.

"Believe me, it gave me no pleasure to type those words," he wrote. "You're disappointed, and you're not alone. My editors and publishers are disappointed, HBO is disappointed, my agents and foreign publishers and translators are disappointed . . . but no one could possibly be more disappointed than me.

"I can't think of any other instance where the movie or TV show came out as the source material was still being written," Martin wrote later in the post. "So when you ask me, 'will the show spoil the books,' all I can do is say, 'yes and no,' and mumble once again about the butterfly effect. Those pretty little butterflies have grown into mighty dragons. Some of the 'spoilers' you may encounter in season six may not be spoilers at all . . . because the show and the books have diverged, and will continue to do so."

His die-hard fans were left to struggle with remaining optimistic and coming to terms with having to see a version of A Song of Ice and Fire's ending play out onscreen instead of reading it in a lengthy, intricate book. Some discontented fans would hound Martin on his blog or Twitter pages, demanding updates or chastising him for daring to work on other projects (writing or otherwise) when he hadn't yet delivered the next book. Still more fans empathized with the amount of pressure and strain he was surely under, and were resigned to wait patiently until he was able to deliver a manuscript. No one wanted a rushed or trimmed-down version of his story, but that didn't mean the sting of the show finishing first was lessened.

A certain peace comes with accepting the things you cannot

change. There was nothing to be done, no alternate paths or magical solutions. The show couldn't halt production to wait for Martin to catch up, namely because of the young actors on the show and how they were visibly aging at a sometimes alarming pace.

"He's very happy with the show and the showrunners and the popularity it has brought to the series," Antonsson said. "He loves the people who work on it, he really admires it. . . . At the same time I think there's a little bit of 'woulda coulda.' Like if [HBO] just took a bit longer with this maybe he could have caught up." Even if Benioff and Weiss hadn't cut so much from Martin's books, and therefore not run out of his published materials so quickly, there's no way of knowing how much Martin would have been able to write in the intervening years.

Your mileage may vary on how the later seasons of *Game of Thrones* fared without Martin's books as their basis. For many fans, a distinct difference in the writing is noticeable starting in the fifth season. Show-only characters like Olly received a disproportionate amount of vitriol online, and there was severe backlash to the decision of placing Sansa in Winterfell with Ramsay Bolton instead of continuing her story in the Vale as Martin's books are currently doing.

People found Arya's Braavos storyline in the sixth season dissatisfying, in part because she survived several knife jabs to the gut by getting a good night's sleep. To be clear, no fan of *Game of Thrones* or A Song of Ice and Fire *wanted* Arya to die. But this was the first of many times when Benioff and Weiss would put the protagonists of the show into seemingly impossible-to-survive scenarios only to have them miraculously rescued or healed.

"I always like the suspense to be real," Martin said back on that noteworthy 2013 *Conan* appearance. "We've all seen the movies where the hero is in trouble, he's surrounded by twenty people, but you know he's gonna get away because he's the hero. And you don't really feel any fear for him. I want my readers and I want my viewers to be afraid when my characters are in danger."

This particular brand of storytelling was not the one Benioff and Weiss chose to maintain through the later seasons. In season seven's "The Spoils of War," Jaime Lannister charges down Daenerys and Drogon in a rash, heroic move. He is saved at the last moment when Bronn knocks him into the river, and we watch as Jaime sinks to the bottom in his armor in the final moments of the episode. "Did Jaime die?" many people asked in the days before the next episode. He was wearing heavy armor and had sunk, unmoving, into the black depths of the river in an ominous cliffhanger. But the next episode begins with Bronn and Jaime popping up out of the water several hundred feet downstream.

The criticism of unrealistic survival odds came up again after season seven's "Beyond the Wall." Jon Snow and a handful of other named main characters set out on their wight mission, but it is mainly just the unnamed extras accompanying them who die in the ensuing fight. At one point Tormund is dragged by a dozen wights toward the icy water but saved at the last minute by the Hound. Later in the episode, Jon is the one knocked into the frozen lake. Just like Jaime, he inexplicably pops back up a few minutes later.

This is the same episode in which the time line of events is muddled, leading to debates because fans didn't understand how Gendry had time to run back to Eastwatch, send a raven to Daenerys, and then have Daenerys fly up north to rescue Jon and the others all in what seemed like a single night. The episode's director, Alan Taylor, acknowledged that people were paying very close attention to the show's internal logic (or lack thereof).

"What's great is that people are analyzing everything with such detail," Taylor said in an *INSIDER* interview. "It's good people are pouring so much attention into it—sometimes it blows up in our face. Like there's a heated conversation about how fast ravens can fly now because of the story in my episode. Sometimes it's not comfortable to have people analyzing things too closely, but it's cool that they want to.

"We have lizards as big as 747s who can blow fire but the fact that [fans] still want it to be believable and real is great," he continued. "That means they're expecting that, which means they've had a diet of that and it means the show is basically achieving that. And so if they want to get out their maps of Westeros and a protractor and measure the speed of a raven and fight about it, then that's good."

Fans could spend hours debating all the various ways Benioff and Weiss's approach to *Game of Thrones* failed or succeeded in its final hours. The thing to keep in mind is that these two writers had never worked in television before *Game of Thrones*, nor did they pitch an idea to HBO that they were going to be entirely responsible for mapping out. The vision they were so confident in all those years ago was dependent on Martin's intricate source material. They began *Game of Thrones* as a true adaptation of the books but were forced to end it largely on their own.

In some alternate universe, A Song of Ice and Fire was already a completed series of books long before anyone saw Sean Bean step into the role of Ned Stark. Maybe in that time line, Martin sat down at that fated lunch at the Palm and told Benioff and Weiss he loved their ideas and vision for the show, but said that they would need to wait until he finished the books before going into production.

We don't live in that universe, unfortunately. The legacy of both

Game of Thrones and A Song of Ice and Fire will forever include this footnote of the many layers of disappointment and discontent that hovered around the final seasons of HBO's biggest series. Let's now take a closer look at how Benioff and Weiss brought their version of the story to an end and how closely matched it might be to Martin's plan.

HOW SIMILAR WILL THE END OF *GAME OF THRONES* BE TO MARTIN'S BOOKS?

Without time-traveling to Santa Fe at the exact moment when Martin sat down with the *Game of Thrones* writing team and listening in on their conversation, it's impossible to ever know how much of the second half of the series was dictated by Martin. The way Benioff and Weiss have described the details of that meeting have varied over the years, and it's worth looking at exactly what they said about how much Martin was able to reveal. In April 2015, ahead of the fifth season premiere, Benioff and Weiss spoke with *Variety* about how they were forging their own path toward the endgame.

"We've had a lot of conversations with George, and he makes a lot of stuff up as he's writing it," Benioff said. "Even while we talk to him about the ending, it doesn't mean that that ending that he has currently conceived is going to be the ending when he eventually writes it."

"It's like looking at a landscape and saying, 'OK, there's a mountain over there, and I know that I'm getting to that mountain,'" Weiss added. "There's an event that's going to happen, and I know that I'm moving in the general direction of that event, but what's between where I'm standing now and that thing off on the horizon, I'm not totally sure. I'll know when I get there, and then I'll see what the terrain looks like around me and I'll choose my path once I get closer to it."

By July 2017, ahead of the seventh season, Benioff and Weiss were talking openly about the specific things Martin had divulged. "[Between seasons two and three was] when we started talking to George and he was giving us a sense of things he was working on that were to come," Benioff told *Time*. "That's when he told us about the Hodor backstory, and endgame stuff. He had some great stuff that he could share with us, like the Hodor thing, but a lot of it, he wasn't sure yet, because he was writing, and he discovers things by writing."

In this *Time* interview, Benioff and Weiss say they outlined seasons seven and eight together but that they had been discussing the "endgame stuff" ever since that meeting with Martin. "There were some details that were added later—but pretty much the actual endgame, the main climactic moments, we had in mind then," Weiss said. "We had ninety percent of this crucial chunk of the story for the final season, and we were mainly talking to George to see how our notion of where things ended up jibed with his notion."

Of course, at this point *Game of Thrones* had already shifted away from many of Martin's subplots, and characters still alive in his books had been killed off (like Barristan Selmy and Stannis Baratheon).

"The good thing about us diverging at this point is that George's books will still be a surprise for readers who have seen the show," Benioff told *Time*. "Certain things that we learned from George way back in that meeting in Santa Fe are going to happen on the show, but certain things won't. And there's certain things where

George didn't know what was going to happen, so we're going to find them out for the first time too, along with millions of readers when we read those books."

This was the first time the showrunners said there would be events and storylines Martin told them in that meeting that wouldn't happen in their version of the ending. Skipping ahead to the flurry of interviews published before the eighth and final season of the show, things became more complicated than ever.

"I've been so slow with these books," Martin told *Rolling Stone* for a feature on Sophie Turner and Maisie Williams published in March 2019. The writer, Brian Hiatt, noted that Martin spoke "with palpable pain" in his voice. "The major points of the ending will be things I told them five or six years ago," Martin said. "But there may also be changes, and there'll be a lot added."

That same month, *Entertainment Weekly*'s James Hibberd published a feature on how Martin was handling the final season of the show being upon him at last. Hibberd noted that Martin was "somewhat in the dark" when it came to Benioff and Weiss's plan for the finale. "I haven't read the [final-season] scripts and haven't been able to visit the set because I've been working on *Winds*," Martin said. "I know some of the things. But there's a lot of minor-character [arcs] they'll be coming up with on their own. And, of course, they passed me several years ago. There may be important discrepancies."

Benioff and Weiss also told *EW* that they had agreed not to publicly discuss which events in the final season were things Martin had told them. "One thing we've talked to George about is that we're not going to tell people what the differences are," Benioff said. "So when those books come out, people can experience them fresh."

Jumping into April, the very month *Game of Thrones* season eight would premiere, we return once more to that *60 Minutes* interview between Anderson Cooper and Martin. "I don't think Dan and Dave's ending is gonna be that different from my ending because of the conversations we did have," Martin said. "But they may be on certain secondary characters, there may be big differences."

So even though Martin hadn't read the scripts for the final season, he seemed under the impression that Benioff and Weiss hadn't made too many major changes to his endgame outline. But he couldn't know for sure if he wasn't involved at all in the writing or production for the eighth season. Benioff and Weiss had even offered him a cameo in the last season, *EW* revealed, but the writer turned down the offer so as to focus on *The Winds of Winter* and his other projects.

The day after the series finale aired on May 19, 2019, Martin posted again on his blog. "How will it all end? I hear people asking," he wrote. "The same ending as the show? Different? Well . . . yes. And no. And yes. And no. And yes. And no. And yes."

Martin made no mention of any specific plot points unveiled in the final eighty minutes of the show. In fact, he never outright said that he had watched the finale. The blog post was instead a focus on celebrating and mourning the closing of this chapter, and thanking all the hundreds of people at HBO involved in bringing his story to life.

The only concrete confirmation about how the show and book endings will match came from Isaac Hempstead Wright, the young actor who played Bran Stark and was crowned King of the Six Kingdoms in the series finale. "[Creators] David [Benioff] and Dan [Weiss] told me there were two things [author] George R. R. Martin had planned for Bran, and that was the Hodor revelation, and that he would be king," the actor said in a *Making of Game of Thrones* interview. "So that's pretty special to be directly involved in something that is part of George's vision. It was a really nice way to wrap it up."

There are numerous narrative hints in Martin's books about Bran winding up as king. Thematically it matches the way the entire inspiration for A Song of Ice and Fire began with the scene of Bran witnessing an execution and finding direwolves in the snow. The story began in the North and centered on the Starks from the very beginning, so this "time for wolves" ending is an easy fit.

Without comment from either Martin, Benioff and Weiss, or the rest of the cast to go off of, fans are going to have to decide for themselves which other storylines in the final episodes might match with Martin's vision. The thought of Benioff and Weiss killing off any major characters whom Martin plans to keep alive is dubious, which means we likely can count Cersei, Jaime, and Daenerys among the main doomed protagonists in A Song of Ice and Fire.

The manner of their deaths might differ, though again it feels unlikely that Benioff and Weiss would stage the dramatic scene of Jon killing Daenerys himself if that wasn't prescribed by Martin. Her descent into problematic moral territory is also thematically in line with Dany's current arc in A Song of Ice and Fire. Her arrival to Westeros in his books will most certainly result in the decimation of armies and cities, even if she believes she is acting on behalf of a greater good.

"The Iron Throne" was indeed an episode laced with bittersweet moments. Daenerys is finally able to stand before the Iron Throne, the seat of power her ancestors once built, but the dream is ripped from her before she could fully realize it. Drogon melts the twisted chair, doing his part to "break the wheel" his mother sought to destroy, and flies away with her body. His survival means not all traces of magic are gone from the world.

Jon Snow's end is also very Martin-esque. We know Martin admires Tolkien and worked Lord of the Rings themes into his ASOIAF characters. Jon not only has the narrative potential of an Aragorn, a hidden king-to-be who would act as a catalyst in the fight for humankind's survival, but also the emotional burden of a Frodo, a good-hearted person who reluctantly shoulders the weight of responsibility. Jon's goodbye to his family and journey into the true North is a parallel to the way Frodo parts with his hobbit friends at the end of *The Return of the King*, sailing into Valinor, the Undying Lands.

There is also a bittersweetness in Brienne sitting at the Lord Commander of the Kingsguard's table as she reflects on Jaime's life, and in Grey Worm sailing away from Westeros without Missandei by his side as he journeys to her birthplace. Arya and Sansa Stark don't just survive, they thrive in the final hours of *Game of Thrones*, and if that's not a bittersweet ending then who knows what is.

Without knowing for certain what Martin's planned ending is, fans will debate about these characters right up until the moment *The Winds of Winter* and *A Dream of Spring* are (hopefully) published. Until then, we're left shuffling the thousands of puzzle pieces contained in A Song of Ice and Fire to see where they might fit into that indelible series finale of *Game of Thrones*.

CHAPTER 17

✦✧✦✧✦✧✦✧✦✧✦✧✦✧✦✧✦✧✦✧✦

The FUTURE of GAME of THRONES

Where will *Game of Thrones* land in the history books? How do we contend with this massive series coming to an end? What comes next for fans of the show? These were the questions on everyone's minds as we reached that dream of spring in 2019.

Thanks to its long off-season and status as *the* water-cooler topic of the decade, *Game of Thrones* drew in more viewers than ever before for its final season. People wanted to join in the hype and see what all the fuss was about before the pop culture behemoth was put to bed. On April 17, 2011, the pilot aired to an audience of around 2.2 million people. The series finale was watched by 18.4 million people on May 19, 2019, a new record for HBO. When you include the many more who streamed or downloaded the episode illegally, and take into account the penchant for massive *Game of Thrones* viewing parties where groups of people gathered around one TV, that audience number gets exponentially larger. This was a series finale that marked one of the last times so many millions of us would sit down and experience a TV show together all at once.

This extra attention on the final six episodes created an overwhelming level of conversation and debate, the strain of which was almost too much to bear, depending on which corners of the internet you spent time in. People took to just calling it "The Discourse," as if the push and pull of criticism and praise and musings was its own separate, beastly entity.

The eighth season of *Game of Thrones* was a complicated, many-layered cake. Some of those layers were things everyone could universally agree were delectable—the score, sound design, costuming, production design, and performances were all top-notch. Folks took the most issue with the writing and pacing of the last run of episodes, shining additional light on Benioff and Weiss and their storytelling choices made in the absence of Martin's completed novels.

Benioff and Weiss had, of their own volition, decided on seventy-three as their goal number for total episodes. The first six seasons were consistently ten episodes in about ten hours (give or take). By the time the sixth season finale had aired, Benioff and Weiss started talking openly about their plans to wind the show down, telling *Deadline* in 2019 that the plan was to finish the show in seventy to seventy-five hours. That limit was not dictated by budget or HBO executives or anything other than the vision Benioff and Weiss had for *Game of Thrones*.

"HBO would have been happy for the show to keep going, to have more episodes in the final season," Benioff told *Entertainment Weekly* in a pre–season eight interview. "We always believed it was about 73 hours, and it will be roughly that. As much as they wanted more, they understood that this is where the story ends."

For the two showrunners, it seemed important not to overstay their welcome or reach a point of oversaturation with Westeros. Going out on a high note would certainly be preferential to fading into the background of pop culture—but unfortunately the final season of *Game of Thrones* landed somewhere in the middle. Benioff and Weiss had tried to avoid padding out the story for the sake of filling a ten-hour season, but it turns out that was exactly what many fans wanted.

Maybe Benioff and Weiss worried those quieter character moments, most of which would have just required a small interior set and no VFX, would bore people. Or perhaps they believed all the previous sixty-plus hours of character development was enough to carry the ending over the finish line without adding more exposition or exploration of lore and magic. It's even possible that many fans didn't realize how essential or important those stage-setting episodes had been in earlier years until they saw what a season of almost nonstop "epic action" looked like, without the added time given to get inside the minds and motivations of these various characters.

The overwhelming adoration for "A Knight of the Seven Kingdoms" showed how much fans cherished the emotional impact of scenes that needed no expensive CGI dragon or hundreds of extras or months and months of grueling night shoots. And yet it was those ambitious and exhausting set pieces that Benioff and Weiss placed the most emphasis on for the final season.

Even though the final season had the longest-ever production time in the show's history, with almost eight months of filming, and just as much time spent on post-production, people still found many odd discrepancies or mistakes in either the script or the aired episode. When a coffee cup from the craft services cart in Belfast wound up sitting on the table in front of Daenerys in a Winterfell feast scene, almost a week's worth of articles and commentary made the rounds in the news. In that same episode, fans of Martin's books noticed that Gendry said his bastard last name was Rivers, even though it should have been Waters. (Rivers is the surname given to bastards born in the Riverlands—not the Crownlands, where Gendry was born in King's Landing.) By the time the finale aired, folks once again spotted an anachronism when two plastic water bottles were visible in the dragonpit council scene.

More internal logic was made screwy then, too, when people were left wondering how Samwell Tarly could be named Grand Maester if he had a wife and children when maesters were supposed to take vows of celibacy. There are many more examples that can lead you down a rabbit hole, and that provided fodder for people who believed the show had done the opposite of overstay its welcome, but instead seemed to hurriedly run out the door with its shoes halfway tied.

Nobody could fairly claim that Benioff, Weiss, and the entire cast and crew of *Game of Thrones* hadn't given the last six episodes every iota of energy they possessed, working themselves into the ground to bring the show to a close. The debate was instead about whether those efforts were misappropriated for a set of scripts that had issues no amount of flawless execution could overcome.

There was never going to be an ending of *Game of Thrones* that left everybody happy. Not with this many millions of fans or the high bar of expectation the earlier seasons had set. Emotions were running at an all-time high, making the debates and criticisms and defenses of Dany's downward spiral or the Night King's narrative purpose a fraught territory.

The fact that this series wrought such engagement and passion is in itself an achievement, even if the people who made the show

might've hoped for the loudest faction of viewers to be the people who loved it. For two months, the whole world stopped every Sunday night at 9 p.m. ET. People who didn't watch the show would still turn on the news or head to Twitter or even just walk down the hallways of their apartment complex and hear the iconic "dun dun, dun dun dun dun, dun dun dun" opening-credits score. *Game of Thrones* was inescapable. Until the very end, it was the ruler of the zeitgeist, untouchable by anything else.

Before the eighth season was done, HBO had already begun exploring options for continuing to build out Martin's world and stories onscreen. After a few different teams of writers put together ideas for spinoff or prequel shows, the executives eventually greenlit a pilot from Jane Goldman, a British screenwriter and producer. Goldman's most notable works have included movies like *Kick-Ass*, *X-Men: First Class*, and the *Kingsman* action movie franchise. Goldman also wrote the screenplay for Disney's live-action version of *The Little Mermaid*, which was in development by 2018.

This first prequel was said to take place "thousands of years before the events of *Game of Thrones*," and chart "the world's descent from the golden Age of Heroes into its darkest hour," according to an HBO press release. This meant it was likely we'd see even more about the origin of the White Walkers and how the first Long Night came about.

People clamor for an Arya Stark adventure spinoff series or a more pointed prequel like the tale of Robert's Rebellion was fruitless. All of the characters made famous by Benioff and Weiss in *Game of Thrones* would be contained to that show, and weren't the subjects of any working spinoff series. Martin preferred using the term "successor shows" when describing them, though he was not involved in any of their productions aside from consulting with the various teams on the initial ideas and scripts.

When the series finale of *Game of Thrones* aired, Martin was still toiling away at *The Winds of Winter*, promising he was at work on it but giving no projected finish time. Benioff and Weiss, who would also not be involved with any version of the spinoffs or prequels, already had their next major franchise project lined up. They were tapped by Disney to write and produce a new Star Wars trilogy, scheduled to be the first set of movies set in a galaxy far, far away after the Skywalker saga ends in December 2019.

As for fans, the trending hashtags and new podcast episodes and group chats about *Game of Thrones* slowly waned. Obsessively loving the show would no longer mean experiencing the annual sprint of emotions collectively experienced by the world at the same time, but instead a more intimate relationship with the fictional realm of Westeros. There were rewatch marathons, fan conventions, and more of Martin's writing on the horizon.

And so *Game of Thrones* itself ends just as it began. Rangers setting forth from the icy cold passageway beneath the Wall, making their way north. But this time, it's not men of the Night's Watch venturing toward their doom, those noble but weary rangers who had long forgotten their true purpose at the edge of the world stumbling upon the existential threat of the White Walkers.

Now we see Jon Snow departing from Castle Black, the Free Folk surrounding him, the very people once hunted down by the Night's Watch. They make their way out from underneath the barrier that once kept their kind away from the safety of Westeros. The Free Folk had once risked everything to get as far south as possible, but now they walk into the true North with no fears plaguing them. And the man who once only ever wanted to find glory ranging beyond the Wall now finds himself leading a new people toward a peace they've never known, in the lands that once represented an unknown horror and seemingly insurmountable set of trials.

The world of Westeros is cyclical, like our own. Seats of power, times of war, systems of abuse—the future seemed such a tenuous thing, a distant dream of bloodless days and warm nights. In this fantasy realm, the unpredictable seasons mean even more uncertainty, with long summers and longer winters. But there, in the final minutes, we see the hint of spring at last. No longer a dream, a sprig of green emerges from the snow, not unlike the once King in the North who bloomed in spite of the cold tundra and found himself capable of shouldering a burden he never wanted.

In this end, everything returns to the children. The future is in those maps Arya holds, and in the stitching of Queen Sansa's gown. The promise of contentment is in the small smiles and lighthearted gaits of the littlest wildlings walking on either side of Jon Snow, the King Beyond the Wall. Together they represent a new respite from the wars that ravaged their lives. We have seen the repercussions of just one selfish or treacherous act, and how it reverberates for generations. We know the weight of promises and terror of war, the fleeting comfort of love and harsh hand of injustice. These children know it, too.

Like Jon, we watch one passageway close and turn our sights forward to a melancholy optimism. His was the song of ice and fire, and we shall never see its like again.

A NOTE ON SOURCES

Putting together this unofficial guide would not have been possible without many *Game of Thrones* reporters and critics who came before me. In my research, Joanna Robinson's work for *Vanity Fair* and James Hibberd's reporting in *Entertainment Weekly* were particularly influential several chapters in this book. Mikal Gilmore's 2014 interview with George R. R. Martin for *Rolling Stone* is an essential read for anyone looking for a core understanding of *Game of Thrones*, A Song of Ice and Fire, and the man who made them both possible. Outlets including *The Hollywood Reporter*, *The Ringer*, *Collider*, *Deadline*, *Variety*, and, of course, my own homes of *INSIDER* and *Business Insider* have done excellent and essential coverage of the show for almost a decade.

Bryan Cogman's book written in partnership with HBO, the first edition of *Inside Game of Thrones*, was also incredibly helpful and a fantastic resource for information about the early creation of the series. Martin's own prolific blogging on both the Live-Journal-hosted *Not a Blog* and his new self-hosted site provided an additional bounty of information, as did the forum site Westeros .org run by Elio M. García and Linda Antonsson. The reporting done by Susan Miller and the entire *Watchers on the Wall* team has been endlessly helpful and informative.

HBO's massive catalog of behind-the-scenes videos and online features on YouTube and the *Making Game of Thrones* site was key. Thanks are also in order to HBO and David Benioff and D. B. Weiss for making the show bible and many scripts available for perusal at the Writers Guild Foundation Shavelson-Webb Library in Los Angeles, California. Javier and Lauren, the librarians there who helped set me up with iPads and Wi-Fi, were godsends.

The /r/asoiaf Reddit community has been an essential part of my deeper understanding and appreciation of A Song of Ice and Fire and *Game of Thrones* from the very start, as have the fantastic podcasts *Storm of Spoilers* (now called simply *The Storm*), *Not a Podcast*, *Bald Move*, and *Game of Owns*.

ACKNOWLEDGMENTS

This book would not have been possible without all the editors who I worked with over the years at *Business Insider*, *Tech Insider*, and *INSIDER* (the trifecta of Insider Inc. websites). Gus, thank you for being the first person at *BI* to take a chance on me. Kirsten, thank you for showing me the ropes when it came to the CMS and killer headline framing. Caroline, thank you for responding with the simple but encouraging "HELL YEAH!" when I emailed to tell you I was thinking about applying to be a reporter on your team. Jethro, thank you for all you taught me about the entertainment reporting biz, and for helping me shine my way over to the West Coast.

To Insider Inc.'s editor in chief and my mentor, Nich, thank you for being the first person to ever ask me if I wanted to write a book, and for helping me make that hypothetical into a reality. You paved a road for me right when I needed it, and your support at *INSIDER* has meant the world. Which brings me to Eric Nelson, who took over for Nich and first fielded my questions about the publishing process and introduced me to my agent. I wouldn't be here without you taking that time, Eric, and I'm eternally grateful. Thank you to my agent, Tim Wojcik, and LGR, as well as my editor, Matthew Benjamin, and the whole Atria team, who helped make this book sing.

To Megan and Madison, thank you for being down in the muck with me during my first year ever of reporting and writing about *Game of Thrones* professionally. You kept me going and taught me so much about the power of friendship and hard work and loving support and also the real meaning of "h/t." Again, huge thanks.

To my *Game of Thrones* brain-twin, Joanna, thank you for keeping me afloat during the final crush of the final season, and for all your guidance and support and texts in the wee hours of Sunday nights. To all of my dearest friends, especially Castle Slack, thank you for always lifting me up when I needed it most.

Thank you to the ASMR Rooms YouTube channel for creating the hyperspecific video titled "Harry Potter Inspired ASMR - Gryffindor Common Room - Ambience and Animation (rain, fire place)." You helped my productivity when I needed it most. Also, shout-out to the Hollywood Trader Joe's for the steady supply of off-brand takis, coffee, and frozen pizzas that fueled most of my hours of writing.

To all the Burtses and Bowleses, thank you for your kindness and for welcoming me into your family and supporting me so much over the years.

And to Mom, Dad, Julie, Sara, and Boon—I love you so much. Your uplifting texts and letters and gifts and long-distance love has kept me going through this tumultuous and scary and amazing chapter of my life. Thank you for helping make me the person I am today.

Above all, thank you, Mike. You're my Samwell and Samwise, the very best partner anyone could hope for. I never would have made it this far without you by my side each step of the way. After ten years together, you're still finding new ways to blow me away with your unending love and generosity and support. I love you.

Each and every person involved with the creation of *Game of Thrones* has my endless gratitude. I can only imagine the literal blood, sweat, and tears that went into creating this show that helped give me a career. Your hard work and efforts are so appreciated, and I'm so honored to play an infinitesimal role in the massive legacy of the show you brought to life. Thank you for all you have done.

And thank you to George R. R. Martin. Without you, none of this would have come to pass.

ABOUT THE AUTHOR

Kim Renfro is an entertainment correspondent at *INSIDER*. She has published hundreds of articles about *Game of Thrones* that were read by more than seventeen million people during the final two seasons of the show. She's interviewed *Game of Thrones* stars, directors, and production crew over the course of her career. She lives in Los Angeles with her husband, Mike, and two cats, Lily and Zelda. This is her first book.